Shepperton Studios

Shepperton Studios

A visual celebration

southbank
publishing

This edition published in 2005 by Southbank Publishing

21 Great Ormond Street, London, WC1N 3JB
www.southbankpublishing.com

Distributed in the USA by Trafalgar Square Publishing, P.O. Box 257,
Howe Hill Road, North Pomfret, Vermont 05053

The design for the end papers comes from the glass roof located in 'the old house'
at Shepperton

Shepperton film dates appear as production dates, all other film dates will be
release dates

A CIP catalogue record for this book is available from the British Library.

ISBN 1-904915-03-5 (standard edition) ISBN 1-904915-06-X (collector's edition)

2 4 6 8 10 9 7 5 3 1

Text by Morris Bright
Edited by Paul Torjussen
Line Edit by Victor Morrison
Designed by George Lewis
Typeset by Avocet Typeset, Chilton, Aylesbury, Bucks

Printed and bound by SNP Lee Fung Printers (Shenzhen) Co., Ltd

The Cinema and Television Benevolent Fund

Pinewood Shepperton and Southbank Publishing will make
a contribution from the sale of this book to The Cinema and
Television Benevolent Fund. The CTBF are developing
Glebelands, their residential centre in Berkshire, into a
"continuing care community", for retired film and commercial television employees.

Put Britain on the map
by Norman Loudon

With the profits from Flicker Productions Norman Loudon was able to purchase Littleton House and form Sound City Film Studios in 1931. The following is an article written by Norman Loudon in 1933 about the creation of what we now know to be Shepperton Studios.

The chairman and managing director of Sound City Ltd who urges that our studios should get away from flirtatious farce and get down to business of portraying the activities of our everyday life.

"The film is a vivid and a vital medium. Let it show therefore, vivid and vital subjects. British films have for many years remained content to play with the light and flimsy dramatics. Let them get out and beyond four walls and pry into the recesses and the secrets of the drama of mankind.

Let films live! Let them have vigour, action and purpose! Subjects of our national life are crying out for filming. There is no lack of material. It is my firm conviction that there is no lack of public support for such films as these.

When I formed Sound City Film Studios, some eighteen months ago. I had, in mind, the above. Night after night, month after month, I went to picture houses and saw American films that flashed with brilliance the activities of American everyday life.

Here were their universities and their department stores, their speakeasies and their gunmen, their navy and their airforce, their hotels and their homes, their open-air romances and their historical achievements. Too often the British counterpart was a flirtatious farce or a cocktail effervescence.

There was nothing vigorous, dynamic, driving or decisive. A pity in a country that has the finest traditions and history of all times! A pity in a country that is proud to possess soil in every corner of the globe and a coloniser that reads, speaks of and watches the mother country.

I was determined therefore to try to carry into effect something of the convictions that I held. Studios had to be built and a production personnel assembled. Both have been done and Sound City today stands in one of the most unique and beautiful spots for talkie film making that the world could find.

Not only is the newest studio just opened the last word in construction and technique, but 60 acres of ground owned by the company enable outdoor scenery to be used to its varied and fullest extent.

The stage is limited to four walls, but the film is peerless in this respect. I am proud to be able to say that one of our first films showed that we are working along the right lines and that in time we could expect the fulfillment of our ideals.

In *Reunion* we showed the present day through the eyes of an ex-army major reduced by ill fortune to the barest existence. He had fought for his country years before like thousands of others, but the vagaries of peace had baffled his honest purpose. Yet he instantly answers the call to attend his old regiment's reunion dinner, although it means another visit to the pawnbroker and the accumulation of more unpaid bills.

To his men he is still their leader and their hero, although in point of money alone, none are probably in such sore straits. He cannot confide in them his difficulties. There is only one thing he can do. It is to act with the same bravery and optimism that characterised their deeds at the front and to know 'that a man is never deserted until he deserts himself'.

Reunion, I am glad to say, although an unpretentious film and made under difficult conditions has received high praise. This is all the more striking in that the cast is composed entirely of men. No mean achievement when women today are such an essential element at the box office.

Reunion has served to give us an indication of what I believe we should strive for at Sound City. Its predominant note to its sincerity. If you do not believe in a thing you might just as well give up attempting to do it, for you are bound to fail.

Sincerity is honesty and gives firmness and resolve to purpose and action. *Reunion* possesses a definite theme. You may grumble but the man smiling next to you may be a sight worse off than you are.

Optimism does more for a man than a world of doubt and despair. Finally the whole cast is natural and colloquial. You have met them off the screen and what they say is sensible and snappy. Other subjects for filming are waiting in their dozens. One of these we are producing now. It is called *Doss House* and reveals a side of life which few people are cognisant. The characters are for the most part down and outs. But they are an active lot and just as cheerful as their counterparts staying at the finest luxury hotel.

They may even be better off for they have not worries and responsibilities. They have their excitement and their amusements. There is one among them from every walk of life, with as large a fund of anecdote as the best 'raconteur' in the best fireside circle.

They have their position to keep up as well. A workhouse inmate is quite another class. In *Doss House* the characters are simple folk, but they are real. You have passed them in the street many and many a time.

Perhaps in the past they have rolled by in luxurious cars and dined and wined in the best places.

In the film one of them was a great musician, but in time his powers failed him and his hosts of friends soon departed from him. Others in the cosmopolitan crowd are labourers earning large weekly wages, itinerant vendors, shoeblacks, butt-end collectors and rogues. All are collected here. What a chance for real characterisation.

In passing it is interesting to notice that 'doss houses' reflect national life to as great an extent as any other institution. Why, business to day in 'doss houses' is not quite as good as it was a few years ago in the boom days. Some of their best clients or 'steadies', as they are called – one of them has had the same bed for sixteen years – cannot now always afford the prices.

In *Doss House* the story concerns a detective and a newspaper reporter and the capture of an escaped convict. In the other stories that we are now preparing for production at Sound City this summer, are those dealing with the revival of shipping, the romance of the canning industry, the professions, a story round the Tower of London.

America has put its national life on the screen. It has done it without fear or favour. I believe that unless we do likewise at once, Americans will themselves come over to produce in this country and do it for us. The industry is growing up in our midst, potent beyond measure. Let us see that its growth is healthy, vigorous and strong."

Norman Loudon
© Picturegoer Weekly 1933

'The Old House', Shepperton

Shepperton DVD

The following film trailers feature on a DVD included free with the book *Shepperton Studios*, courtesy of CANAL+IMAGE UK LTD.

The Third Man

The Sound Barrier

I'm All Right Jack

A Kind of Loving

Billy Liar

The Servant

Darling

The Great St Trinian's
    Train Robbery

Dr Who and the Daleks

The Family Way

The Wicker Man

The Man Who Fell to Earth

Foreword: Sir John Mills
Introduction: Sir Ridley Scott

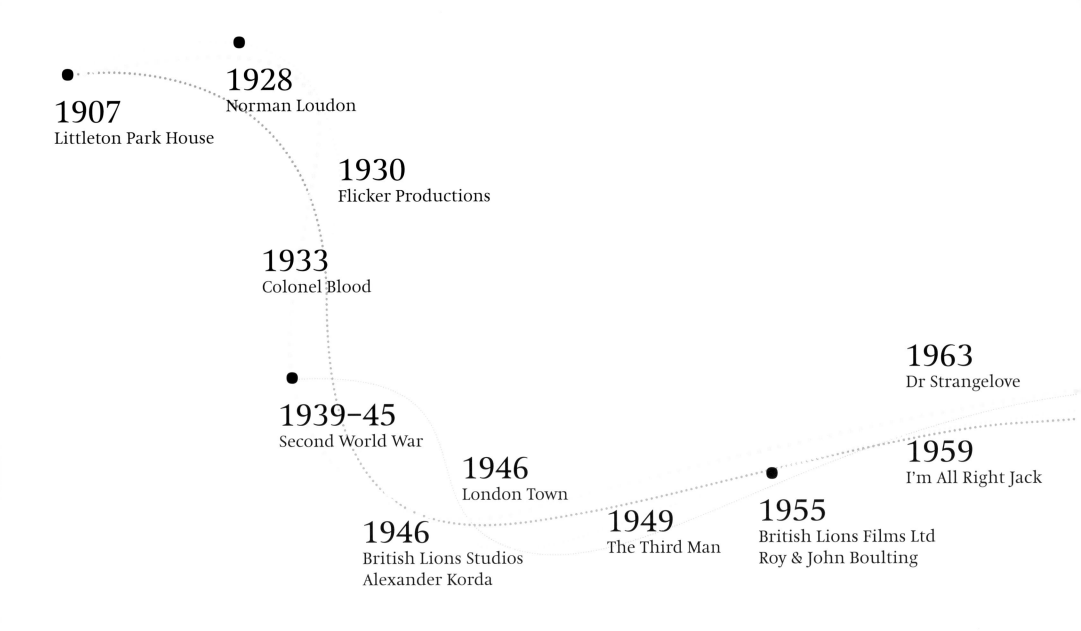

1907
Littleton Park House

1928
Norman Loudon

1930
Flicker Productions

1933
Colonel Blood

1939–45
Second World War

1946
London Town

1946
British Lions Studios
Alexander Korda

1949
The Third Man

1955
British Lions Films Ltd
Roy & John Boulting

1959
I'm All Right Jack

1963
Dr Strangelove

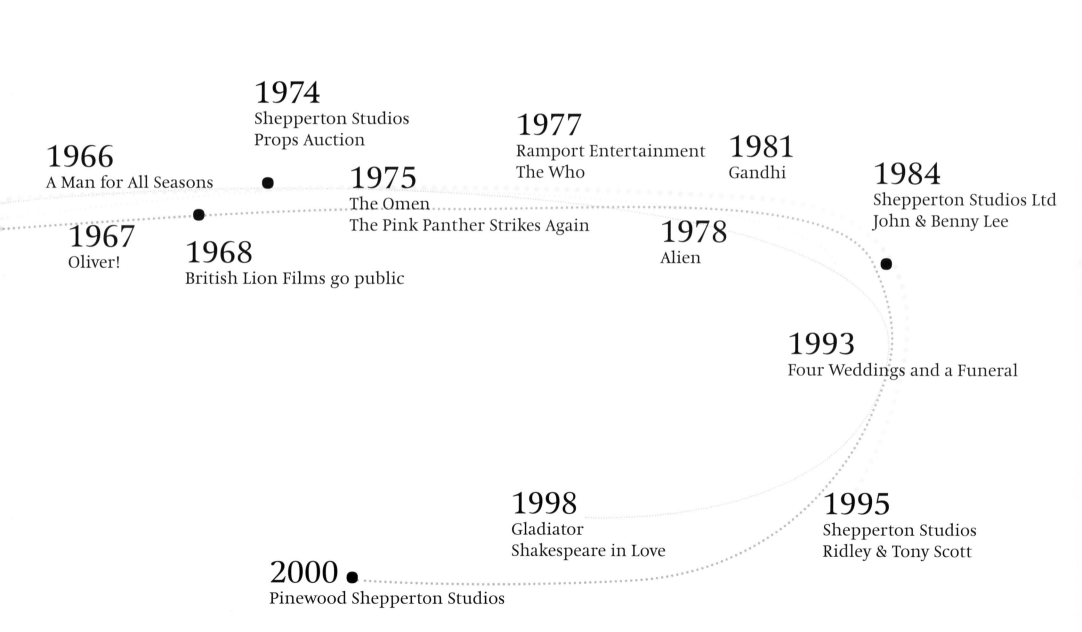

1966
A Man for All Seasons

1967
Oliver!

1968
British Lion Films go public

1974
Shepperton Studios
Props Auction

1975
The Omen
The Pink Panther Strikes Again

1977
Ramport Entertainment
The Who

1978
Alien

1981
Gandhi

1984
Shepperton Studios Ltd
John & Benny Lee

1993
Four Weddings and a Funeral

1995
Shepperton Studios
Ridley & Tony Scott

1998
Gladiator
Shakespeare in Love

2000
Pinewood Shepperton Studios

Shepperton was my favourite studio. I loved all the nonsense of the (Old) House and the big black and white tiled floor, which we had to cross to get to the restaurant and bar. In my day it was a converted conservatory. I remember the story of the dotty lady who threw herself from the gallery into the hall and had died, naturally enough. A lot of actors rather wished that they could follow her course having been to the 'rushes'.

Sir Dirk Bogarde

This book is dedicated to the life of Sir John Mills who died on 21st April 2005 aged 97.

Foreword
by Sir John Mills CBE

The start of my career in film and the early days of production at Shepperton enjoy many similarities.

I made my first film back in the early 1930s. Shepperton Studios saw its first film produced then too. I found myself as a novice in the business swept along by a tide of Government rules which stated that, for every American film being shown, a British one must be shown with it. The same applied to Shepperton. I starred in lots of those "quota quickies," as they became known. Shepperton – like all of our studios at that time – found itself churning out quota quickies by the dozen.

Extraordinarily though, I seemed to work at every other film studios in and around London, with the exception of Shepperton itself, for the best part of two decades. I had started off at Twickenham, and worked at Ealing, Elstree and Pinewood. Indeed it was not until 1953 – some 20 years since my first part in a Jessie Matthews musical, *The Midshipmaid*

(1932) that I finally arrived at the gates of the unforgettable Shepperton Studios in Surrey, to star in what would become probably my favourite film role to date.

The part of Willy Mossop – a white-faced, shy, young Lancashire bootmaker – in the 1953 film *Hobson's Choice* was never meant for me at all. The part had been cast for the distinguished stage and screen actor Robert Donat. The poor man suffered terribly from asthma and was taken ill just a few days before filming was due to begin. This was all unbeknownst to me. At the time, I had been working extremely hard and was delighted when my wife Mary and I were invited to spend a week with Rex and Lilli Harrison at their new villa in Portofino. The holiday was just what we both needed and within a few days we were beginning to feel incredibly spoiled and thoroughly relaxed. Until, that is, a telegram arrived from the renowned and much-admired film director David Lean. It read something along the lines of: "Dear Johnnie, this is an SOS. Can you drop everything and return home immediately? Bob Donat ill. You can't turn down Will Mossop in *Hobson's Choice* can you?" Within a few hours, Mary and I were on the train heading home.

The very next day, there I was, sitting in the make-up chair at Shepperton Studios, my fit and tanned look quickly hidden, to be replaced by a pasty-faced looking chap with shaved eye brows and an awful pudding-basin hair-cut to match.

Now that David Lean had got me there, he was the first to admit that he really thought Bob Donat would have been much better in the role. He was not comparing our acting abilities, but was referring to Bob's stature – he was taller than me – and David had imagined Willy Mossop to be a large and awkward-looking chap. Nothing though was going to spoil my excitement of working with one of the cinema's acting greats – the larger than life Charles Laughton who was to play the turn-of-the-century Salford cobbler Henry Horatio Hobson, at war with his daughters and most of the town it seemed.

Laughton was an extraordinary man. Both David Lean and I were rather in awe of him and whenever he would bellow out his own often eccentric ideas for a particular scene, we would both nod as one, in agreement, though much of the time neither of us were quite sure what he was suggesting. I adored working with the whole cast and crew, especially Brenda de Banzie, who played Hobson's daughter Maggie and, of course, later in the film, my wife.

Hobson's Choice won the British Academy Award for Best British Film in 1954. It was a very proud moment for us all. I was nominated for Best British Actor, the award going, most-deservedly, to my good friend Kenneth More for his role in the hilarious medical comedy, *Doctor in the House* (1954). That didn't detract from my love of the film and of the part of Willy Mossop. It is a role I will always be so proud to have played.

My appearances at Shepperton are a little akin to the proverbial London buses. You don't seem to see one for ages, then a host of them arrive at the same time. No sooner had I worked on *Hobson's Choice*, than I found myself at the Studios again, this time in the emotionally charged war film, *The Colditz Story* (1954). It was a hard film to make, having to recreate the horrors that so many of our gallant soldiers went through in World War II, just ten years after fighting had ceased and with the memories of those times still very much etched in the minds of a shell-shocked generation. The film though stayed true to its cause, was well produced and well received and was also nominated for a BAFTA in 1955. Ironically, the British Academy Award for Best British Film that year went to another Shepperton production, that of my dear friend Laurence Olivier's *Richard III* (1950).

I was back at Shepperton again the next year working with more friends, Dickie Attenborough and Bryan Forbes, shooting the naval comedy *The Baby and The Battleship* (1956). It was during the making of this film that dear Dickie got nick-named "Bunter" by Bryan, because of his endless passion for chocolate. It's funny how one remembers these things with a smile, looking back almost fifty years.

I think that in total I have made around eight films at Shepperton Studios. That may not sound many when I tell you that I have had roles in around 100 films in all, but every one of them remains a production very close to my heart. I have worked with some wonderful directors and actors there, from David Lean to Richard Attenborough, from Kenneth Branagh to working with my own daughter Hayley, in *The Family Way*, back in 1966.

What has always remained with me about working at Shepperton has been the sheer professionalism of everyone, both in front of and behind the camera, to ensure the very best of British film-making for the most particular of audiences – you, our all-important public – who expect no more and no less than the very best this country has to offer by way of cinematic excellence.

I feel privileged to have been a part of Shepperton's history and I am delighted that its long and illustrious history is being celebrated in this book, so full, as it is, of beautiful and striking images from 75 years of independent film production.

If a picture speaks a thousand words, then this book is indeed a weighty tome. I do hope you enjoy it.

Sir John Mills CBE
Denham Village, Buckinghamshire
January 2005

Sir John Mills CBE
22nd February 1908 – 21st April 2005

Introduction by Sir Ridley Scott

As a young man I was more enthusiastic about film than the average teenager. I would try and see everything that I could. I loved Westerns and was a big fan of John Wayne. The biggest question for me was how could I get into this world? They didn't have film schools in those days and you had to find your own way into the business.

The late 1950s saw a whole new wave of films hit our screens in Britain. I never gave up on John Wayne but now my essential cinema fodder had changed. Suddenly my eyes were opened to the works of Michael Powell, David Lean and Tony Richardson. They got me noticing films at a different level. I watched Richard Burton and Richard Harris, young, fresh and very real – *Look Back In Anger* (1959), *Saturday Night and Sunday Morning* (1960). This was all great inspirational stuff to an aspiring director.

There were maybe 250 directors in London in those days. Now there are more than 1,000 – which is probably about 600 too many. I didn't end up in film straightaway. Like so many of my peers, such as Alan Parker and Hugh Hudson, the magic of the movies came second to the alluring pull of the world of commercials. Which is how I ended up at Shepperton in the first place. Shepperton became the home to my studio-based filming work around 15 years before I actually made a film there – my second feature, *Alien* (1978).

From the moment I entered Shepperton, I knew the place was special. Anywhere that had had within its walls Carol Reed directing Orson Welles in *The Third Man* (1949), was going to mean a great deal to me. It is true that there was a touch of "them" and "us" at the studios in the 1960s. "We" were making commercials, "they" were making films. But that snobbery has always existed – it still does – and I wasn't troubled by it.

What did trouble me was the decline of Shepperton in the 1970s as the British film industry took one of its many

knocks over the years. The studios started to resemble a shabby uncle – much loved but in need of some care and attention. I carried on working there regardless, because I don't give a damn whether a studio is decrepit or not, so long as I've got a good camera and a good script and a good crew – because then I know what I'm doing and I'm enjoying myself.

There were just six productions made at Shepperton in 1978. It meant that there was no shortage of space for me to make *Alien* there and I will always be delighted that I did. I was so struck by the sheer professionalism of everyone who worked at the studios and I still am. Shepperton has some of the best artisans and craftsmen in the industry and so when I came to make *Gladiator* (1998) some 20 years later, there could only really be one place from which I sourced all the props. We filmed a great deal of *Gladiator* in Malta, but every piece of armour and sword, chariot and tent, furniture and Roman column came from Shepperton. What a great plaster cast and fibre-glass room they've got there. I was so indebted to them all.

Shepperton has always been renowned for its expertise. I've been in and out of the studios for over four decades and that's still the case today. I believe it is that expertise which has helped keep the studios alive at its most difficult times. When the studios came up for sale in the mid-1990s, my brother Tony and I knew that we had to try and buy it. The previous owners, the Lee Brothers, had done a great job of face-lifting the studios in the years before we took over. I believe they cared deeply about the studios' survival and we had a tough act to follow. They had passed on this "valuable ball" to us, that we had to keep polished and shiny, and this is what we have done. Money was invested, stages were refur-

bished and re-built, and a long-term plan put in place for the future. Even then, when we took over Shepperton we already had our eyes on Pinewood. We tried to buy it twice. Our thinking was, that once you get one big film into a studio, you can lose as many as eight big stages – out of, say, the 17 that Shepperton has – which is good news on the one hand, but means you can't take on another big film because all the plum stages have been booked. But to have the combination of two studios – some 38 stages – where you can straddle two or three large productions, must be better business. We never got to buy Pinewood, but others had the same fore-sight and I am delighted that the merger between the two studios has now happened. The value to the industry of having Pinewood and Shepperton together is huge. Look at a map of Europe and ask yourself, where is there anything else like it. That must be good for this country's film industry.

We are now witnessing a super demand for entertainment material in whatever form, be it film, DVD or television. It's all got to be made. Sometimes you can make it on location, sometimes you can't. And when you can't, you can make it at Shepperton.

I hope I have played some part in securing the short and medium future of this very special place. There were those who thought that the advent of computer-generated imagery would see the end to traditional ways of making movies. But that hasn't been the case. There has been a resurrection of the traditional methods of building a set for most films, and so you need stages. I've always believed that. I went into Shepperton with that thought and I know it's not going away.

Of course the British film industry will continue to fluctu-ate. That's to be expected. Yet I'm more confident about its future now, than I have ever been. I'm not in London enough anymore and I miss it. It seems that I tend to shoot everywhere in the world except the US and England. I hope to be back soon.

There will always be those who believe that this industry is just one big party, but those of us who are in it, day in and day out, will know just how hard we all work. On set at 6.30 in the morning, often not finishing before 11 at night. In the film industry, whatever level you're at, for the most part, if you're serious, you work like a dog. It's a passion, not a vocation.

I would like to thank everyone who has helped assist me and my productions at Shepperton over the years. The "shabby uncle" has been well cared for and is now revived, once again holding his head up high. So many people have played a part in making that happen. This book is a tribute to those who have been involved, either in front of the camera or behind it, on over seven hundred productions filmed at Shepperton since 1931.

Sir Ridley Scott
California, USA

History

Right
Sir Edward Nicholl, a wealthy
shipping tycoon and Member of
Parliament, who lived at Littleton
Park until 1928

The site of Shepperton Studios dates back to the late seventeenth century when local nobleman Thomas Wood built Littleton Park, the mansion house which still stands at the centre of the 60-acre Surrey studios site more than 300 years later. The Woods lived at Littleton Park for the best part of two centuries. Their home was grandiose and played host to many royal visitors; from William IV, who enjoyed relaxing in the summer house by the edge of the River Thames, to the Prince of Wales – later Edward VII – who found the grounds' close proximity to London extremely useful, allowing him to indulge in one of his favoured pastimes of hunting without having to stray too far into the countryside, away from official duties.

A fire in 1876 put paid to such visits for many years and it was almost 25 years before the house was fully restored by Sir Richard Burbridge at that time the managing director of the world famous store, Harrods. Burbridge had an eye for the resplendent, with useful contacts to boot. Using timber from the original Houses of Parliament and marbles depicting the great battles of Nelson and Wellington, Littleton Park soon felt and looked positively palatial.

Following Burbridges's death in 1917, the whole estate was bought by Sir Edward Nicholl, a wealthy shipping tycoon and Member of Parliament who lived there until 1928.

The site was then bought by Norman Loudon, a young wealthy Scottish businessman whose newest venture – producing "flicker" books for children – was proving financially rather successful. "Flickers," as they were known, were made up of dozens of consecutive single frame photos that gave the impression of movement as a child literally flicked through the book. Suddenly one could see a cricketer bowling a ball or a golfer swinging his iron. It was all very exciting and, more importantly for Loudon, very profitable. A facsimile of a 'flicker' book is included in the collectors' edition of this book. Seeing this as a portent that he should delve further into the world of film-making, Loudon bought Littleton Park with the profits of Flicker Productions. The house and its surrounding grounds cost him just £5,000; some 70 years later, the same site was sold for around £35 million.

And so it was, in the winter of 1931, that Shepperton Film Studios – or Sound City Film Producing & Recording Studios as it was then known – was born. Loudon was ecstatic. In an article for *Picturegoer Weekly* in May 1933, he explained why the studios were so important to him: "Let films live! Let them have vigour, action and purpose!"

"When I formed Sound City Film Studios, I had, in mind, the above. Night after night, month after month, I went to picture houses and saw American films that flashed with brilliance, the activities of American everyday life.

Loudon knew that if he was to be taken seriously and was to attract film business his way, he needed sound stages to be built for film production. There was certainly no shortage of film studios for producers to choose from at that time. There were several dozen working studios in and around London at the beginning of the 1930s. The advantage Loudon had over his business opponents was that theirs had all been built during the silent era and were hastily being refurbished to take into account the advent of sound at the end of the 1920s. Hitchcock's 1930 thriller *Blackmail*, for example, had originally started production at Elstree as a silent movie, with sound having to be quickly added as the success of such films in America spread across the Atlantic.

Opposite
Two of the three Korda brothers –
Alexander and Vincent

Right
Colonel Blood (1933)
Directed by W P Lipscomb

So while Elstree and others had to be refurbished, the appropriately named Sound City was able to start from scratch, erecting two purpose-built sound-proofed stages within six months. Littleton Park offered new, modern and fast-expanding production facilities. Loudon was proud of his work: "I was determined to try to carry into effect something of the convictions that I held. Studios had to be built and production personnel assembled. Both have been done and Sound City today [1933] stands in one of the most unique and beautiful spots for talkie film making that the world could find. Not only is the newest studio just opened the last word in construction and technique, but the 60 acres of ground owned by the company enable outdoor scenery to be used to its varied and fullest extent."

By the end of 1932, Sound City's increasingly popular facilities had seen the production of no less than seven films, two full-length features and five shorts.

Littleton Park's grandiose mansion along with the conservatory, ballroom, and acres of parkland, and its ability to turn films around quickly, soon attracted production companies away from other London studios. Big name producers of the time who defected to Sound City included the Wainright Brothers and Embassy Pictures.

The Studios also became a breeding ground for young and up-and-coming film directors, establishing itself even then as the home for independent film-makers – a tradition which has stayed with the Studios throughout its lifetime. Among them was John Baxter, a confirmed Christian Socialist, who as a producer-director led the way in making gritty rough-and-ready dramas to prick the social consciences of

the viewers. His first film, *Doss House* (1932) centred on an escaped convict who is followed and eventually caught by a newspaper reporter and detective posing as tramps. Everyone at Sound City predicted the film would be a huge failure – declaring that the theme was not one that people would want to pay good money to go and see on a good night out. Whilst it didn't exactly have audiences rolling in the aisles, it did leave a lasting impression on the huge numbers who flocked to see it.

John Paddy Carstairs, at just 21, also became one of Sound City's first directorial shining lights. He made

his first film at Shepperton, *Paris Place*, in 1933. Later he would be closely linked with a host of well-known British films of the 1940s and 1950s and, specifically as director on several of Norman Wisdom's comedy films.

Some 12 features were made at Sound City in 1933 and Loudon knew it was time to expand. The original £5,000 he paid for the 60-acre site had proved a worthy investment. By mid-1933 he registered Sound City as having a capital of £175,000. However, not everything that Loudon was to touch would turn to gold. Carried away with his own exuberance, he was soon to witness the studios' first big film being produced, promptly released, and then flopping at the box office! With a budget of around £60,000 (or £1 million in today's money) *Colonel Blood* (1933) was written and directed by author W P Lipscomb. The film had looked grand enough, and the sets built for its filming included a reconstruction of the Tower of London in the studios' tank. Its failure at the cinemas gave Loudon a jolt. Lipscomb moved shortly afterwards to Hollywood where some of his other works, such as *Clive of India* (1934) and *A Tale of Two Cities* (1935), were better received. Indeed by the time Lipscomb won an Oscar® for his writing work on the British film *Pygmalion* (1938) in 1938, his early failure was all but forgotten.

Not so by Loudon who knew that if there was to be occasional box-office failure, it must not be allowed to bring down his studios. His insurance policy was The Cinematograph Films Act of 1927. This enthusiastic and pro-film piece of legislation had been rushed through Parliament to help save a dying film industry, that had plenty of studios but was under intense pressure from America. The Act ruled that an increasing number of British films should be made and released on a sliding scale over a ten year period, their number to total at least 20 per cent of all film output by the end of the 1930s. The Act also set out the percentages of staff employed on a production that had to be of British origin. This led to a surge in films being made quickly and cheaply to meet the terms of the quota. These films became known as "quota quickies." While they did much to stabilize and then substantially increase the rate of British film production, the quickies did little to improve the industry's reputation. With the definition of "British" extending to anywhere within the then resplendent Empire, some very peculiar oddities were offered for screening from the far flung corners of the world, including several silent productions from India which had cost little more than £500 per film to make.

Most of the quota quickies did not make a profit. Several made a small loss. But the sheer number produced offset worries of a huge financial disaster. Additionally, and far more importantly, they were a good training ground for up-and-coming actors, writers, technicians, producers and directors.

With the Act also encouraging American studios to set up operations in Britain and feed their own home markets by producing films cheaply over here for consumption over there, the industry was soon back on its feet again.

Norman Loudon used the Act to his and Sound City's advantage. Concerned more about his company's financial worth than the aesthetic pleasures of many of the cheap productions he was churning out, Shepperton went from strength to strength. After a short closure for modernization and further expansion, the Studios re-opened with seven sound stages, a dozen editing rooms, three viewing theatres and large numbers of prop and scene workshops. Additionally, the old house was opened as a hotel and restaurant, providing all the services on one site that stars – particularly the Americans – had come to expect.

Among those attracted to Sound City and its huge facilities and riverside location were the Korda Brothers – Alexander, Zoltan and Vincent. Of Hungarian descent, the brothers were a formidable film-making force and, fortuitously, would in time develop their relationship with Shepperton much further. For now, Studio City was to be their base for 1934 and 1935 as they worked on the ambitious *Sanders of the River*.

Opposite

British film star Anna Neagle cuts a cake at the 1946 Shepperton staff Christmas party – Studios owner Alexander Korda and Neagle's husband, director Herbert Wilcox, are sitting behind her. Wilcox and his wife were at the Studios making the classic, *The Courtneys of Curzon Street*. A young David Niven can be seen in the background next to Wilcox

Above
Popular wartime comedian Sid Field, takes the lead role of provincial comic Jerry, in one of the first films to be made at Shepperton Studios after World War II, *London Town* (1946)

Opposite
Welsh music-hall favourite Tessie O'Shea – billed as Two Ton Tessie after her signature tune – in the musical comedy *London Town* (1946)

The Studios continued to improve and expand and by the late 1930s, with Sound City booming, Loudon – never one to stand still – announced his most ambitious project to date. Recognising that sound stages only took up part of the land he owned, aware of Sound City's beautiful riverside views, and knowing just how close to the metropolis the site was, Loudon hit on the idea of a zoo and pleasure park. Almost two decades before Walt Disney was to open his first theme park in America, Norman Loudon announced his ideas for a theme park in the studio grounds at Shepperton, named Wonderland.

The idea was vast. Loudon had a model of his Wonderland erected in the studios original sound stage "L", employing the designing skills of the former assistant curator to London's Regents Park Zoo, Alan Best, to draw up the plans. Looking to attract private investment, Loudon had a prospectus published, explaining how the theme park would look and work alongside the current studio production facilities.

Loudon's Sound City Zoo and Wonderland, with its planned 15 themed areas and a Noah's ark of 100 species of animal, could, he predicted, be built and open to the paying public by 1940. The project would be more ambitious, popular and long-lasting than anything yet seen in this country. At least that was the plan. Then Germany invaded Poland.

The outbreak of World War II caused major problems for film studios in and around London. Huge sound stages, the size of aircraft hangers, were ideal for a government that needed space to – among other things – store much needed food supplies for a nation under bombardment. Shepperton was not alone in being requisitioned by the government for war work. Pinewood, Elstree, Nettlefold, Worton Hall, Islington and Beaconsfield Studios all had to hand over space to the War Office and Board of Trade for the duration.

Originally, Sound City looked as though it may have been spared the requisition. Indeed, for a short while production of films continued both at Shepperton and at other British studios. Patriotic flag-wavers were

of warplanes attacked the capital and its outskirts. Air raid sirens would sound and whoever you were and wherever you were in a studio, you had to get down to the shelters quickly. Stars of the day like George Formby and Thora Hird would find themselves sitting next to a girl from the canteen shelling peas for lunch.

The Ministry of Defence finally requisitioned Sound City in 1941. Four of the five sound stages were used for storing supplies of sugar. Then, when the Vickers factory nearby took a huge hit and was severely damaged, the sugar was packed into just two sound stages, with the other two being used by Vickers workers to make bomber parts and spares.

Sound City's designers and prop hands were not left idle, but instead of building sets for films, their talents were employed to build hundreds of decoy planes, imitation landing barges, fake guns and landing strips. Made mostly of wood and canvas, these decoys played an enormous part in convincing the Germans that Britain's strength and the positioning of our forces were not as it first appeared.

The fact that the end of the war did not mean the end of the sound stage requisitions was incredibly frustrating for studio owners and producers alike. Cinema attendances had peaked by the end of the war, hitting a staggering 31 million a week. Yet just twenty per cent of films that people went to see were British.

Alexander Korda led calls for the government to start releasing stages back to the industry. His efforts were partially successful. Studios across the country began to operate again. By September 1945, Sound City had re-opened with two of its large stages and one small stage ready for action. Ironically, its first major film was to be an import from Pinewood, where the Rank Organisation found they hadn't yet been released enough space to make a big British musical, *London Town*. The film cost over £1 million to make, the size of its budget being surpassed only by the size of its failure. The film was a huge disaster. *London Town*

Laurence Olivier enjoyed recalling Korda's own words to actors and actresses: "I want you to become a star because it will help make you rich, but even more so because it will help make me rich."

needed to keep up the morale of the country. From Noel Coward's serious and heart-rending story of a torpedoed destroyer and its crew *In Which We Serve* (1942) to the hilarious antics of everyone's favourite bumbling professor and incompetent spy, Will Hay, in *The Black Sheep of Whitehall* (1941) or *The Goose Steps Out* (1942) – whether serious and sad, or funny and mad, audiences needed something to watch, to take their minds of the constant and often devastating bombardments from the air.

Filming wasn't easy. Productions – like every other business – were regularly interrupted as another wave

"Anyone who gets a raw deal in a film studios is no more deserving of pity than someone who gets beaten up in a brothel. A gentleman has no business in either place."

(1946) seemed finally to push Norman Loudon over the edge. Now, some seven years after he had to relinquish control of his studios and his grand plans for a zoo and theme park, his company's return to the world of cinema had been an embarrassing and frustrating flop. Enough was enough for this canny entrepreneur. He was getting out. His opportunity to go came with Alexander Korda's purchase of British Lion in April 1946. This bought a controlling share in Sound City and with that controlling share came Shepperton Studios.

After he paid off his debts, it is alleged that Loudon left Shepperton with nothing but the clothes he was wearing, but that wasn't true. Littleton Park House may have been his home but he had invested in other properties in Beaulieu, Hampshire, and a 75-acre site, Tite House estate, in Runnymede. It was there that Loudon tried to rejuvenate his theme park idea, but again to no avail. This time he was to be thwarted by the shortage of money and materials that post-war Britain had, or rather didn't have, to offer.

Alexander Korda was nothing like Norman Loudon. Born in Hungary in 1893, Korda first worked in films in his home country, then across Europe before coming to England in 1931. He had an early success with *The Private Life of Henry VIII* (1933) that won an Oscar® for its star Charles Laughton; Korda himself was nominated for an award in the Best Picture category. The film did much to improve the reputation of British cinema, while catapulting Korda to the forefront of the industry. The financial rewards of *Henry VIII* allowed him to build Denham Studios in 1934. Large organisations such as the Prudential Assurance Company, were keen to invest – as it turned out unwisely – in Korda's "English Hollywood." Korda quickly started to lose money, a position that he was unable to reverse until the late 1940s. An internal memo from a regretful Prudential Assurance Company noted at the time: "His engaging personality and charm of manner must be resisted. His promises, even when they are sincere, are worthless. A very dominant man and very dangerous to converse with owing to (among other things) his powers of persuasion."

With his two talented brothers by his side – Zoltan, also a director, and Vincent, an art director – Alexander Korda was a film-making force to be reckoned with. Stars loved him and loathed him in equal numbers. But all recognised his ability to make a good film, even if his productions didn't always make a good profit. Ralph Richardson, who appeared to great critical acclaim in several of Korda's works, most notably *Things to Come* (1936), *The Four Feathers* (1939) and *The Sound Barrier* (1952) exclaimed: "Alexander Korda continuously makes people do things against their will but seldom against their interest." Laurence Olivier enjoyed recalling Korda's own words to actors and actresses: "I want you to become a star because it will help make you rich, but even more so because it will help make me rich."

Korda was knighted by Churchill in 1942, partly in gratitude for wartime services to Britain and mainly as a thank you for being the man who was widely regarded as having saved the British film industry. Linking up with such names as independent film producer David Selznick ensured large-scale films with even larger appeal. Selznick, responsible for such American classics as *Gone With the Wind* (1939) and *Rebecca* (1940), found Korda a joy to work with. Their joint work, *The Third Man* (1949), remains one of the most universally loved films of all time, a match made in cinematic heaven and one that re-ignited both the industry's finances and Korda's too. Money which Korda immediately plumbed back into films: "I'm not afraid of spending big money on big pictures," was a phrase he did not use lightly.

Unfortunately, the new peacetime era had also seen a new government in charge at Westminster. With it came policies not exactly designed to halt the British film industry in its tracks, but which led to that outcome anyway. Labour's President of the Board of Trade was a very young Harold Wilson, some 20 years before he was to become Prime Minister. With his stewardship in June 1948 a new quota for films was introduced. Under the terms of the new Cinematograph Films Act, 45 per cent of first features had to be British and 25 per cent of the second features or

Above

Film poster for, *A King in New York* (1957), the only film that Charlie Chaplin made at Shepperton

Opposite

The Sound Barrier (1952)

Opposite and this page
Saint Joan (1957) Jean Seberg was selected from a
final list of 3000 candidates, interviewed by director
Otto Preminger.
During the filming of the execution scene, Seberg
suffered burns during a special effects accident.
There was a delay lighting the gas and the excess
provided more flames than anticiptated. Jean Seberg
was burnt, but luckily not badly

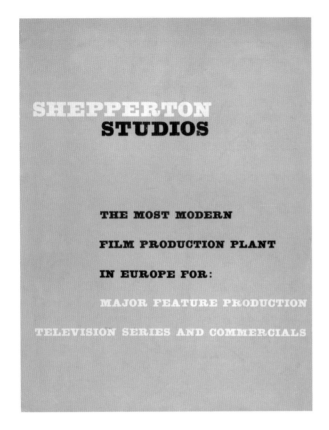

SHEPPERTON
STUDIOS

THE MOST MODERN

FILM PRODUCTION PLANT

IN EUROPE FOR:

MAJOR FEATURE PRODUCTION

TELEVISION SERIES AND COMMERCIALS

Above
The Boulting brothers

Above, left
The cover of a Shepperton
Studios brochure from the sixties

Opposite
The Shepperton set for *The Guns of
Navarone* (1960)

supporting programmes. The figures were far too high. The industry was unprepared and unable to meet those targets. To compound the problem further, there was a lack of money being invested in films. Banks and other institutions, that had been badly hit by a near collapse of the industry before the war, were now scared of dipping their toes in the water once again. Within weeks, by the winter of 1948 a dozen studios were laid empty and the government's original plans, to promote and advance the British film industry, had to be re-examined to see if ways could be found of keeping it alive and afloat.

Once again it was Sir Alexander Korda who would be seen to be saving the day. Using the same charm and persuasion so expertly heaped on the Prudential Assurance Company a decade earlier, Korda praised and wholly supported the government's introduction of the National Film Finance Corporation and promptly secured a loan of around £3 million to finance future production by the British Lion Film Corporation. Korda himself was not a beneficiary. Indeed, the government loan to British Lion via the NFFC accelerated his decision to step down from producing and directing at the time of the post-1948 film industry recovery. During his last seven years –until his death in 1956 – Korda acted as an overseeing executive producer and studios administrator, using his charm until the very end to cajole some of the country's best loved and renowned film makers to switch away from organisations such as Rank and move to British Lion at Shepperton. Among them were Carol Reed, David Lean, the Boulting Brothers – Roy and John – and Laurence Olivier. As Graham Greene once said of Korda: "His human wisdom was always greater than his film wisdom." Borne out perhaps by Korda's own words: "When all my friends and I were young in Hungary, we all dreamed of being poets. And what did we become? We became politicians and advertisement men and film producers."

With these producers came a cinematic golden age for Shepperton. Behind the scenes, Korda was fighting hard to keep his company British Lion solvent, a battle he was to lose before his death. But on the sound stages themselves pure silver-screen magic was now

being conjured up for audiences who wanted films to excite, enthrall and, following the depths of wartime depression, to make them smile.

With around 15 productions made at Shepperton in 1952, it is hard to imagine that while the sound stages continued to overflow with work, the finances of Sir Alexander Korda's British Lion continued to decline. The breakdown of a relationship with the Republic Pictures Corporation of America a few years earlier didn't help the state of the balance sheets. High production losses continued and in 1954 the National Film Finance Corporation decided to call in their £3 million loan. A receiver was appointed and it soon became clear that British Lion's share capital of over £1 million had been lost. A new company, British Lion Films Limited, was immediately set up in January 1955 to take control of the assets of its predecessor. The new company was to oversee film distribution and provide financial guarantees for its independent producers. There was a shake-up at board level. Korda was out. The new board comprised, among others, film-makers Roy and John Boulting – another set of brothers who would soon take charge at the helm of Shepperton Studios.

Sir Alexander Korda died of a heart attack in January 1956. Even though he had lost his company he was heavily involved in film production at the studios until the very end. If he was bitter about the way things had worked out, no one would have known. He bore it all with his usual grace and flamboyance. As the wise showman himself once declared: "Anyone who gets a raw deal in a film studios is no more deserving of pity than someone who gets beaten up in a brothel. A gentleman has no business in either place."

John Boulting and his twin brother Roy were an inseparable director-producer team throughout their careers. Inseparable and interchangeable, to the extent whereby they would alternate on films, one taking on production, the other direction and then swapping for their next feature. Their films became known as simply those of "the Boulting Brothers,"

thinking of them as a whole rather than two separate talents. Together, the Boultings brought biting and hysterical satire to the screen. Their comedies of the late 1950s are renowned for their casting of some of the great comedy acting talents of a generation: Ian Carmichael, Richard Attenborough, Terry-Thomas, Irene Handl, Peter Sellers, and others. The films took swipes at this country's "great" institutions – mocking the Church, the Army, Civil Service and, in the widely-acclaimed and still highly-regarded unions/upper class bashing farce, *I'm Alright Jack* (1959).

It was the Brothers' down-to-earth, tell-it-as-it-is atti-tude that made them attractive to a new board of directors in need of impressive independent film-making talent. It was generally perceived that if the new British Lion was to have a future, it needed people like the Boultings on board to give it a push. Shepperton, and more importantly British Lion, needed their skills and those of the fellow film-making team Frank Launder and Sidney Gilliat not just for their production prowess, but also for their business acumen and knowledge of what had become a very difficult market for both the company and the Studios.

Alexander Korda may have cleverly persuaded the Government to part with vast sums of money in the late 1940s, but there had never been a long term game plan to combat the problems independent film-makers had to try to overcome in order to distribute their films. What is known and already stated is that the NFFC gave Korda a £3 million loan. What was little understood was that, whilst the loan was seen as an encouragement to stimulate independent film production in Britain, there had also been another reason for handing over the cash. The President of the

Back on the road again after ten years, Bob Hope and Bing Crosby reunite – this time in Britain – to make the seventh and last film in their musical comedy series, *The Road to Hong Kong* (1961)

Board of Trade, Harold Wilson, was concerned that the distribution of films – which cinemas showed which films, where and when – was controlled by two big players, Rank and the Associated British Picture Company (ABPC). Rank owned Pinewood Studios and ABPC owned Elstree. They also, between them, controlled the three largest cinema circuits in the country. This meant that they could make and distribute films and ensure that their own films got the best billing at cinemas, giving them more chance of financial success at the box office. Additionally, with the power they could lever through their cinema arms, Rank and ABPC could pick and choose the best films to come in from America to play on their screens. At one stage Universal Pictures and Columbia had tied up attractive distribution deals with Rank, while MGM and Warners had done a similar deal with ABPC.

British Lion and Shepperton felt left out in the cold. For, whilst British Lion may have made and distributed its films and owned Shepperton Studios, it owned no cinema circuits. That meant the showing of its films was at the behest of what some thought – including the Government – were its commercial competitors. Harold Wilson felt that was unfair and hoped a huge cash injection would allow independent film-makers and studios like Shepperton a little more room to grow and to survive as a production and distribution force of its own.

Wilson also introduced a levy – devised by Wilfred Eady at the Treasury – on cinema tickets, to be distributed to film-makers in direct proportion to the popularity of a film. The more bottoms on seats, the more money a producer made, which could then be ploughed back into film-making. At least that was the plan. In fact, for a while this bonus for producers or tax on going to the cinema – whichever way you wanted to look at it – had the interesting effect of increasing the number of films which Hollywood made in Britain.

The government may have had the best of intentions, but these two financial shots in the arm provided only temporary respite for independent producers

and studios. There was still too much power in too few hands. Cinema admissions continued to fall and television fever hit Britain. These were not the best portents for the Boultings and their colleagues to jump on board at British Lion. But if they were nervous, they certainly weren't showing it.

Throughout the late 1950s and into the 1960s, they tried to find ways of keeping the Studios viable. Large budget productions including *The Guns of Navarone* (1960), *The Day of the Triffids* (1961) and *The Day the Earth Caught Fire* (1961), pointed the way to a reversal in Shepperton's financial decline. In time, takings increased and the financial standing of British Lion Films Limited continued to improve. Much of this new success was down to the foresight of David Kingsley, who had been the Managing Director of the Government's NFCC and who had taken over the running of British Lion on the departure of Alexander Korda. No one was better placed to understand the problems that independent film producers were facing and Kingsley was as keen as any film-maker to ensure the future of British Lion and independent production. Indeed such was Kingsley's faith that he persuaded the government to inject a further £600,000 (over £5 million in today's money) into the company. Knowing that this was not nearly enough, Kingsley went to the financial institutions and managed to secure a further £3 million against the assets of the company, which included Shepperton and its film library.

British Lion soldiered on but box office failures still outweighed successes. It was then that Kingsley hit on the idea of bringing producers onto the board. Kingsley was a financial man and not a producer. Why not engage the talents of the film-makers? Put them in charge of their own budgets and make them responsible for taking day-to-day, and often hard, production decisions. Rank or ABPC didn't do it. They allowed accountants and money-men to be the final arbiters over what films were and were not made. Kingsley did the opposite; he invited producers to come on board and promised them a stake in any financial success. He made his motives very clear as

Roy Boulting recounted: "He was, I remember, very frank... he needed people who could guide and advise the board on film-making, the talent to be encouraged, the scripts that should be made into films... Ours had always been a two-man operation. We had fought for, and largely achieved, complete competitive freedom. To what extent would answering to a board inhibit that? So the issue was simple: our freedom, or a battle to help save and promote British Lion as an independent third force in its unequal struggle with the Rank-ABPC cartel. Could we, whose voices had for long been raised in protest – to Parliament, the press, on radio and television – now stand by merely to watch as the combines administered the last rites? The answer was obvious; we phone David Kingsley to say, in effect: 'Let battle commence!'"

Commence it did. Between 1958 and 1961 the fortunes of British Lion were turned around. The company went from being a huge loss-making enterprise to break even, and within two years was actually making money. In 1963, the company announced its fourth year of profit and that it had repaid the most recent loan of £600,000 back to the government. In return the government instructed the NFCC to sell Shepperton. British Lion had become a victim of its own success. Enough money had been lent over the years and now seemed as good a time as any to quit while they were, if not exactly ahead, then certainly in a better position than before.

The sale wasn't all bad news for the five executive directors, who saw their own shares bought out at a vastly higher rate than they originally paid for them. The Boultings, Launder & Gilliat and David Kingsley received almost £160,000 each (around £1.5 million in today's money) for shares for which they had paid £1,800 (the equivalent today of around £22,000) less than six years previously.

Several groups expressed an interest in buying the Studios, some from within the industry and others from outside who saw it as a potential long term investment. But the Board of Trade stipulated that there was to be no benefit of future tax relief available, until such time as the government had been paid back the £2 million that was still outstanding from previous loans. That whittled the interested parties down to just two, and finally on 31 March 1964 British Lion was sold to a consortium headed by former director and chief of production at Ealing Studios, Sir Michael Balcon.

The uncertainty over the future of Shepperton took its toll on earnings and as Balcon took over, profits dropped 80 per cent. David Kingsley and Roy Boulting resigned from the board. Whether or not they resigned because of falling profits or out of protest at being taken over is difficult to know. Certainly the British film industry as a whole seems to have been opposed to the sale. Putting Shepperton back into the bear pit of private industry was regarded by independent film-makers as a huge retrograde step. Whatever the motive behind Kingsley and Boulting's decision, they weren't the last to go. Profits continued to drop and in September 1965, Balcon himself stood down from the board.

The financial ups and downs that had plagued Shepperton from its founding days, did little to stop the continuing impetus of fresh, new, independent talent. Increased demand for filming space brought two new stages to Shepperton and few could have anticipated the slump which was to follow in the next decade. For now, Shepperton was on a roll. An increase in British Lion's profits was announced in 1967. John Boulting, who had stayed on the Board was now managing director and things appeared to be going very well. Yet, within a very short space of time what had been thought of as a healthy trading situation had turned around 180 degrees. The number of new films being distributed started to decline from a healthy 27 in 1969 to just seven in 1971. By 1979, this figure had dropped to just two films made at Shepperton that year. This catastrophic fall was less about Shepperton's facilities or the running of the studios and more to do with lack of investment incentives being offered by the government and the increasingly parlous state of the world economy. The 1970s were plagued by strikes, fuel shortages and power cuts.

The advent of colour television didn't help matters; audiences stayed at home in great numbers to watch their favourite programmes, on the small screen.

Once again Shepperton changed hands. The board of British Lion had no choice but to accept an offer by financier John Bentley who, along with Barclay Securities, took over the company in April 1972. The board were unhappy that the move had been forced upon them but were more than aware that plummeting stage rentals left a huge hole in the company's finances, which was unlikely to be filled. Selling up was the only way to try and keep the studios alive. It also meant that the directors would not leave empty-handed. Waiting for an upturn in the industry was likely to have meant that they could have walked away penniless. The name of the new overseeing company was Lion International.

Within weeks, Bentley appeared to be ringing the death knell for Shepperton. The man who had built up a reputation for asset-stripping – taking over a company at a low price and then selling off assets piecemeal – seemed to be studying the component parts that were British Lion far too closely for the industry's liking. Bentley identified that British Lion comprised a production and distribution company, a film library (though much of that had been sold to the BBC in 1968), an advertising company, a property company, and a studio-owning company. Bentley's own estimates were that separately these assets were worth £20 million; Barclay Securities had just paid £5.5 million for the whole lot. In an interview for *Cinema TV Today* in May 1972, Bentley said: "At the moment we have a programme of films at Shepperton until September, with John Boulting in charge, and no changes will be made until then. It has been suggested that Shepperton could occupy less space than it does. That is one hypothesis. Another hypothesis is, why should Shepperton not be merged with Pinewood? We have 400 people at Shepperton earning high salaries and not being used throughout the year. Pinewood has the better studios but Shepperton has excellent equipment and it could be that the men and equipment could be moved there."

The suggestion was preposterous and it soon became clear that Bentley wanted Shepperton shut and the land used for housing development. British Lion's accounts for the year ended 31 March 1972 showed the value of the Studios as being around £1.7 million. As housing development land it was calculated that the value would be nearer £3.5 million. With Shepperton said to be losing £12,000 a week, Bentley was keen to make the argument for a quick sell off.

For once the British film industry pulled together. It was not prepared to see an important part of itself threatened by an outsider intent on destroying its heritage just to realise a profit on a short-term investment. After all, if this could happen to British Lion and Shepperton, who might be next at this difficult time? Representations were made to the Department of Trade and Industry and the NFFC. Not persuaded by the arguments put forward by Bentley that the studios had little viability, the NFFC reported to the DTI that it believed the Studios could be run, through time, without making a loss. A stalemate was reached. The NFFC's findings ensured that there could be no selling of the studios' property. At the same time it had no power to prevent owners Barclay Securities from just closing the whole place down, which it was threatening to do. A compromise needed to be found.

Eventually, after a series of high-level meetings, a compromise was proposed in November 1972. The plan was to reduce the size of the studios from 60 acres to around 15 acres. Stages "A", "B", "C" and "D" would stay and there would be workshops, a dubbing theatre and an area for a backlot. Permission would be requested to allow the building of some new offices to service the studios and a selection of other ancillary services deemed necessary by the industry. That would take up another five acres, which left 40 acres for the owners to dispose of for their own purposes. The "new" studios would be covered by a detailed covenant to prevent any further threat to its survival. The plans went out to consultation to all the interested parties.

While the consultation was taking place, films continued to be made and ironically, after an appalling year in 1971, some 18 films went into production at Shepperton during 1972 – the second highest number at the site since the war. Critics of both the new company and the new plans for the site pointed to these figures and questioned why there were such prophecies of financial doom and gloom and threats of imminent closure for Shepperton.

Rumours as to the future of the studios continued to abound. Speculation grew that the BBC would buy the site when it vacated Ealing Studios in 1973. Eventually, agreement was reached for a 20-acre studios which kept stages "E", "F" and "G" but meant the selling off of the backlot. Bentley also guaranteed a voluntary redundancy scheme for staff and three-year job protection for those who wished to continue at work. Ironically, Barclay Securities agreed in principle to these plans even though they themselves had been taken over by another financial group, Vavasseur and Co, two weeks earlier. Just as one campaign looked like it had been won, another needed to be fought. Indeed it took until November of 1973 before an agreement over the studios was finally reached, in which Shepperton would now keep eight stages on a 22 acre-site and with no redundancies. Everyone seemed happy.

As if in direct contrast to the huge sigh of relief across the industry, production levels at Shepperton plummeted again. The upsurge of 1972 ran out of steam, with only six films being made at the Studios in 1973.

In these circumstances, getting money in was all important and a huge clearout of equipment and props (amounting to 3,000 lots) was auctioned over five days in September 1974. Film fans, historians and industry workers were angered as great swathes of British cinema heritage went under the hammer for knock-down prices. A Surrey man paid £55 for a Triffid and some lucky person got Oliver's begging bowl for the just £28.

Slowly, the omens for the studios began to look better. Lion International sold its interest in the studios to a company backed by five banks and controlled by the managing directors of British Lion films. This meant that British Lion was once again an independent film-making company and even if Shepperton was not as busy and thriving as it had been once, it was still very much alive, although production remained low – with just three films in 1976 and a few more in 1977.

In the early 1980s the studios were being run by Mills and Allen International – the new name for Lion International – which had bought the majority shareholding in Shepperton back in 1975. Some excellent films were produced at the studios in this period; nevertheless, Mills and Allen decided that it wanted to relinquish its hold over Shepperton and it was generally agreed that the Lee Group would be the ideal company to take over. The Lee Group (two brothers, John and Benny) hired out lighting equipment to the makers of commercials and documentaries, a flourishing business that had strong links with the Studios. John Lee remembers: "We knew Shepperton was going through a bad time and we asked if we could buy it. We offered £4 million and our offer was accepted. The Studios needed lots of work. But the deal wasn't that easy. The rock group, The Who, owned the old mansion house, and the old "H" stage was owned by the Council who had bought it in the 1970s for housing development. We negotiated a price for The Who to get out of the mansion house – I think it was around £500,000 – and then we negotiated with the council to buy back "H" stage before they had time to knock it down and develop on it. I think we paid the Council £1 million for that though we didn't get that deal finally done until 1987."

With the purchase of Shepperton Studios in 1984, the Lees found themselves owning more sound stages in Britain than either of their two main competitors, Pinewood and Elstree. The company immediately set about giving the studios a much needed facelift as Gary Stone, who had moved with the Lees across to Shepperton, recalls: "Lee Lighting and Lee International Studios had a great reputation. They gave everything. They painted the studios from top to bottom and redecorated the whole place. The Lees reputation encouraged commercials and film to

Above

Ron and Benny Lee meeting Prince Charles with Shepperton M.D. Dennis Carrigan far left.

come in and use the facilities. The idea was to spend £15 million on Shepperton to upgrade it."

What the Lees had identified very early on, was that owning studios by themselves was unlikely to make money but if the studio owner was able to oblige incoming tenants and production companies to lease the in-house facilities then profits could be made.

Sadly, a mixture of the stock market crash on "Black Monday" in October 1987, an American scriptwriters strike in 1988, and accusations that a senior employee in Lee International had been "fiddling the books," saw John and Benny Lee lose control over their empire. Investment bankers Warburg-Pincus stepped in to take over their companies for $60 million. The Lees were devastated and John Lee is still very sad at the way things turned out: "If you ask 'did we make any money at Shepperton?' I'll tell you, 'yes'. Why did we get out? We had no choice. We were fiddled out of our money. And the company had to go. The Americans took it over. It wasn't what we wanted. But we had no choice."

At the end of the 1980s there was a huge increase in the amount of television programmes and commercials being produced at Shepperton in place of film. Gary Stone, who became the studio manager in 1989, points out: "There was a huge commercials industry in this country. It was 80 per cent of our stage rental income but we still had a great reputation and a lot of loyalty, and we slowly but surely started to hit our targets."

Five films were made at Shepperton during 1990, and at the same time no less than nine television series. Although many in the industry felt uncomfortable with a studio being run by a bank, clients remained loyal and production continued.

By the time 1995 arrived, the studios were buoyant once again. Question marks over the future of the studios appeared to be subsiding. Then, in February that year, news came that a consortium led by British film directors and long term tenants at Shepperton,

Ridley and Tony Scott, had bought the Studios. Fears for the future evaporated completely. Suddenly, Shepperton was in the hands of two highly respected and, more importantly, successful film industry players. This fourth set of brothers to own and run Shepperton promised that there would be major investment in the studios. Ridley Scott is the first to admit that the foundations for the future survival of the studios had been firmly laid in place by the hard work of the Lee brothers back in the 1980s: "The Lee Brothers had done a great job of face-lifting the Studios in the years before us coming in. We wanted to carry that hard work forward. One thing we tried to introduce was an apprenticeship scheme – not for writers or directors – but for craftsmen, plasterers, and all the trade skills and artisans of the film industry."

"Buying Shepperton was the right thing to do for me and Tony. I had been making commercials there since the 1960s. The studios had been kind to me. It was almost like pay back time." And pay back they did, as Gary Stone recalls: "They were true to their word. There was at least £15 million investment in the studios after the Scotts took over; new dubbing theatres, "J" & "K" sound stages built, new offices, wardrobe departments, and general facilities. The Studios bought a backlot of 22 acres of field land for £1 million. The roads around the studios were upgraded. The cafeteria was refurbished. There was big investment. It was very exciting. People were delighted that Ridley and Tony were running it – people from the industry rather than a bank."

With 10 features made at Shepperton in 1999 and a further 14 in 2000, as well as the continuous production of commercials and television films and series, it felt that Shepperton's resurgence and resurrection was complete. Production companies who had had happy experiences working at the studios were returning to make sequels.

Almost five years to the day after Ridley and Tony Scott took over, the announcement came that Shepperton was to merge with what had been, up to

that point, its biggest commercial competitor in the British film industry, Pinewood Studios. Two years before, Pinewood itself had been bought out from its owners Rank by a consortium led by Ivan Dunleavy, Michael Grade and venture capitalists, 3I. Like Shepperton, Pinewood had experienced great peaks and troughs as the industry gained and suffered from cyclical highs and lows. In the early 1990s there was a time when Pinewood had no films at all. For Pinewood's new owners and its managing director Steve Jaggs, it seemed only logical to seek to merge with its biggest competitor. Steve Jaggs explains: "When Michael Grade and Ivan Dunleavy came into the business at Pinewood, one of the first things we discussed was how to grow our television production arm. We then set about looking at other opportunities to expand and within one year we had bought Shepperton. We realised that if we had Shepperton as well as Pinewood we would have 36 stages and that by managing the estate properly we could take in at least one extra film than the two could separately. For example, a production may have wanted five stages, and there were three empty at Pinewood and three empty at Shepperton. So neither of us could take the film. By merging, and with good management, we can now get that feature in. That's one more film made in Britain, which has to be good for this country's industry."

The merger had its critics. Life-long supporters of Shepperton were concerned that the studios would lose its reputation of being a haven for independent film production and that the two entities that were Pinewood and Shepperton could not easily be mixed. The new management were quick to act to assuage those fears, admitting that each studio, though part of the same company, could have its own style while sharing the same ethos. Steve Jaggs has never pretended that one size fits all: "Studios will always feel different because they are set out differently but it is the way we treat our clients that matters. We've put some stability and continuity into Shepperton. The client can see what we're doing, where we're going with both studios. More stages at Pinewood and Shepperton. We are a studio group now that has 36 stages. That's a big studio compared to anywhere in the world. There's comfort in that. Shepperton's future is more secure than it ever has been. It has seen many owners. I think we've got it right because we have both studios."

Film industry big hitters now seem happy to give the merger the thumbs up. Tim Bevan of Working Title believes that Pinewood Shepperton augurs well for the British film industry: "The merger of Pinewood and Shepperton has probably helped our industry. The fact that the two are working in sync and that you can cross-schedule big films now and that there is no competition between the two of them is a good thing. We've not yet made a movie where we need to use both studios, but I'm sure that time will come." Veteran director and long-time campaigner for the British film industry, Richard Attenborough, agrees: "I think the merger has been very good. This industry is dependent to a certain extent on what is fashionable. Movies go through fashions, depending on what people want to go and see. So there is always the possibility that there will be a fallow period for our industry. I believe that if you can juggle productions and films between the two studios where say one has too much space and one doesn't have enough at any given time, then that works very well for everyone concerned."

Some forty years after he first ventured through Shepperton's gates, Ridley Scott feels that the future of the studios is more secure now than at any time in its history as Sir Ridley Scott said in the introduction of this book: "There was a time, not so long ago, when people thought that big studios would become dinosaurs, particularly because of the advances in computer-generated imagery. Yet, in recent years there has been a resurrection of the valuation of the traditional methods of building a set for most films and so you need stages. I've always believed that was the case. I went into Shepperton with the thought that this isn't going away. The combination of the value of Pinewood and Shepperton together is huge. The merger could not have made the studios any stronger. Just look at a map of Europe and ask yourself where is there anywhere else like it."

Opposite
Studio set for, *Bonnie Prince Charlie* (1947)

Right
A modern studio set showing Stewart Craig –
Production Designer, on the set of, *Notting Hill* (1998)

Enthusiasm such as that has kept Shepperton alive at times when it seemed that it had no chance of survival. Impending threats of asset-stripping, sell-offs and housing development have hung over it for most of its 75-year history. Finally though, Shepperton seems to be facing a stronger, healthier and more positive future. And while this book happily celebrates Shepperton's illustrious and proud past, it is to the future that all lovers of the industry must look to ensure that these issues do not threaten its survival again. This belief, shared across the British film industry, is summed up by Shepperton's new owners. Steve Jaggs is planning for Shepperton's long-term success: "We must never forget our history and the track record of all the great films that have been made at Shepperton over the past 75 years. However the future is just as important as the past. This industry will still be going in the decades ahead. People will still want to be entertained with the moving image. The next 75 years are as important as the ones that have gone. I may be dead and buried by then. But I know that Shepperton will still be here."

Left
Aerial view of Shepperton
Studios

George Frost
Make-Up

Humphrey Bogart, Katherine Hepburn, Errol Flynn, Orson Welles, Ava Gardner, Richard Burton, Gregory Peck, Vivien Leigh, John Hurt, Jane Fonda, Sean Connery, James Mason, Paul Newman, Vanessa Redgrave are just some of the great names who have sat in "my chair" over a career spanning 50 years.

We were commonly known as powder monkeys and were a necessary evil of the film business, not unlike soundmen! I arrived at Shepperton in 1946 at the time when the Kordas controlled the studios. I started as a trainee in the make-up department at £5 a week. I was 24. I don't know why I ended up in this department, it just seemed the right thing to do. I was on trial for three months.

Opposite
George Frost with Gregory Peck, during the making of *The Guns of Navarone* (1960)

My first film was called *A Man About the House* (1947), directed by Leslie Arlis and starring Dulcie Gray. I worked on the crowd scenes and using a sponge and some brownish-black make up, had to make the crowd look dirty. Luckily I was part of a team and having been thrown in at the deep end, I copied what the others were doing and was given regular training sessions "off set" which allowed me to gain useful experience. I went on to *An Ideal Husband* in 1947 and *Bonnie Prince Charlie* in 1948 as an assistant.

In 1949 I was to get my break and be put in charge of make-up on *The Third Man*. It's rewarding to think that after all this time, *The Third Man* has become such a classic, and indeed a top ten favourite of many people. Those were heady days and I just happened to be in the right place at the right time.

I knew Jack Cardiff reasonably well when putting a crew together for *The African Queen*. We spent three months in the Congo, an experience that I think was to set me up for life in the film world. No matter how tough conditions might be on future films, they would not exceed what we went through making that film.

I was never phased by stardom and having worked with many of the major names it is perhaps just as well. For some it could be very daunting to enter a room where a big name actor would be waiting to be made up (quite often it was the other way around) but I think they appreciated the fact that I was not in awe of them and that I treated them like anyone else.

One of my most enjoyable tasks was working on the film *Oliver!* with Ron Moody. At the end of the shoot he gave me a wallet as a present. However there was one proviso, "that I should give it back when it was full!"

I worked in the film business for 50 years, and I completed over 100 productions. Luckily for me some were amongst the most successful films ever made and many were Shepperton-based.

I have seen many changes, none more so than the studio dress code. Group photos 50 years ago were all suits and ties. How things have changed.

Pat Eustace

Stand-in

My film career began in 1947 at Walton-on-Thames studios. My mother secured a place for me as a film extra on *The First Gentleman*, starring Cecil Parker, Athene Seyler and Margaretta Scott. It was strange that I should have begun my career at Walton as it was there that my mother had begun hers, back in the days of silent film. My mother would be taken out of school by Cecil Hepworth to work with such stars as Chrissy White and Alma Taylor.

Although working as a film extra may sound glamorous, it had more than its fair share of unglamorous moments. Hours could be spent out in the freezing cold or queuing for make-up and hairdressing, in addition to many very early starts. You had to be prepared to to anything, at pretty much anytime. Film extras belonged to a union, Film Artists Association, and to an agent. Your agent would categorise

Opposite
Cast and crew of *Britannia Mews*, made at Shepperton in 1949. Pat is sitting in the front row, first from the left

you according to height, age, colouring, whether you could dance, play a musical instrument, drive a car, ride a horse, speak a foreign language, whether your wardrobe was smart casual or rough. This information was essential for an agent so that when you called each day, he could tell you whether there had been a request for film extras that matched your particular categories.

It was during the very first experience of being a film extra in *The First Gentleman* that I was fortunate enough to be chosen to be Margaretta Scott's stand-in. The job of stand-in was to be on the set to watch the artist rehearse a scene with the director and lighting cameraman. When they were satisfied, the artist would leave the set (for the hairdressing and make-up departments) and be replaced on set by the stand-in, wearing identical outfits worn by the artist. The scene would be repeated, during which the lighting and camera positions would be set. This could take several hours, depending on the duration of the scene.

The next memorable stand-in role I had was with Maureen O'Hara. I had been working at Shepperton Studios as a film

extra in the Herbert Wilcox film, *Elizabeth of Ladymead* (1948).
As the production was nearing its end the next one, *Britannia
Mews* (1949), starring Maureen O'Hara was being set up. The
first assistant from the crew, Guy Hamilton (who went on to
direct five Bond films, including *Goldfinger* (1964)) introduced
me to the lighting cameraman, George Perinaux and it was
agreed that I would make a suitable stand-in for Miss O'Hara.
I did not have beautiful red hair, alas, and had to resort to a
wig!

I was to make many films at Shepperton and have now lived
close to the studios for over forty years. I was also a stand-in
for Ingrid Bergman on *Murder on the Orient Express* and
appeared in a varied list of films throughout my career,
including *Moulin Rouge* (1953), *Mahler* (1974), *Carry on Henry*
(1970) and Ken Russell's *The Devils* (1971).

Early
Classics

"In Italy for thirty years under the Borgias, they had warfare, terror, murder, bloodshed, and they produced Michaelangelo, Leonardo da Vinci, and the Renaissance. In Switzerland they had brotherly love, five hundred years of democracy and peace, and what did they produce? The cuckoo clock."

Harry Lime in *The Third Man*

The word "classic" is used a lot when it comes to films, even though very few films actually turn out to be classics. The dictionary defines the word "classic" as meaning: being "of the highest class especially in art or literature," "serving as a model of its kind; definitive," and "of lasting interest or significance." These definitions prove helpful if only to justify why, among the hundreds of films made at Shepperton in its first twenty-five years, very few are regarded as genuine classics, with one or two on this very short list barely remembered, if at all.

Shepperton's early cinematic output was riddled by the quota quickies, which sought to keep the UK film industry afloat by legally dictating the amount of cinema product that had to be made and shown in which there was British involvement. For studio owners like Shepperton's Norman Loudon, this law proved most equitable. For budding film-makers it proved equally as useful as they were forced to learn and hone their craft quickly and within very tight financial and timing constraints. One such director was Christian Scientist, John Baxter. Baxter was to become renowned for producing and directing rough-and-ready dramas and comedies in the 1930s and 1940s, which paved the way to the new wave of gritty realism that hit screens at the end of the 1950s.

Born in 1896, Baxter was the associate director on the very first feature made at Shepperton's Sound City in 1932, *Reunion*. He immediately went on to directing his own films and the next year made what is regarded as an early classic of British cinema, *Doss House*. The story follows a group of characters who take refuge for the night in London lodgings. Baxter had wanted to make the documentary-style film for some time and in a letter to Sound City boss, Norman Loudon, in December 1932 declared: "I feel sure you will appreciate its tremendous possibilities, not so much from story value, but as a chapter from life. There is no need whatever to dwell on the squalor and lousiness of a doss house as I am told that most of them are under strict London County Council inspection."

From the outset, the media found the subject unusual, not at all what they had come to expect from film-makers. Many were surprised that such a subject would even be considered as suitable material to attract a cinema-going audience wanting an evening of fun, with the latest Jimmy Cagney crime thriller or Laurel and Hardy comedy vying for their attention. Just days before the film went into production, Baxter toured some of London's doss houses with a reporter from the *Evening Standard*, Ernest Betts, in tow. In a piece on 27 March 1933, Betts wrote: "Down below there was an interesting collection of doss-house types. A man in a bowler hat, with a stub pipe, was reading a thriller at the table. Some were playing cards. There were very old men, still and thoughtful, and young bods in caps and pullovers reading the betting news. Mr Baxter viewed this new kind of glamour with pleasure. I could see the camera angles racing in his mind."

Opposite
On the set of *Doss House* (1933) directed by John Baxter

The phrase "unsung saga of courage and efficiency" could as equally have been referring to the film's production. Originally titled Bosambo, Sanders was based at Worton Hall studios in Isleworth, west London. Sound City's proximity to the river made it an ideal location at which to construct a village, alongside the waters, to double as its African counterpart.

Doss House had the most extraordinary of London releases. Distributor Metro-Goldwyn-Mayer considered the film to be just another quota quickie and treated it as such, using it as a support feature to a new Laurel and Hardy two-reeler. Critics and audiences though, immediately took to the drama. Left-wing documentary maker and union activist Ralph Bond wrote in September 1933: "*Doss House* almost marks a revolution in British film production. We had difficulty in believing our eyes... When do they turn on the sex appeal, we asked ourselves. But there was no sex appeal, not even a single woman, and no cabaret. Instead we had a poignant character study of some of London's down-and-outs who are permitted by a generous society to take shelter in the night provided they can raise the sum of ninepence."

Doss House is generally regarded as a classic film if not for its production values which with the limited budget available and the short time in which it had to be made, are not as high as many first features of the time. Yet for the manner in which Baxter pursued the subject, honestly attempting to portray life out on the streets of the capital in the early 1930s, it does, fulfil the definition of a classic – that of "serving as a model of its kind; definitive," and "of lasting interest or significance."

Sound City saw around 90 films made at its studios in Shepperton, between its opening at the beginning of the 1930s and the outbreak of World War II – which all but halted production until 1946. Besides *Doss House*, the only other pre-war film which could be regarded a classic would be the 1934 production *Sanders of the River*. Starring Leslie Banks and Paul Robeson the film tells the story of the problems experienced by a British colonial officer with the local tribes in Africa. Made by London Films, it was an ambitious project headed by Hungarian producers and brothers, Alexander, Zoltan and Vincent Korda.

Sanders of the River used its opening credits to play up the excitement awaiting the audiences who had queued to come and watch the film: "Africa... Tens of millions of natives under British rule, each tribe with

its own chieftain, governed and protected by a handful of white men whose everyday work is an unsung saga of courage and efficiency. One of them is Commissioner Sanders."

The phrase "unsung saga of courage and efficiency" could as equally have been referring to the film's production. Originally titled *Bosambo*, *Sanders* was based at Worton Hall studios in Isleworth, west London. Sound City's proximity to the river made it an ideal location at which to construct a village, alongside the waters, to double as its African counterpart. Cast and crew spent six months at Sound City. Some 300 black extras were brought in to play the "natives" and an encampment was built to house them in tents in what is now the car park at the back of the Mansion House that adjoins the river. It was not reasonable to expect the extras to sleep out in tents for the many months that sequences were being shot at Sound City, so the extras were regularly bussed between Shepperton and a more permanent housing base many miles away, in Cardiff's Tiger Bay area.

The film was a great success, thanks in no small part to the personality of the popular African American actor and singer Paul Robeson, as the escaped convict Bosambo. His singing of the "native" chants made him a favourite of audiences and music hall impressionists, who spent many years afterwards mimicking Robeson in their acts.

Sanders of the River although dated still holds up as an historical document of the perception of British rule in Africa. At the time, *Variety* declared: "It will interest those who are sincerely interested in the cinema as an art form, but it will suffer the hazards of all pioneers."

Acclaimed cinema pioneer, director Carol Reed, once told James Mason: "Making a film is like going down a film mine for eight weeks." In the case of Reed's *The Third Man*, one could easily be forgiven for replacing the word "mine" with "sewer." Certainly, most of the actors involved in the underground filming in Vienna found the weeks of location work during the bleak

Austrian autumn and winter of 1948 equally as horrible as two months in Reed's hypothetical hell.

The Third Man is still rated as one of the top films of all time. It is a classic of the thriller genre and has been often imitated though never bettered. The film is set in post-World War II Vienna and tells the story of a novelist, Holly Martins (Joseph Cotten), who discovers that his friend, Harry Lime (Orson Welles), whom he believed to be dead, is still very much alive and is running a drugs racket in the city. Martins teams up with a British army officer, Major Calloway (Trevor Howard), to capture Lime, much to the distress and angst of Harry's lover, Anna Schmidt (Alida Valli).

Following the war, Alexander Korda had continually expressed great interest in making a film in Vienna but was short on ideas for a suitable story. Korda approached writer Graham Greene – with whom he had already successfully worked on two earlier projects. Greene scribbled down a few lines on the back of an envelope which he read to Korda: "I had paid my last farewell to Harry a week ago, when his coffin was lowered into the frozen February ground, so that it was with incredulity that I saw him pass by, without a sign of recognition, among the host of strangers in the Strand." Korda was entranced by this kernel of a plot and immediately dispatched Greene to Austria in search of further ideas and inspiration. Greene remained uninspired until, by chance, he found himself in the company of a British intelligence officer who recounted the problems that were being experienced with illicit trading in penicillin, and the patrolling of the city's sewer systems by the police. It was the breakthrough that Greene and Korda needed. Greene's screenplay was soon ready, though director Carol Reed was to make many changes during filming. Originally Alida Valli is kidnapped by the Russian police. Reed replaced that scene with one of her slowly walking past Joseph Cotten and away from the cemetery, accompanied by the haunting zither music of Anton Karas. Reed had stumbled across Karas performing in a Viennese café just days before filming began. Many critics insist that the *The Third Man* would not have become the classic that it is without the

Above

Nina Mae McKinney (Lilongo) and Paul Robeson (Bosambo) in the early Shepperton classic, *Sanders of the River* (1934)

Opposite

Shepperton studios doubling up for colonial Nigeria, for the filming of *Sanders of the River* (1934)

melodies created by Karas. Korda must therefore have been very pleased that he was able to snap up the rights to the music for just £300.

The use of a cat to introduce Harry Lime in the shadows was devised by director Carol Reed. Three different cats had to be "employed" for shooting the scene and the only way they could be persuaded to brush against Lime was by spreading sardine oil on Orson Welles' trousers. Welles was not happy, but then he hadn't been happy from the moment he arrived in Austria. The actor was a great admirer of Carol Reed and initially had welcomed the role of Harry Lime. Also, by his own admission, Welles needed the money that the role would earn him as he prepared to fund his own production of *Othello*. At the last minute, he panicked. He thought the part of Harry Lime was too small for him and would damage his reputation as a lead actor. On the day he was due to film his first scene, Welles turned up on set and announced that he was pulling out. It took Reed's huge powers of persuasion to coax him back. For the rest of the time that Welles worked on the *The Third Man*, he divided his time equally between moaning about the cold and depressing conditions he was having to film in, and offering advice to Reed and cinematographer Robert Krasker on the best angles to shoot or the lighting of a particular scene. Reed was in some awe of Welles' performing abilities and was happy to listen and occasionally use the actor's ideas. One such brainwave was to allow Harry Lime to speak the following lines, which at the time Graham Greene thought Welles himself had written, but which actually came from a long-forgotten Hungarian play: "In Italy for thirty years under the Borgias, they had warfare, terror, murder, bloodshed, and they produced Michaelangelo, Leonardo da Vinci, and the Renaissance. In Switzerland they had brotherly love, five hundred years of democracy and peace, and what did they produce? The cuckoo clock." Brilliant, even if cuckoo clocks originate from Germany.

Shooting of *The Third Man* ended in Vienna in early December 1948. Filming at Shepperton started a few weeks later in January 1949. The studio sets were

designed by Alexander Korda's brother, Vincent who, with backdrop painter Ferdinand Bellan, recreated the Vienna cemetery and the infamous Ferris wheel ride's cabin interior. Due to Welles' behaviour on location in the real Austrian sewers, Reed didn't have all the material that he needed. This meant that in addition to the sets already constructed, a set identical to the Austrian sewer they had filmed in weeks before, also had to be reproduced at Shepperton for scenes to be extended or re-shot. Cast members were brought in to shoot the interior scenes and additional sequences. These cast members included various Austrian actors who had originally been contracted only to work in their homeland and who were now having to be flown to England to work on scenes which would have been completed on location, had Welles not forced the production to stop. On set, Welles, who was having an unhappy time in his private life, had an even shorter temper than usual. He exploded when Lady Clarissa Churchill, wife of Sir Anthony Eden, visited the sound stage with some of her debutante friends. Laughing, giggling and failing to observe the cardinal rules of silence on set while filming, their behaviour caused Welles to freeze in the middle of a scene. He demanded that they be escorted off the set immediately and in so doing caused upset both to the Edens and Winston Churchill.

The Third Man received its London premiere on 2 September 1949. The rest is history, though very few people know that the film was almost history before ever being released. While being edited during the summer of 1949, a fire broke out in the cutting rooms at Shepperton that destroyed seven out of the twelve edited reels. Carol Reed set about repairing the loss by bringing in a second editing team to help reconstruct the film using only the sound track as their guide.

Shepperton's next early classic, *The African Queen*, was first identified as potential cinema material in 1938. An adaptation of the C S Forester novel was on the cards after Warner Bros bought the rights to the story. At the time, Bette Davis and David Niven were said by some to be in the frame for the lead roles of the prim missionary Rose Sayer, and gin-drinking

Opposite

The Third Man, co-stars Joseph Cotten (left) and Orson Welles (right) share a joke during the making of the film

Above

Orson Welles as Harry Lime in *The Third Man*

Bottom right

The replica sewers built at Shepperton Studios

river trader Charlie Allnut, thrown together for a dangerous boat trip in Africa in 1915. With the onset of the World War II, the film was shelved. The project resurfaced in 1947 but it took some time to get the film off the ground. Several stars turned down the roles – further delaying the production – including Charles Laughton and Elsa Lanchester, the aforementioned Bette Davis and David Niven, and John Mills and Deborah Kerr. The roles of the "psalm-singing skinny old maid" and the "wretched, sleazy, absurd, brave little man" were finally accepted by Katherine Hepburn and Humphrey Bogart. By now it was 1951, and a British production company Romulus Films, run by brothers John and James Woolf, had teamed up with the American production company Horizon, run by Sam Spiegel, to finally get the film made. It was Romulus who signed up Hepburn, Bogart, Spiegel and the film's director, John Huston. The project was a huge gamble for Romulus, as Sir John Woolf recalls: "Alexander Korda, who had been an old friend of my father's, warned me against a film about two old people going up and down a river in Africa, with a director whose last film was a disaster. If it had failed it would probably have been the end of Romulus." Korda, was perhaps being a little unfair to the American director. Huston was something of an eccentric who had made his name by writing hard-hitting thrillers and melodramas in the 1930s, before branching out to direction of such classics as *The Maltese Falcon* in 1941 and *The Treasure of Sierre Madre* in 1948 – both of which starred Humphrey Bogart.

Before the film arrived at Shepperton for the studios-based shooting, the cast and crew first had to spend many weeks in Africa. Huston had travelled some 25,000 miles across the continent before he was satisfied that he had found the right location – a 1,000-mile stretch of the Congo near Ruiki. Conditions out on location were not easy. Filming was regularly disrupted by, among other things, herds of charging elephants, crocodiles, and infestations of soldier ants. Many of the crew, including cinematographer Jack Cardiff, fell ill. Some caught malaria. Hepburn herself became terribly sick, as she remembers: "I lost 20 pounds and I was thin to begin with. It was weird. The

doctor on the boat was totally confused. He had analyzed the water tank – it was OK. Finally he put everyone on bottled water. Still disaster. Finally, we lost so many of the crew that they said to me, 'For God's sake, lie down. We're insured if you're sick.'" Ironically Huston and Bogart seemed to escape the malaise, thanks, it is claimed, to their preference for alcohol rather than polluted bottled water.

It was with some relief then, that the cast and crew finally decamped to England. Shooting was divided between small studios at Isleworth and the larger Shepperton, whose adjoining river was cleverly decorated to allow it to double for the same African river that the cast and crew had been filming on and in, just days before. While most of the film was recorded in Africa there was a handful of crucial scenes that were just too dangerous to attempt in the black, infested waters of the Congo. One was a scene where Bogart and Hepburn had to swim underwater to fix the African Queen's broken propeller. Another, saw the pair having to wade through the water dragging the African Queen through the reeds. The scene which Bogart disliked filming the most was the one where his body is covered in leeches, as Katherine Hepburn recalls: "They brought in some real leeches – poor Bogie. They are really repellent. A glass full of slimy things. 'What's the matter, Bogie – you scared of a leech? Try one,' I said. 'You try it first, kid.' Well, ugh, I just couldn't. They are revolting. And he had to be covered with them." Bogart was understandably concerned about being hurt by the live leeches. The Shepperton art and props department spent a considerable amount of time trying to find a material that they could use which would look like leeches and that would adhere to Bogart's skin in the same way. They eventually succeeded. Bogart was much relieved when out of the many leeches that were 'attached' to his body in that particular sequence, only two of them were real.

Ever the practical joker, director John Huston decided to get his own back on Bogart's cowardice. This he did during the filming of a scene where the actor had to sit under a blanket while torrential rain flooded in

through the roof of the boat. Huston scheduled the scene for shooting just a few minutes before the one o'clock lunch call. The actors got into their places. Bogart was ensconced under the blanket beneath the split canvass roof of the African Queen. The camera was positioned for a close up shot and the rain machine was turned on. And it was left on. The film's cinematographer Jack Cardiff was there: "Huston made gestures to us all. Instead of saying 'Cut,' we all quietly left the studio. When Bogie realised, he was furious, he was screaming all the things he'd do to us. Eventually, he got the joke."

Filming at Shepperton was a far happier and easier experience than it had been for the cast and crew who had struggled with the harshest of elements in Africa. Jack Cardiff has no regrets: "Every time I see the film, I wince at the recollection of our sufferings, but I still marvel at John Huston's magical touches as a director and the truly perfect performances of Katie and Bogie. I know whatever the painful difficulties were, it was well worth it." It was certainly worth it for Humphrey Bogart who won a Best Actor Oscar® the only one in his long and much-admired career.

It was originally Alexander Korda who had suggested to David Lean that he consider producing an adaptation of Harold Brighouse's 1915 stage comedy, *Hobson's Choice*, for the big screen. The play had been filmed twice before, in 1920 and 1931. David Lean had established his career under the tutelage of Rank at Pinewood Studios. He had cut his directorial teeth co-directing, alongside Noel Coward, in *In Which We Serve* in 1942 and in his own productions of, among others, *Great Expectations* in 1946 and *Oliver Twist* in 1948. Following two less successful outings with *The Passionate Friends* and *Madeleine* at the end of the 1940s, Alexander Korda had not found it too difficult to persuade Lean to switch studios.

Lean never rushed a production, and his eye for meticulous detail of character and set were essential for his own success and the success of his films. Indeed, following his move from Pinewood to Shepperton, it took

Above
Katherine Hepburn in *The African Queen* (1952)

Right
Humphrey Bogart in *The African Queen* (1952)

Opposite
Director John Huston (right) with cinematographer Jack Cardiff on set of *The African Queen* (1952)

Above
Hobson's Choice (1954)

Opposite
John Mills and Charles Laughton
in *Hobson's Choice*

(1935) and *The Hunchback of Notre Dame* (1939). But Laughton's troubled private life, including insecurity about his physical appearance, appeared to blight his film career in the 1940s and 1950s. Neither Lean nor Korda had any doubt though that Laughton was the right person to play the title role in *Hobson's Choice*.

Also lined up for the film was British actor Robert Donat, due to play the put-upon, shy, and slightly simple cobbler, Willy Mossop, who finds love and a home with Hobson's eldest daughter, the brash and no-nonsense Maggie. Some two decades earlier, Donat had also appeared in *The Private Life of Henry VIII* and both he and Laughton – who had stayed friends – were looking forward to being reunited on the big screen. Just days before filming was due to begin at Shepperton, however, Donat had to pull out after another crippling attack of asthma which had plagued his career and ironically, had been largely responsible for his distinctive and appealing voice. Lean was in a quandary, needing to find a replacement for Donat immediately. Within 24 hours, John Mills was sat in a make-up chair at Shepperton having his hair shaved and his newly acquired suntan well hidden under the pasty make-up needed for the part.

By now, Lean and Mills were highly experienced in their respective crafts of film-making and acting, yet director and actor were both phased by Laughton, as John Mills remembers: "I was excited at the idea of acting with Charles Laughton whom I had always regarded as a great and most brilliant actor. Poor David had never worked with an international name before and I think he was slightly in awe of him. Laughton seemed a bit eccentric – though rather likeable I thought. He had a tendency to express himself in a somewhat peculiar way which would throw both David and myself. I remember one scene when we were all in the kitchen together for a big comedy moment and Charles told David and myself that he thought the scene when played back should appear to be like 'star shells and rockets' going off. Dear David looked thoughtful and replied after a moment; 'Yes, Mr Laughton, that was

Lean two years to complete his first film for Korda, *The Sound Barrier*, released in 1952.

The lead in *Hobson's Choice* was to be Charles Laughton. The larger-than-life actor had played the part of the self-important Lancashire bootmaker many years earlier – when a teenager in Scarborough. Laughton had also already made several successful films for Korda, including *The Private Life of Henry VIII*, in 1933, for which he won a best actor Oscar®. Laughton's career continued to shine during the 1930s, in productions like *The Barretts of Wimpole Street* (1934), *Mutiny on the Bounty* (1935), *Les Miserables*

The film won a BAFTA for Best British Film as well as the Golden Berlin Bear award at the Berlin International Film Festival in 1954. Such is the affection for the film in the Mills' own household, that 50 years after *Hobson's Choice* was made, and on Sir John Mills' ninety-sixth birthday, he was given a cake in the shape of two of Willy Mossop's old black boots.

Back in 1949 Alexander Korda had encouraged Laurence Olivier to set up his own film production company. Together with Korda's London Films, Olivier produced a film version of Shakespeare's *Richard III* at Shepperton studios in 1954. As in his previously highly-acclaimed productions of *Henry V* in 1944 and *Hamlet* in 1948, Olivier was to produce and direct the film, as well as star in the lead role. His superb performance as the deformed and bitter king drew much from his earlier playing of the role on stage at the Old Vic during World War II. Always one to ensure that he had the best of acting talents around him, the cast for *Richard III* included Ralph Richardson, John Gielgud, Stanley Baker and Claire Bloom. The film broke new ground by allowing the lead character to speak directly to the camera, as if bringing the audience in on Richard's dastardly plans and making them his accomplice. It was all very daring for the mid-1950s, as was the portrayal of the lead character, whose striking walk was said to be based on Jed Harris, a Broadway actor, along with touches of the almost manic petulance of Adolf Hitler, whom Olivier had carefully studied on wartime newsreels.

Above
Spanish surrealist painter Salador Dali (left) on the set of *Richard III* with Laurence Olivier

Opposite
Laurence Olivier in costume preparing another sequence for *Richard III*

exactly what I had in mind.' Yet neither of us had the slightest idea what he was talking about."

Once up and running, production on *Hobson's Choice* went smoothly. Even though he was not the original choice for the role of Willy Mossop, John Mills' performance is still regarded by audiences, critics and the actor himself, as one of the best he has ever given on screen. There is no doubt that the talents of the actors seemed to lift each others' performances and though Laughton did not get on with Brenda de Banzie, and was upset that Donat wasn't playing the part of his son-in-law, he too put on a dazzling show.

The film's battle scenes could not be filmed at Shepperton – there was not the space or suitable land on which to recreate them. The ideal setting for the battle of Bosworth Field which was historically correct, was in Leicestershire, England. However, this had proved unsuitable as the area had been dissected by a canal and a railway. Olivier felt he had no choice but to send the film's co-producer, Anthony Bushell, to scout for a suitable location in Spain. Finding somewhere green enough and reminiscent of the traditional English landscape did not prove as easy as Olivier would have liked. The Spanish authorities were most

helpful and suggested Andalucia, a green region which was also covered in cactus. Olivier joined Bushell in Spain and soon they agreed on a marshy terrain in the Escorial area. The grass was silvery grey but the assurances were that come September the autumn rains would change the colour to a far richer green, which thankfully they did.

As in *Henry V* (1944), Olivier was injured during shooting on location. An arrow destined for a cork protector on the flank of his horse, actually hit him and embedded itself in his calf. Olivier completed the scene before having the arrow removed.

Following the Spanish location filming in September 1954, Olivier, his cast and crew, began 13 weeks of shooting at Shepperton. The actor-producer-director thoroughly enjoyed making the film but was never happy about the battle scene, which he found very disappointing: "I adored every moment of the picture's making and have always felt quite happy about the result – with the exception of one pretty important element, the battle sequence. Somehow, after *Henry V*, I couldn't find another battle in me. I could only show as well as I could the happenings, as history tells us they took place on that day on Bosworth Field, with the usual hideous problem of trying to make 500 men look like 60,000 – this time on a widescreen."

Olivier also had Alexander Korda constantly breathing down his neck about costs. The Hungarian was quoted by Olivier on many occasions as having said: "Larry, you must cut, you know? You ruin me, you know." Olivier showed an early print of the film to *The Third Man* director Carol Reed, who, after a while and looking slightly perplexed, asked Olivier: "Why on earth didn't you invent some Shakepearean-sounding lines to help the audience understand better what was going on, such as 'Go to thy furthest westest with the utmostest speedest!' I bet you've done it before, often." Olivier was the first to admit that in the past that is exactly what he had done: "He was right, I had, but here when it was most essential I went and got all prim and orthodox. Infuriating. I fear that when they occasionally revive it, out of some misguided respect it is always shown in its full-length version, though I actually prefer it cut, particularly the battle sequence. So Alex was right after all: so much cheaper to leave it off the negative at the outset than on the cutting-room floor."

The film's distributor, Paramount, gave the film a simultaneous premiere at cinemas and on television in America. Some 40 million viewers watched the NBC screening – more than all the audiences in the play's previous 350-year history added together. Sadly, *Richard III* was not a hit at the box office and Olivier was unable afterwards to raise the money he needed to film his adaptation of *Macbeth*.

Yet ironically, the film was a critical success – winning three BAFTAs and a fifth best actor Oscar® nomination for Olivier. Proof, if proof were needed, that *Richard III* is a clever and highly professional production. The camera work, beautiful sets and excellent acting, came together to turn a classic Shakespeare play into a classic Shepperton film and one which is still regarded, some half a century later, as being the last of the studios early classic productions.

Opposite

Director, as well as, screenwriter and actor in *Richard III*, Laurence Olivier checks the camera for the next scene

Sybil and Keith on their wedding
day, 28th January 1950.

Keith Robinson
Sound Production
Sybil Robinson
Stills Department

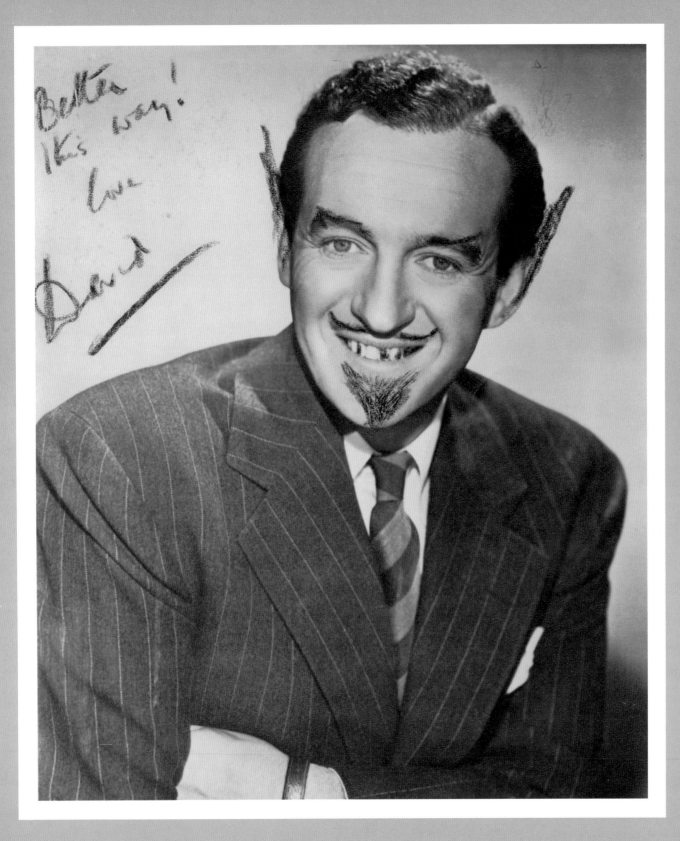

Better this way! Love David
A signed photograph from
David Niven to Sybil

Keith Robinson

In my teens I had worked in cinemas and, luckily, a career developed for me within the film business itself. In 1947, after three years at Elstree Studios, I got a job in the projection department at Shepperton Studios. We showed rushes and film for special effects and cutting editors to see how their work was progressing. Sometimes they would ask our opinion and we would happily give it in any of the five preview theatres that were available at the time.

Peter Sellers was playing the part of a projectionist in a comedy called *The Smallest Show on Earth* (1957). A technician asked us how a projectionist would behave in a cinema. One tip was that after putting on the last reel of the film a projectionist would always put on his hat and coat, ready to dive out of the door as soon as the National Anthem had finished. Peter Sellers portrayed this to perfection, but we didn't get a script credit!

I worked on *The Third Man*. One night the cutting rooms caught fire and most of the film was lost. Carol Reed, the director, was in despair, saying "The film will never be the same". "Yes it will be even better," I replied, and the subsequent history of the film bears this out. It regularly appears in the list of top ten films ever made.

Post Sync: Sometimes the dialogue wasn't clear because of background noise and a different voice to the actor in the action would be used. The actor would look at the action on the screen and synchronise his dialogue to the movement of the actor's mouth on screen. This was recorded. The same procedure takes place in the music scoring stage when an orchestra and its conductor would provide appropriate music for the sequence. This was done over and over again until it was perfect, at which point a recording was made.

Sybil Robinson

I started work in the film industry in 1947 in the general office at Shepperton studios. We typed call sheets, scripts and shoot schedules on stencils and printed them off on a duplicating machine. No copying machines or computers in those days! I met my husband, who was a projectionist, a few days after my career began at Shepperton.

The studios were owned by Sir Alexander Korda and most of us including technicians were employed by British Lion, there were very few freelance staff. It is true to say we were one big happy family. There was a great social club and Sir Alex always gave us marvellous Christmas parties. I remember the day the head of the make-up department rang the office and asked for volunteers for their trainees to practice on. My friend and I volunteered. Two 19-year-olds were made-up to look 75. Later they gave us a glamour make-up and we went back to the office looking like a couple of starlets. We experienced first hand, the skill and dedication of those often-unsung heroes behind the scenes.

In 1948 I got a job in the stills department as secretary/receptionist. My boss was Ted Reed, one of the best photographers in the business. My duties were to make out orders for the darkroom, send weekly returns to the accounts department and, best of all, ordering tea, taxis or anything else the stars might require when they visited the studio for a portrait session.

I met such stars as David Niven, who had a very different take for a signed photograph, Trevor Howard, Albert Finney, Jane Russell, Anna Neagle, Ava Gardner, to mention a few. Apparently David Niven liked to say

Dubbing: All the recorded loops of film from post sync, such as dialogue, bird sounds, footsteps, trains, aeroplanes, in fact any sound that was needed for the film, plus the music, had to be recorded on one track.

In the dubbing projection room the action was run on the projector, showing the picture on the screen. There were maybe four dialogues, three music tracks, and three effects which have to be run on separate sound heads. All have special start marks and the dubbing mixer on the console in the theatre knows when a certain dialogue on a certain head can be brought up to be heard by a footage number shown under the screen. All tracks were done in the same way and it was all recorded onto one track, known as the married print. This print would be previewed in the studio theatre.

In 1967 I had been in charge of my own preview theatre for two years when, John Green, the musical director of *Oliver!* wanted his own preview theatre and staff for the making of the film. He chose mine and had brand new equipment fitted for the production. We worked on *Oliver!* for two years. John Cox, head of the sound department, and the dubbing mixers Red Law and Bob Jones, won an Oscar® for *Oliver!*

I worked at Shepperton until 1974 and had such stars as Katherine Hepburn, Kim Novak, Howard Keel, Bing Crosby, Bob Hope, Orson Welles, Richard Widmark, Trevor Howard, Oliver Reed, Mickey Rooney and Richard Harris visit my studio.

Also, I met my wife Sybil at Shepperton Studios and we often remember our happy times there.

what he considered to be a rude word just before the shutter was released. He claimed it gave a sparkle to his eyes! He asked the make-up and wardrobe ladies to leave before he said it. I received a telephone message for him and crept into the studio just as he said, "Dick." The shutter clicked, the portrait was taken. He turned and saw me, "Oh not another one," he groaned.

Technology moved forward and 35mm still cameras were used instead of the old 10x8 cut film cameras. So the portrait studio was rarely used. In 1962 I decided to go freelance as a publicity secretary on a film called *Two Left Feet* (1963), starring Michael Crawford, Julia Foster, Nyree Dawn Porter and David Hemmings. It was a first for several of us including my boss the publicist Gordon Arnell who ended up as publicity director for the Bond films at Pinewood. We worked together on another film at Shepperton called *A Jolly Bad Fellow* (1964), starring Janet Munro and Leo McKern. One day I went on the set with a message. The red light was off which tells anyone outside that the studio isn't filming. However, there had been very little filming at all as the days shooting had run into difficulties. As I arrived on set there was a deathly hush and a very tense atmosphere. I was unsure what to do. All of a sudden there was a tapping noise and the director, Don Chaffey said, "Oh, no Leo". Leo was tapping his glass eye with a pencil to relieve the tension. It did. Everyone relaxed and filming commenced.

I spent most of my career at Shepperton and recall working on many great films. I have many happy memories of this great studio.

Gritty Realism

Billy Liar (1962)

The 1950s was a fairly predictable time for British cinema. The tastes of the viewing public seemed to alternate between wanting, on the one hand, to be reminded of the country's outstanding achievements in World War II, and on the other, a chance to forget it all and escape the horrors of war by having a good old-fashioned laugh. A study of the top money-making films for each year of the decade seems to bear this theory out. For five of those years the highest earner was a comedy; four of those being medical laughter-makers (three *Doctor* films and *Carry On Nurse* (1959)), and a frenetic British farce starring Alastair Sim and George Cole, *Laughter in Paradise* (1951); one was a family film about the adventures of an East African game warden called *Where No Vultures Fly* (1951). The other four top earners of their year were all war films: *The Cruel Sea* (1953), *The Dam Busters* (1954), *Reach for the Sky* (1956) and *The Bridge on the River Kwai* (1956) – reminding us all of the mettle and steel of a nation that really did help to keep the "great" in Great Britain.

Over in America, the types of films people were going to see couldn't have been more different. In the same period, the highest earning films at the US box-office included *The Greatest Show on Earth* (1952), *The Ten Commandments* (1956), *Ben Hur* (1959) and *White Christmas* (1954). Only once in that decade did our trans-atlantic viewing tastes coincide, with *The Bridge on the River Kwai* making it to the top in 1958, both here and in the USA.

It was while out filming on location in a desert that very same year, for yet another Rank war suspense film, *Sea of Sand* (1958), that Richard Attenborough felt it was time for a change. Attenborough, already an acting star, had tired of the direction that British cinema appeared to be taking in the mid-to-late 1950s. He blamed much of the blandness of productions on the need for British films to find favour with American audiences. This, he said, involved making editorial concessions: "A number of us who placed aesthetic considerations high on our agenda were concerned that the fundamental quality of much of what we were doing was in question and that the wrong priorities were being addressed. Commercial success, presentation and promotion were everything, while the actual kernel of the thing was very often not what it ought to be." This from a man who had been involved in over 20 films during the 1950s. He knew what he was talking about.

Attenborough wanted a challenging subject to get his production teeth into and to challenge the British cinema-visiting public at the same time. And it was in that most unlikely of settings – a sand-drenched desert location in the middle of nowhere – that the increasingly disgruntled Attenborough was to be presented with a fascinating idea for a film, which immediately whetted his creative appetite. He overheard a story from his *Sea of Sand* co-star, Michael Craig. The story was of a factory hand who falls out with his union and is "sent to Coventry" when he refuses to join his colleagues on strike. Craig himself had first heard about the real-life plight of the worker from York when he was in repertory theatre just after the war, and the story had stayed with him ever since.

Michael Craig was under contract to Rank. He too felt his acting career was stalling by continually being asked – or rather instructed by studio bosses – to play the tall and handsome, but quite boring characters, demanded of lead men in many watchable but ultimately forgettable late-1950s productions; from hospital melodramas such as *Life in Emergency Ward 10* to the oft-repeated themes in domestic comedies such as *Upstairs and Downstairs*.

Opposite and above
Tom Curtis (Richard Attenborough) votes not to strike, against the advice of work colleague and friend Joe Wallace (Michael Craig), in the ground-breaking melodrama, *The Angry Silence* (1959)

While both men were bemoaning the state of the British film industry in general and their acting careers in particular, Craig openly remarked within earshot of *Sea of Sand* director Guy Green that he simply couldn't understand why it was that over a decade after the war had ended, producers were still making pictures about it. Attenborough was sufficiently enthused by both the actor's gall and the story he had been told to invite Craig to work on a draft screenplay. Guy Green was tentatively offered the directorship if the project ever got off the ground.

Meanwhile, back in England and unknown to them all, Attenborough's close friend, the actor and writer Bryan Forbes, was also getting tired and frustrated with the work he was being asked to produce. Forbes, a very talented man, had even at that time – not yet in his mid-30s – become a respected actor, producer and screenwriter having worked on and/or starred in such 1950s classics as *The Wooden Horse* (1950), *The Colditz Story* (1955) and *I Was Monty's Double* (1958). Later, Forbes was to add director, head of production at EMI's Elstree Studios, and novelist to his long list of industry credits. Co-incidentally, his wife, actress Nanette Newman, had just read a news story of a railwayman who had been sent to Coventry by his work mates and, after three years of harassment, had committed suicide. Returning shortly afterwards from their location work on *Sea of Sand*, Attenborough and Forbes met to discuss what ideas they could potentially produce under the banner of their new production company, Beaver Films. It was soon agreed that they would pool their ideas of an isolated union worker, get Craig and his brother, Richard Gregson, to write the script, and Guy Green to direct, while they would attempt to find the funding and produce the project.

Made in 1959, *The Angry Silence* was a tough film. Unlike its satiric equivalent, *I'm All Right Jack* (1959), which was made at Shepperton the same year, the film's punches were not side-swipes at the unions and the establishment. They were very real attacks on institutions that drove a young, honest hardworking man to the brink of killing himself. Neither the British film industry nor cinema-goers had ever seen anything quite like it before. Forbes knew it was a very different type of British feature. "It was a watershed film, perhaps ahead of its time. I didn't have to research trade unions to write the screenplay, I knew enough from my own experience of them. There was anarchy in the industry at the time. Some of the unions were very militant. Very often they'd pull the breakers on you. If I wanted to take the quarter – that is, film until half past five instead of 5.15 – the union had to have a meeting at lunchtime to discuss it. We then had to apply for the extension and they either granted it or didn't. Everyone was supposed to work until half past five but there was washing up time which meant they could stop earlier. No one washed up anything. They just left as quickly as they could. But this was just the film industry and it didn't matter because it didn't bring the country to a standstill.

"We made *The Angry Silence* a very tough film. The unions hated it. Dickie and I were accused of exaggerating the story. We even received death threats. To this day, some people have never forgiven us."

The film almost wasn't made at all. Attenborough and Forbes had terrible trouble raising the finance. It seemed that social conscience, while highly regarded, was not considered strong enough box-office, and the necessary investment was not forthcoming. Indeed the only reason that Richard Attenborough himself ended up playing the lead role, was that there wasn't enough money to employ big acting names such as Kenneth More, who had been one of the first choices to star in the film. Everyone involved in the project agreed to a salary of just £1,000 each (less than £15,000 in today's money) with a percentage of any profits, if any were to be made. No one really expected the film to be a hit, but such was the commitment from all those involved that the relatively paltry sums on offer were accepted with grace – the money playing second fiddle to the unanimous feeling that this film needed to be made.

That commitment was duly rewarded with three

A KIND OF LOVING THAT KNEW NO WRONG UNTIL IT WAS TOO LATE!

A JOSEPH JANNI PRODUCTION.

ALAN BATES
in
A KIND OF LOVING 'X'

with
THORA HIRD
introducing
JUNE RITCHIE

Screenplay by WILLIS HALL and KEITH WATERHOUSE
Adapted from a novel by STAN BARSTOW
Produced by JOSEPH JANNI
Associate Producer JACK HANBURY Directed by JOHN SCHLESINGER

ANGLO AMALGAMATED FILM DISTRIBUTORS LTD.

TOP PRIZE WINNER
BERLIN INTERNATIONAL
FILM FESTIVAL

Oscar® nominations – for Forbes, Craig and Gregson – and a British Academy award for Forbes for best British screenplay. At the time, renowned film critic Dilys Powell commented: "This is a film made by people who care about the screen and care what they are saying on it". There could have been no finer plaudit for Attenborough and Forbes who had started off just trying "to do something that had contemporary social awareness." In doing just that and more, *The Angry Silence* is generally regarded as introducing a new wave of gritty realism to our screens – a movement which lasted the best part of a decade and which saw some fine cinematic gems produced from the Shepperton stable.

Forbes is more modest and attributed the "new wave" of British cinema to the likes of John Osborne, whose play *Look Back in Anger* – the story of a young man with a grudge against life and the government – was filmed with Richard Burton in the lead role the same year as *The Angry Silence*; and to *Saturday Night and Sunday Morning*, made in 1960, about a man who has an affair with a married woman (Rachel Roberts) before settling down for a quieter life. In truth they all played their part in heralding a new age to our screens.

Certainly audiences appeared to lap these films up and the productions won their fair share of awards and award nominations both here and across the Atlantic.

Almost overnight, young actors were to become stars of the big screen: including Burton, Finney, Tom Courtenay and Alan Bates. New, fresh faces, portraying the deep confusion and misunderstanding of an unfolding post-war world, with a new generation asking after all the suffering the nation went through: "Is this it?". It seemed a question that many were asking and they went to the cinemas in droves to find out if any answers were out there.

The answers – like the films – were often contrasting. In *Saturday Night and Sunday Morning*, the main character rebels and then settles down to a conventional life. *A Kind of Loving* was equally blunt and melodramatic, though it was a completely different set of

Almost overnight, young actors were to become stars of the big screen: including Burton, Finney, Tom Courtenay and Alan Bates. New, fresh faces, portraying the deep confusion and misunderstanding of an unfolding post-war world, ...

circumstances that ultimately led the main character to attempt to settle down.

A Kind of Loving was made at Shepperton in 1961 and starred Alan Bates as Vic Brown, a young draughtsman who is forced into marriage when he gets a girl pregnant. He can't afford to rent or buy a property and so ends up living with his new bride and her harridan of a mother. To make matters worse, his wife Ingrid suffers a miscarriage and he now finds himself stuck in a loveless marriage in an unhappy home. The film was directed by 35-year-old John Schlesinger who was to become the most prolific of the young directors who brought their own very personal innate sensibilities to British cinema's new realism. His films were heartfelt and compassionate, and he always got the best performances out of his actors. Certainly the audience felt sorry for Vic Brown

– he wasn't in any way rebellious. Unlike Finney's character Arthur Seaton in *Saturday Night and Sunday Morning*, Bates' Vic Brown was just the nice guy next door, as Bates himself recalled: "It had a lot of human understanding, a lot of awareness of young people's problems and their blindness and the whole pot-luck chance of life… It wasn't brutal. It was absolutely life as it was lived. It wasn't about exceptional folk, it was really about everyday people and their struggles". Perhaps because of that, the film, which is strikingly shot among urban grime and suburban conformity, has to have its main character settling for conformity in the end. Vic Brown is a good man who believes in doing the right thing. He may well – after a drunken binge and ritually puking on the carpet – have stormed out of his mother-in-law's house promising never to return, but he is a married man and one who, though forced into walking down the aisle,

Left and Opposite
The relationship between Vic (Alan Bates) and Ingrid (June Ritchie) becomes complicated – the stark image from the film also used for the poster for *A Kind of Loving* (1961)

Right
A stunning publicity shot of Julie Christie as
Liz, taken to promote *Billy Liar*, in 1962

actually takes his vows seriously enough to give it
another go with Ingrid. He decides to try and make it
work, because that's what people did in those days.
That was the realism of it all. No fairytale ending
there.

No fairytale endings didn't mean that the characters
in these gritty films couldn't fantasize about a different or better life. That was certainly true of Billy
Fisher, the undertaker's assistant who escapes his
mundane existence by transporting himself to the
fantasyland of Ambrosia, where he is ruler over everyone and everything. *Billy Liar* had been a huge hit on
stage. Written by Keith Waterhouse and Willis Hall,
the story was brought to the big screen by John
Schlesinger after he had finished *A Kind of Loving*. On
stage, the part of Billy had originally been created by
Albert Finney, but later in the run and when the show
went on tour of the provinces the role was taken over
by Finney's friend, Tom Courtenay, who early in 1962,
while performing in *Billy Liar* at night was also filming
his much-acclaimed debut cinematic role in *The
Loneliness of the Long Distance Runner*. Schlesinger was
very keen to have Courtenay as the lead for the film.
This appeared to suit everyone concerned as Finney's
time was to be taken up filming *Tom Jones* (1963).

Left and below
Tom Courtenay plays daydreaming
undertaker's assistant, Billy Fisher,
in *Billy Liar* (1962)

The intense strength of Courtenay's performance (even though he often said he thought he "looked a bit raw in some of it") was beautifully matched by Julie Christie as Liz, one of the three women in Billy's life. With grit and grime appearing inextricably linked with the phrase "social realism," Julie Christie brought to the production a much-needed, welcome, warm, and fun-loving sensuality which seemed to have been a missing ingredient in these films until then. In *Billy Liar*, sex was portrayed as possibly being rather fun, as opposed to, say, a sleazy quickie with your friend's wife as in *Saturday Night and Sunday Morning*, or a sullen one-off act which led to unwanted pregnancy and even less-wanted marriage as in *A Kind of Loving*. Ironically, Julie Christie claims to have been very unlike the free-spirited Liz, "Despite the fact I thought of myself as a rebel, I was very shy, and Liz wasn't shy. She was also a very different class from me, so that when she got lifts from lorry drivers she had the confidence of equality, whereas I would have been absolutely paralyzed by my awful middle-classness and unable to say anything at all. In a way it was her class that gave her strength and I didn't have that class."

Certainly Julie Christie brought an air of perceived permissiveness to the screen which had only been hinted at in previous films. That, along with Cinemascope in which the film was shot, made the production feel much brighter than the dreariness of *A Kind of Loving*. Yet for all that, *Billy Liar* never lost its identity and never let go of its roots of realism. Indeed, the film was accused of having an unnecessarily downbeat ending – Billy deciding to stay in his fantasy world and not escape his drab life. Schlesinger disagreed: "I don't think it is a downbeat ending at all, because Billy stayed with his fantasy. He funked going to London, missed his opportunity with the girl and with life and everything else, but he still had his fantasy and he returned in triumph to his house, marching along with that invisible army. I thought that was wonderful." Wonderful it was. It still is. But perhaps the film's ending was a contributory factor in *Billy Liar* losing out at the Oscars® and the BAFTAs to *Tom Jones*, which picked up best film and best adapted

Above
Director John Schlesinger (holding clapperboard) with Tom Courtenay (sitting centre) on location, during the filming of *Billy Liar*, in 1962

Opposite
Director John Schlesinger planning his next shot, during the filming of *Billy Liar* (1962)

screenplay. Critics do tend to like happy endings, don't they?

Bryan Forbes found further international acclaim with his 1962 Shepperton production of *The L-Shaped Room*, for which he was both writer and director. Set in the world of shabby bedsits of the early 1960s, it has Leslie Caron playing the part of Jane Fosset, an unmarried girl who falls pregnant and, while deciding whether or not to have an abortion, takes a room – in the shape of the film's title – in a grubby London suburban house, frequented by a host of different characters. An interesting bunch they were too – a middle-aged matronly lesbian, a struggling author, a couple of prostitutes and a black jazz musician. The setting of the film is exceptionally bleak, and the situations that the characters are in appear even bleaker. Yet Forbes is a talented writer and he draws out the warmth and the wit that so often comes with despair.

Caron's performance was outstanding. At the age of 22, a decade earlier, the French-American actress and dancer had been nominated for an Oscar® for her performance in *Lili*. Now she was nominated again for her role in *The L-Shaped Room*. She lost out to Patricia Neal who had given a barn-storming performance in the American film about life on a Texas ranch, *Hud*. But Caron's acting skills were not totally overlooked and she was awarded the Golden Globe for best motion picture actress in a drama in 1963.

The L-Shaped Room divided critics in Britain. All were impressed by the acting of Caron and her co-stars, including Tom Bell, Cicely Courtneidge and Bernard Lee. Yet a few felt that some of the realism was lost in what they considered to be an attempt to create a hit by bringing together such an assortment of characters under one roof. As one critic exclaimed: "It would be hard to imagine a more unlikely, or commercially more sure-fire group of lodgers living under a single roof. Made under the watchful eye of Richard Attenborough and Forbes' second production company, Romulus films, it certainly did seem to have something for everyone to think about back in

Opposite

Unmarried mother-to-be, Jane Fosset (Leslie Caron), checks to see if she is showing with her illegitimate child, in *The L-Shaped Room* (1962)

Left

The L-Shaped Room (1962)

Below

Bryan Forbes (left) directing Leslie Caron and Tom Bell, on the Shepperton set of *The L-Shaped Room* (1962)

1962. Indeed its themes of abortion, homosexuality, race and class are equally as powerful over 40 years later.

One of the acting casualties of the new wave of realism to hit our screens, was the most popular of 1950s film actors, Kenneth More. After a slow start, his rise to the top of British film stardom was very swift. But it was not to last. Born in 1914, More started working life as an engineer's apprentice and as a fur trapper in Canada. He took a bit part in a Gracie Fields' film called *Look Up and Laugh* in 1935. A series of small roles in plays and films followed, before he joined the Royal Navy where he served during World War II. After the war, he again attempted a career in films, but though he had an easy-going manner, which proved valuable in both comic and more adventurous roles, it wasn't until he hit 40 that suddenly Kenneth More became a star, all thanks to two very British comedies – *Genevieve* (1953) and *Doctor in the House* (1954). In the first he played a flirty and boasting upper-class chappie enjoying the single life while quietly lusting after the married contentment enjoyed by his middle-class friends, whom he ends up racing back to London from the Brighton veteran car rally. In the second he played a somewhat confused medical student for which he won the British Academy award for best actor in 1954. Suddenly More was in huge demand. He appeared in some of the biggest films of the era, most notably as World War II hero Douglas Bader in *Reach for the Sky* in 1956, the title character in *The Admirable Crichton* in 1957, the first mate on the Titanic in *A Night to Remember* in 1958, and the director of naval operations in *Sink the Bismark!* in 1960.

The fashion for the stiff-upper-lipped heroes which had made More such a box-office winner, declined rapidly, as the swinging sixties began, and with it, so did the number and quality of roles he was being offered. More must surely have regretted turning down the lead role in *The Angry Silence* when offered it by Richard Attenborough and Bryan Forbes in 1959. They obviously saw that his acting potential extended much further than the naval officer types he was

Young and star-struck Fay
(Angela Douglas) starts an affair
with older rep actor Chick Byrd
(Kenneth More), in Alvin Rakoff's
The Comedy Man in 1963

being called on to play. But at the time, Attenborough was asking a huge box-office earner to star in a production for next to no money. More made what he felt was the best decision for himself. The rest, as far as *The Angry Silence* goes, is history.

No doubt still smarting from missing out on a role that could have proved of far greater worth to an actor than simply financial reward, and with offers for film work starting to dry up, More embraced the role of Chick Byrd in *The Comedy Man* in 1963. The film follows the life of a down-on-his-luck middle-age repertory actor who spends his days dreaming of a big break into the business. Byrd eventually finds his fortune through, of all things, a TV commercial, but turns his back on the money and the fame to concentrate on his "serious" acting career.

A film which deglamourised trying to be a star was a huge gamble, made that much more realistic by the themes running through it which were mirroring More's own life at the time, as a middle-age actor touching 50, finding good work harder to come by. More had been there before and it was looking like he might be going there again. The critics saw the irony in it, the *Evening News* declaring the film: "A merciless and accurate picture of the brave band of actors who live from hand to mouth and commute between the Salisbury Arms pub and the Poland Street labour exchange." Of course, to make the film as wholly convincing as it was, a talented band of actors was needed to communicate the frustration of the situation and the bonhomie among out-of-work thespians. The excellent cast included veteran actor Dennis Price, Billie Whitelaw and Frank Finlay. And there was also the young Angela Douglas, just 21 years old.

In *The Comedy Man*, More's Chick Byrd and Douglas's Fay start a relationship and share a bed. Chick refers to Fay as "Shrimp." Kenneth More and Angela Douglas started a real-life affair while making the film and their bedroom moments seem that much more real now that we know what was going on behind the scenes. The couple were tortured by the fact that More was married and by the large age difference between them. More thought less for himself than for his girl-

friend who was trying to establish herself on the acting industry ladder. He said to her after the affair had begun: "Angela, you must promise me one thing. At the end of the film when we all go back to London, there'll be no phone calls, no letters, nothing. No contact. Promise me."

After a difficult divorce and their being shunned by the film and television industry for most of the rest of the 1960s, they were still together, as husband and wife, when More passed away from Parkinson's disease in 1982. He was 67 and she was 40, and until his very last day, he was still calling her "Shrimp."

Julie Christie's stunning performance in John Schlesinger's *Billy Liar*, had found her overnight fame and put her very much in high demand for film work. She was to go on to star in some of the most coveted female roles throughout the rest of the sixties. Her place in the industry's affections was sealed in her second film for Schlesinger, *Darling* (1964), which also catapulted Christie to international fame and fortune.

Darling is the story of the shallowness of celebrity and the gullibility of the public. The film follows the life of an ambitious woman, Diana Scott, who will stop at nothing to become famous, jumping from one relationship – and bed – to another. She leaves behind a trail of used and disappointed men – from her journalist mentor to a company director, an effeminate photographer to an Italian prince. The film provides a wicked insight into a sham world which is still relevant some four decades on. We all know how empty the world of a "celebrity" can be, but we still love to read about it and watch their often seedy goings-on. The tabloids – which we bought in their millions daily – survive and thrive on it all nowadays. Yet in the 1960s, this new openness and sexual honesty was quite a shock to the viewing public's system. It was a different type of realism to the grime and downbeat working-class scenarios audiences had been watching until then. It was still real even though it wasn't happening in their world. Somehow the character's come-uppance was welcomed. For once in this new wave of realism you didn't feel sorry for anyone; you felt they all deserved what they got.

Considered an important and groundbreaking film, *The Servant* (1963) tells the story of a Cockney servant (Dirk Bogarde) trading roles with his master (James Fox) an aristocrat. Directed by Joseph Losey the film won British Academy Awards for Best Actor (Bogarde), Most Promising Newcomer (Fox) and Best Cinematography (Douglas Slocombe).

Top right
Sarah Miles is the beautiful Vera,
in *The Servant*

Top left
Director of *The Servant*, Joseph Losey

Opposite
A scene from *The Servant,* with Sarah
Miles and James Fox

Dirk Bogarde as Robert Gold
and Julie Christie as Diana Scott –
roles which won them both a
Bafta and Julie Christie an Oscar®
in John Schlesinger's 1964 drama,
Darling

Schlesinger picked up the kernel of the idea for the film from a journalist friend, who had told him the story of a girl who had been kept by a syndicate of show business types who all chipped in to buy her a flat and keep her on as their respective mistress. Eventually the girl killed herself. Schlesinger thought the subject was interesting but a little nasty. So he did not pursue it from that angle, allowing instead the writer Frederic Raphael to follow his own instincts and write a screenplay from his own imagination. Any similarities in the storyline were coincidental, Schlesinger insisted.

The cast for the film was impressive. Julie Christie was more than ably assisted by British acting heart-throbs Laurence Harvey and Dirk Bogarde. *Darling* was a huge critical success, but not in all quarters. It won two Oscars®, best actress for Julie Christie and best screenplay for Frederic Raphael; three BAFTAs – Julie Christie and Dirk Bogarde taking best actress and best actor, and Frederic Raphael another writing award; and it won a Golden Globe for best English Language Foreign Film. Yet the British critics gave it a bit of a rough ride, one proclaiming it: "As empty of meaning and mind as the empty life it's exposing." John Schlesinger recalled that some of their views may well have been not far off the mark: "The British critics, who were very unpleasant about it, were probably right, although I think they were probably influenced by its American success. They are a very nasty lot. But it's far too pleased with itself. It's something to do with the script, something to do with the way we shot it; they're not very deep people." Julie Christie seemed to agree: "I think it is a film of its time. I'd call it very good source material for the 60s... It's a bit too slick, not naturalistic. I think one would have to wait a bit longer to see it as a product on its own and whether it holds up as a period piece."

Schlesinger and Christie worked together again on a genuine period piece, *Far From the Madding Crowd*, in 1967. This also starred Alan Bates – the second of four successful outings that the actor and director would share together. All three would be reunited for the

last time for a television adaptation of Terence Rattigan's *Separate Tables* in the 1980s.

The high-life and bright lights of the world that was *Darling* could not have been more different from the next Shepperton entry on an increasingly impressive list of gritty, realistic productions. For, just as *Darling* opened up the world of showbusiness to scrutiny for a cinema-going public unused to witnessing such things; at the other end of the spectrum along came a film which would shock them even more by challenging any preconceptions they may have had about the world they were watching.

The Spy Who Came in from the Cold, a gruelling adaptation of John Le Carre's novel about spying in Eastern Europe during the Cold War, was made in 1965, and starred Richard Burton and Claire Bloom. Burton played a disillusioned British master spy, Alec Leamas, who, in an attempt to get one over his East German opponent, allows it to be thought that he has been sacked by his own government and is open to recruitment by other powers who may want his services and need his knowledge. The film is gripping but very downbeat. It is harshly photographed, and both Burton's character and the film itself ooze bitterness at the position Leamas finds himself in.

This all came as a bit of a surprise to a viewing public which, by the mid-60s, was living and breathing the exploits of everyone's favourite spy, James Bond. In both 1963 and 1964 the films which more people went to see than any others in Britain were Bond films; *From Russia with Love* and *Goldfinger* respectively. Suddenly, everyone thought being a spy was cool and hip – tall, good looking, frequently travelling to warm and exotic locations, laden with gadgets, shooting the baddies and getting the girls. Most men wanted to be Sean Connery or 007; some wanted to be Michael Caine or his character, the bespectacled Harry Palmer from the 1965 film, *The Ipcress File*. Few wanted to be a genuine spy. No one really knew what that entailed. *The Spy Who Came in from the Cold* seemed to put that right, portraying as it did a far different, more realistic and harsher life altogether – one which few people would want to voluntarily sign up to .

The film gave Burton one of his best cinematic opportunities to show what a genuinely great actor he was, though he did not find the role easy. Burton was used to launching into speeches of great passion and allowing his deep Celtic tones to stir up emotion, both inside him and inside those who witnessed his performances. But the role of Alec Leamas did not afford him that opportunity. In what is effectively an essay on loneliness, Leamas is reduced almost to monosyllabic comments and retorts. As Burton commented at the time: "The others do all the acting. As Leamas, I just react." Burton found the part both rewarding and challenging in equal measures. At times he also found it tortuous. He worked long days in the cold and wet, from the back streets of Dublin to the snows of Bavaria. Fast approaching 40, Burton found he had quite a bit in common with Leamas and some of the moribund nature of the character appeared to rub off on him.

Yet it wasn't all doom and gloom. Burton had the chance to work with some favoured acting chums including Robert Hardy and a still relatively unknown Warren Mitchell. He also got to spend two months in the penthouse suite in Dublin's Gresham Hotel with his wife Elizabeth Taylor. Such was the fame of the couple, that crash barriers to hold back the crowds had to be erected for Burton's night time shooting on Dublin's streets.

The Spy Who Came in from the Cold was rapturously received by public and critics alike, providing an exceptionally realistic snapshot of the Cold War era. The film received four Oscar® nominations, but failed to win any of the awards. Burton did lift up one of the four BAFTAs which the film picked up in 1965. Alexander Walker wrote in the *Evening Standard*: "Richard Burton's performance completely rehabilitates him as an actor to respect. Playing the most difficult part of a character who can only react to things that are done to him, he succeeds in giving Leamas the impressiveness of a burned-out volcano."

If cinema-goers found the worlds of showbusiness and spying difficult subjects to comprehend, they were unlikely to find any difficulty understanding the problems to beset a marriage between two young

Left
Richard Burton, as cold war spy
Alec Leamas, crossing an Allied
checkpoint behind the Iron
Curtain – this scene from *The Spy
Who Came in from the Cold* (1965)
was filmed on a specially
constructed set at Shepperton

Above
Two scenes from filming on *The
Spy Who Came in from the Cold*
(1965)

Right
A scene from *The Family Way*

Below
Hywel Bennett

to his new bride Jenny while his Dad and family are all crammed in downstairs drinking and carousing, would be very funny if it wasn't so sad and touching. Theirs is a small terraced house with paper-thin walls. Sex is an expected but unspoken part of marital life. Arthur's inability to perform his conjugal responsibilities soon means that the subject becomes the major topic of conversation, both in the Fitton household and beyond. As each day passes and the news of Arthur's inadequacy spreads, the pressure on him and his marriage grows.

The two main leads play the roles perfectly but are upstaged by Hayley's real-life father John Mills, who plays Ezra Fitton, Arthur's dad. John Mills recalls landing the part of Ezra: "The last really great part that had come my way was Colonel Barrow in *Tunes of Glory* (1960) and I was hungry for something good to get my teeth into. Then out of the blue came a phone call which not only provided me with the part I was looking for but also had a profound effect on our lives. When Roy [Boulting] offered me the part of Ezra, I jumped at it. I'd seen Bernard Miles play it at the Mermaid Theatre and I knew that it was right up my street. The other plus, as far as I was concerned, was the fact that the Boulting twins offered Hayley a part in the picture, which was exactly what she needed at that time to help her step out of the 'little girl' image." The film certainly did that in more ways than one. Hayley fell in love with the director Roy Boulting who was 33 years her senior. They were married from 1971 to 1976. Of *The Family Way*, Hayley Mills has only happy memories. "It was a wonderful part for me – it was like going back to the beginning, working with my father, who was so lovely as Ezra. And Marjorie Rhodes was great, and darling Avril Angers as my mum. It was a darling film. I absolutely adored it. I wasn't really enjoying acting, but I did enjoy making that film. Perhaps if I hadn't fallen madly in love with Roy Boulting I might well have given it up. Roy was a wonderful director with actors, one of the best I've ever worked with."

working-class sweethearts. *The Family Way* was filmed at Shepperton and on location in Lancashire in 1966. Made by the brilliant film-making team of Roy and John Boulting – known to the industry as "the terrible twins" – *The Family Way* was the cinema version of a one-hour play called *All In Good Time* by Bill Naughton, in which a young groom finds himself unable to consummate his marriage with his attractive young bride. The film was risqué for its time, and though purporting to be a gentle comedy, dealt with sexual matters which were still quite taboo in the 1960s. Unlike its gritty counterparts earlier in the decade, this film was made in colour and boasted a musical score by Paul McCartney.

The parts of the newly-weds were played by Hayley Mills and Hywel Bennett, whose immediate on-screen chemistry saw them paired together again on two more productions in the coming two years. Off screen as well as on, a friendship blossomed, with Hywel Bennett becoming godfather to Hayley Mills' eldest son.

The Family Way derived its realism by recounting the experiences of many newlyweds in the 1960s, who found themselves sharing a home with their in-laws for much of the early years of their marriage. Watching Arthur Fitton as he tries to make love for the first time

Authorities on the subject, and those in the know, will tell you that "realism" is a style of film which

The **BOULTING BROTHERS'** production

Hayley **MILLS**
Hywel **BENNETT**

John **MILLS**
Marjorie **RHODES**

AVRIL ANGERS
LIZ FRASER
WILFRED PICKLES

JOHN COMER
BARRY FOSTER
MURRAY HEAD

THE FAMILY WAY

MUSIC BY
Paul McCARTNEY

FROM
BILL ('ALFIE') NAUGHTON'S
"ALL IN GOOD TIME"

EASTMAN COLOUR

X

SCREENPLAY BY BILL NAUGHTON · ADAPTATION BY ROY BOULTING & JEFFREY DELL · A BRITISH LION PRESENTATION THROUGH B.L.C.

attempts "to depict the real world in an accurate and objective manner with as little idealization or distortion as possible; its aim is often to increase our awareness of social conditions." Ironic then, that the film can be classified both as being the most realistic of arts – by being able to faithfully recreate moving images with sound – while at the same time seeming to be the most divorced from reality. Certainly, Shepperton's output from the late 1950s to the late 1960s could be seen to endorse both sides of the argument. On one sound stage at Shepperton in 1959, for example, when the "new wave" of film-making was just beginning, one could have watched the shooting of, say, *The Angry Silence* (1959) or *Room At the Top* (1959), while on another stage one could witness the production of *Tarzan's Greatest Adventure* (1959) or *The Night We Sprang A Leak!* Some seven years later when *The Family Way* was being produced at Shepperton, one could have dropped in elsewhere in the studios to watch the filming of *Calamity the Cow* (1967) or *The Spy with a Cold Nose* (1966). Which just goes to show that, while gritty realism played a hugely important part in the history of British cinema, some producers, never really lost sight of what kept them, the studios and the cinemas afloat; getting bums on seats with popular escapist entertainment.

A new era of film-making had arrived and Shepperton Studios provided the base where these, often daring film-makers, felt able to produce their modern and innovative work.

Above
Hayley Mills and Hywel Bennett,
in a scene from *The Family Way*

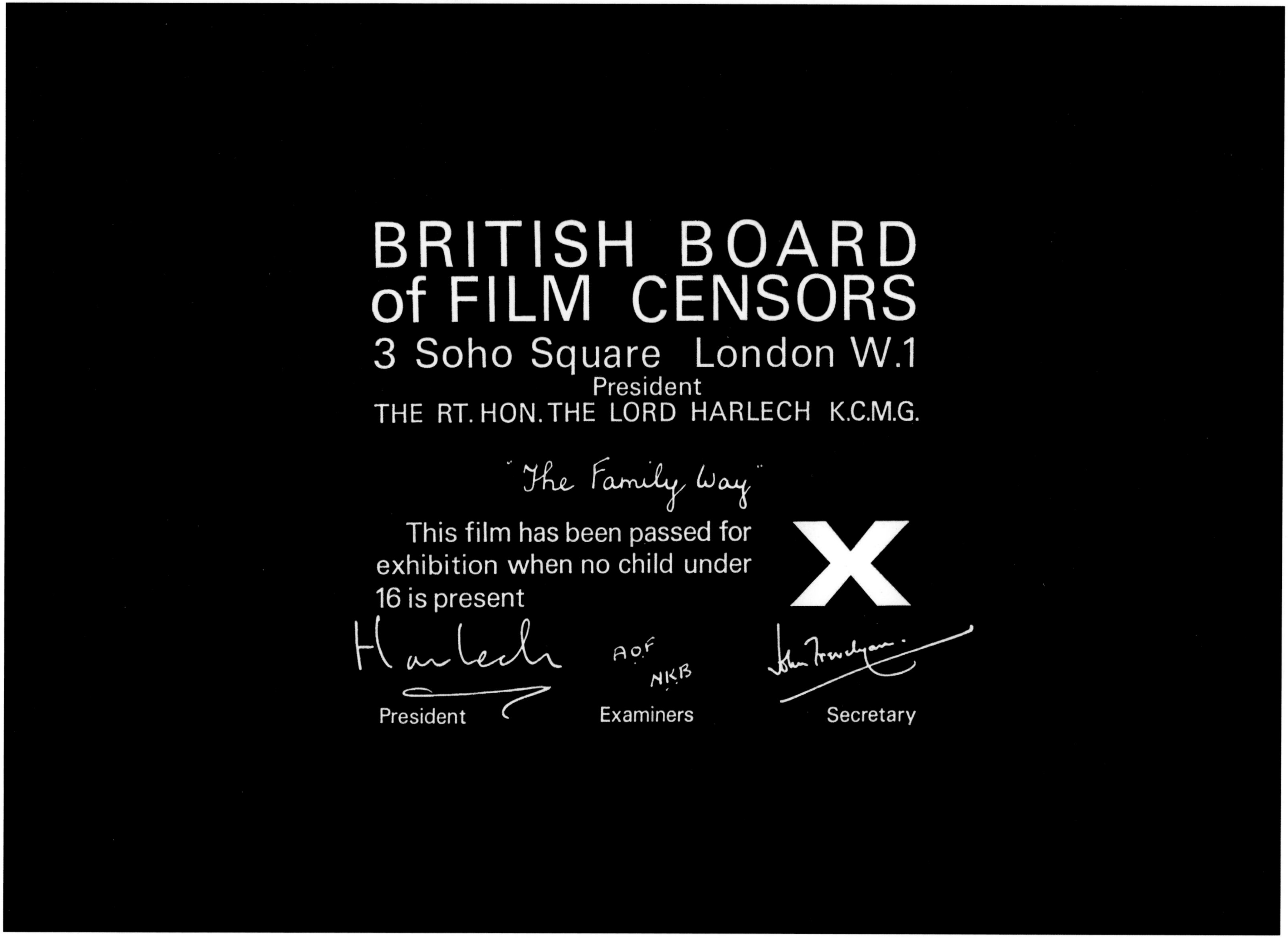

BRITISH BOARD
of FILM CENSORS
3 Soho Square London W.1
President
THE RT. HON. THE LORD HARLECH K.C.M.G.

"The Family Way"

This film has been passed for
exhibition when no child under
16 is present

X

Harlech
President

A.O.F
N.K.B.
Examiners

John Trevelyan
Secretary

In Memory
of
Eddie T. Swindells server 1938-40
Killed in air raid on Sound City Studios
next to this Church.

21st October 1940 aged 15
Not forgotten by his fellow servers
21st October 1990.

Above
A plaque to commemorate Eddie Swindells, located in
St Mary Magdelene church next to Shepperton Studios

In 1938 at 14 years of age, I left school and started work at Sound City Studios Shepperton, in the General Stores.

In the 1930s jobs were very scarce and hard to come by. My father was a painter there and had worked on films such as *Sanders of the River* and *Mill on the Floss*.

In those so called good old days the studios were known as Sound City and men waiting for work, had to wait outside the gate in all weathers. They were owned by Mr Loudon with Percy Bell, an ex-electrician as Studio Manager, who ran the five studios with a small administrative staff. Had it not been for the war, Mr Loudon had planned to turn the backlot and river area into a zoo.

The Old House, which is now in use as offices, was at the time, a hotel restaurant and bar and the stars would stay there until their films were completed. Part of the back lot now occupied by housing, were used as the locations for scenes from films like *Sanders of the River* (1936). At that time the river flowing through the grounds was kept very clean and many scenes were shot in and around the area. The Mermaid Statue, sitting in the middle of the river, was used in several films and can still be seen from the road bridge.

After starting work at Sound City in 1938, I worked there until joining HM Forces in 1941. The four stages "A" "B" "C" and "D" were taken over by the Government as a food emergency supply depot. Tate and Lyle Ltd. then filled the four stages with sugar.

Roy Pembroke
Props Manager

During the early part of the war the studios were bombed during daylight hours and two fourteen-year-old boys evacuated from London, who had not long started to work there, were killed. One of the bombs hit the corner of "C" stage where they were standing. One night later on in the war, a time bomb became buried under "D" stage and had to be dug out by the Army Royal Engineers. The Queen Mary Reservoir next to the studios had many bombs and mines dropped on it. At the top of the Old House, there was a man on duty, whose job it was to put a flag up and blow a whistle as a warning of German aircraft approaching, whilst all personnel ran for cover until the raid was over and the 'All Clear' given.

When the Vickers Aircraft Works at Weybridge was bombed, "A" and "B" stages were emptied of the sugar and Vickers moved in to make parts for Wellington bombers.

Whilst all this was going on, Mr Loudon and Percy Bell were organising the manufacture of dummy tanks, guns and aeroplanes, made out of canvas and wood and then camouflaged. These were used in the Middle East to convince the enemy that resources were greater than they were. This deception played a major part in the success of the campaign in the Middle East.

Every night of the war there were at least ten members of staff on all night fire duty and the hotel bar was a useful haven between air raids. When the Americans came into the war the guns of an Ack-Ack site at Addlestone were taken to help defend New York and they were replaced by dummy guns made at Shepperton studios. Many of our aircraft flying over enemy territory were nominated and given names of film stars who had worked in the studio.

In 1941, I left the studios and joined the Middlesex Regiment until getting demobbed in 1946. I returned to Shepperton and joined the Property Department, working on films such as *The Ideal Husband, The Four Feathers* and James Cagney's last film, *Ragtime*.

Working in the Property Department requires a comprehensive knowledge of a wide variety of subjects. They have a script and breakdown to enable them to cover the shooting programme scene by scene. An experienced props department is an essential element, for any production, as quick solutions are required as scenes develop and problems inevitably occur. When retakes are required, sometimes weeks later, the set has to be recreated exactly the same way using the same props, to ensure effective continuity.

Best Sellers

"You never know how far you'll go. It could all end tomorrow. It could all go on. You never know with this business... which is one of the good things about it."

Peter Sellers on the set of *Dr Strangelove*, 1963

Peter Sellers was the most extraordinary of comedy actors, yet he had the most ordinary of faces. He has been likened by many to the original "man with no face" of British cinema, Alec Guinness, whose ability to morph into the characters he played, made him the most admired film actor of his generation. Indeed Sellers started his hugely successful cinematic career alongside Alec Guinness in the 1955 Ealing Studios' classic, *The Ladykillers* – as the inept criminal spiv, Harry. Sellers studied Guinness carefully. He watched as this most plain and mild-looking actor became the convincing thief and murdering mastermind by using little more than a pair of red-rimmed glasses, some false teeth and a leering voice which Sellers admitted later, turned him "emerald with envy." Guinness spotted Sellers' talent immediately.

Sellers understood their similarity. Both had exceptional vocal abilities, and both were generally thought of as looking just the opposite – quite unexceptional. Yet, as the years were to progress it would become evident that Sellers' physical ordinariness – like Guinness's – would prove a huge boost to his career in film, enabling him to mould his plain features into a vast number of memorable characters, each with an extraordinary voice to match. "Never play the same kind of role twice over," was the advice that Alec Guinness gave Peter Sellers at the time, and with the exception of the long-running Pink Panther series, it appears the advice was heeded. Across more than 60 films, Sellers created a host of treasured characters and left behind him a legacy of comedy creations unrivalled by any film actor, before or since.

Richard Henry Sellers was born on 8 September 1925 to Peg and Bill Sellers in Southsea, Hampshire, England. He was called Peter in memory of his stillborn older brother. Within days of being born, Sellers made his first theatrical appearance, carried on stage at the King's Theatre in the arms of his parents, who were seasoned vaudeville entertainers. The bug must have bitten and Sellers' early years were taken up with drama and dancing classes before he was drafted into the Royal Air Force, where he became an official concert entertainer from 1943 until the end of World War II. While performing for the forces Sellers first met and worked with Spike Milligan.

It was Sellers' unusual gift for voice mimicry that pointed him in the direction of BBC radio. With the post-war years came a glut of comedy shows – on stage and radio – with established and new talent in high demand to help lift the nation's spirits following wartime triumph. Yet more than two years after hostilities had ended, Sellers, despite attending several auditions, still hadn't succeeded in joining the Beeb. Increasingly desperate, he decided to take matters into his own hands. One of the most popular shows of its time was *Much Binding in the Marsh*, a radio comedy set in a fictitious air force base, starring big name entertainers Kenneth Horne and Richard Murdoch. The show's producer was Roy Speer, who received a phone call one morning from Kenneth Horne. In his rich, deep, plummy voice, Horne waxed lyrically about a "first-rate chappy" he'd seen the week before at London's notorious Windmill Theatre. Speer reached for a pen and paper and asked Horne where he could find this Peter Sellers person. There was a pause at the end of the line

John Lewis (Peter Sellers) in Bryan Forbes *Only Two Can Play* (1961)

Right

Peter Sellers as Prime Minister Count Mountjoy –
one of three roles that he played in the 1959
comedy, *The Mouse That Roared*

Opposite

I'm All Right Jack (1959)

and then Kenneth Horne's voiced turned back to Sellers' own. "Actually this is Peter Sellers. Neither Mr Horne nor Mr Murdoch know anything about this call!" Sellers begged for an audition, claiming that the phone call surely proved he was a man who had the talent to impersonate. Sellers often claimed that the next few seconds lasted a lifetime as Speer thought through the deception, reflected on the deceit and then, quite wisely as it turned out, pushed his personal feelings to one side: "You're a cheeky bastard... but I suppose I've got to see you."

Sellers was given a five minute slot on a variety programme showcasing new talent enticingly called... *Show Time*. He used every second to run through his now well-rehearsed list of radio and film personality "voices." On 10 July 1948, the radio critic of the *Evening News* declared: "This mimic is the tops." Suddenly Sellers was in demand.

BBC radio's *The Goon Show* beckoned, reuniting him with wartime performer and friend Spike Milligan, along with Harry Secombe and in the show's early years, Michael Bentine. The Goons established Sellers as a character actor without rival. His outlandish characters, including Major Bloodnok and Bluebottle, are etched in the collective minds of a generation of radio audiences, and have been recognised as the precursor for the shenanigans and over-the-top tomfoolery of the Monty Python team.

It became obvious quite quickly that Sellers' voice appeared to be his biggest asset. His first "serious"

film work was dubbing voices, characters, and even animal noises onto soundtracks, including the uncredited role of a parrot in the 1954 Joan Collins' vehicle *Our Girl Friday* and even some of Humphrey Bogart's lines in *Beat the Devil*, the same year.

Peter Sellers made around a quarter of his films at Shepperton Studios. He appeared in 16 productions there, playing no less than 26 different characters – and that takes no account of the many "aliases" created by his cinematic alter-ego, the incompetent policeman, Inspector Jacques Clouseau, in the three Shepperton-based Pink Panther films. His list of dressing-up credits in these films alone includes a priest, drag artist, Mafia boss, hunchback, and "telefurn"-repairman.

Sellers' first Shepperton appearance, in 1957, came some two years after he had appeared in *The Ladykillers* (1955). The Ealing comedy had been a great success, though not for Sellers' own film career prospects. Perhaps the industry felt that one Alec Guinness was enough to be going on with. No one was more surprised and frustrated than Sellers himself, who in a 1956 interview declared, "Do you know what the powers of showbusiness call me? That man who does funny voices." So when the opportunity arrived to allow Sellers to show that his ability extended beyond his obvious vocal talents, he was to wholeheartedly embrace the role of Percy Quill, the 68 year old befuddled projectionist in a fleapit cinema in Frank Launder and Sidney Gilliat's Shepperton comedy, *The Smallest Show on Earth*. Because of Sellers' age, just 32, the producers had trouble visualizing this relative newcomer convincingly portraying the doddery old-timer opposite distinguished film actors Margaret Rutherford and Bernard Miles, both of whom were a generation older than him. In fact, Sellers' age was more akin to the stars of the film, Bill Travers and Virginia McKenna, who played the parts of the young couple who inherit the run-down loss-making venue. Sellers convinced the producers he had the voice, but did he have the look? Launder and Gilliat were shown an edition of the television show *Idiot Weekly* in which Sellers was playing the part of an old fuddy-duddy, William Cobblers. They hastily arranged make-up

tests and soon after Sellers was offered the part of Percy Quill. While a lot of Sellers' performance was trimmed in the cutting rooms before the film was released – much to the actor's annoyance – his portrayal was strong enough to ensure that he would finally be recognised as a very talented character actor on the big screen.

Sellers' next Shepperton outing was for John and Roy Boulting, who had achieved great success in the 1950s with biting satires on the legal profession, the army and universities in their hilarious and well-observed social comedies: *Brothers In Law* (1957), *Private's Progress* (1956) and *Lucky Jim* (1957). Having observed Sellers' work, particularly his regular appearances on the increasingly popular medium of television, they felt he was the right person to join a select group of respected acting talents who often starred in their productions. That treasured band included Terry-Thomas, Richard Attenborough, Ian Carmichael, Dennis Price and Irene Handl.

The Boultings put Sellers on a five-year, non-exclusive contract, which allowed the actor to work on other productions but meant that any time taken out from working with them would be added to the contract at

Ironically, while the screen test was going on, a seven-man delegation from the Electrical Trades Union was waiting in the wings to see the Boultings with another complaint. None of them recognised Sellers' character as being almost identical to their boss. "They even joined in the applause," remembers Roy Boulting.

the end. Sellers would make films on and off with the brothers for 15 years.

At the beginning, Sellers had problems getting to grips with the character of Prime Minister Amphibulos in his first Boulting's film, the 1958 production, *Carlton-Browne of the F.O.* (1959): "I just don't understand the character," he complained. Roy Boulting sat him down and to the best of his ability recounted the exploits of the Italian entrepreneur Filippo del Guidice, who had been a film promoter for some years and who with guile, cunning and continuous fawning persuasion had managed to find financial backers for, among other, famous British productions, Olivier's *Henry V* (1944) and *Hamlet*. Boulting did his best to put on the accent, which Sellers picked up on immediately and within minutes the character was born.

Carlton-Browne of the F.O. told the story of an incompetent diplomat (Terry-Thomas) fostering poor rather than happy relations in a British colony where valuable minerals are suddenly discovered. It was not a great success, though Sellers did receive some praise as the duplicitous politician.

The Boultings were not troubled. They already had their eyes firmly fixed on their next project, a stinging swipe on the British trade union movement, factory management and outdated shop-floor labour practices, *I'm All Right Jack*. So excited were the brothers at the prospect of Peter Sellers playing the role of the abominable union leader Fred Kite that they sent him the script by special courier. The script was returned equally quickly; Sellers turned it down.

The brothers were furious. They demanded to know

why. Sellers explained that he had read the script and just couldn't find the jokes in it. The Boultings didn't believe him and John Boulting immediately called Sellers over to his house for dinner, to allow both sides to talk through their concerns about the project. As Boulting recalls: "I was determined to be at my most insinuating, not to say insidious – subtly, patiently undermining all his objections." The problem was that many of Sellers' objections were based less on the script and more on his private fears that he could not find the character. The part of this harridan union leader was not in Sellers' realm of experience and he thought the role was beyond him. His final objection was that the role wasn't large enough. This they conceded, but pointed out that it would be the part that everyone remembered. Finally, Sellers agreed to carry out a screen test.

Sellers tried on more than 20 suits before he found the one he wanted – ill-fitting and baggy, yet tight and restricting in places, akin to the Marxist policies that Fred Kite adhered to. The actor began to feel much happier. Unlike Alec Guinness who preferred to create a character from the inside out in his own mind, Sellers preferred creating his characters from the outside in by literally putting the clothes on first and taking it all from there. The Boultings could have saved Sellers some time if they'd admitted to him early on that the bolshie union leader, Fred Kite, was closely based on a difficult shop steward at Shepperton. The "real" Fred was a diehard member of the Electrical Trades Union. He looked and behaved perfectly innocently until he brought the rule book out, when all hell would break loose as he forced fellow members to abide by some draconian regulations which he insisted must be followed to the letter.

There was certainly no shortage of verbal and visual material for Sellers to study in order to build up the character. The late-1950s saw much in the way of industrial strife across Britain as old-style unionists accused "the management" and the Tory government of not caring enough about the workers. Union leaders were never off the news. While the Boultings worked on the satire, Sellers was getting his teeth into the part. He

had his hair cut short and gave the character a Hitler-style moustache. By the time Sellers came to take the screen test he had also conquered the other physical attributes of Fred Kite, particularly his stilted, clipped voice and robotic walk. The test was to be a two minute scene in which Fred Kite berated fellow workers and interrogated one in particular, Stanley Windrush, the boss's incompetent nephew, to be played by Ian Carmichael. The Boultings didn't want to pay Carmichael just to come to Shepperton for Sellers' test, so positioned the assistant director opposite the actor instead, as Sellers let rip. At the end of the barrage there was a deathly silence – as of course there would be on a sound stage which had to remain perfectly still while filming was taking place. Sellers, having no actor to bounce off and feeling nothing coming back, started to look worried. Then the silence broke as John Boulting recalls, "Suddenly there was a gale of laughter, a round of applause from the workers who… were savouring something they'd never dreamed of hearing – their own shop stewards turned into recognisable figures of outrageous fun. Peter got his confidence back in a flash."

Ironically, while the screen test was going on, a seven-man delegation from the Electrical Trades Union was waiting in the wings to see the Boultings with another complaint. None of them recognised Sellers' character as being almost identical to their boss. "They even joined in the applause," remembers Roy Boulting. "That little incident confirmed Peter's wavering faith in our ability to judge what was funny – and what was best for him. It was an inestimable advantage… for the time it lasted."

I'm All Right Jack was a huge hit and won Peter Sellers the British Academy Award for best British actor of 1959. A review of the time by Leonard Mosley of the *Daily Express* seemed to sum up the reactions of both critics and audience to Sellers: "I saw a great British clown shed his comic mask and become an actor to be reckoned with. It is Peter Sellers who gives the film its touch of distinction. Where all the rest are just playing for humour, he is playing for the harder and more rewarding kind of humour – the kind that comes from observation of the way people behave." Such was

Above
A bearded Richard Attenborough as poet Gareth Probert, and Peter Sellers as frustrated husband John Lewis, in *Only Two Can Play* (1961)

Opposite Top
The point of no return for would be adultress John Lewis (Peter Sellers) tempted by unhappily married Elizabeth Gruffydd-Williams (Mai Zetterling) in *Only Two Can Play* (1961)

Opposite Bottom
Frank Launder on the set

the power of the film in general, and of Sellers' performance in particular, that 20 years later, when prime minister James Callaghan called an election suddenly in 1979, the BBC cancelled a scheduled screening of *I'm All Right Jack* for fear of being seen to lose its impartiality in such matters. The film had lost none of its power in summing up the problems in British industry, following a winter of strikes and union discontent. The film was again pulled from the schedules during Britain's infamous miners' strike, four years later.

Surprisingly, despite its great success it wasn't to be *I'm All Right Jack* which would find Peter Sellers international acclaim. That plaudit was to be bestowed on his next Shepperton production, *The Mouse That Roared*, the 1959 comedy directed by Jack Arnold and produced by future Beatles' films producer Walter Shenson. The film revolved around a small European country that decides to declare war on the United States in order that it can surrender and so become entitled to vast amounts of aid. Sellers played three roles in the film: that of the wily prime minister, Count Rupert Mountjoy; the grand old dame, Grand Duchess Gloriana; and the shy army chief, Tully Bascombe. *The Mouse That Roared* aspired to the coziness of the best of the Ealing comedies, with Sellers once again appearing to be copying Alec Guinness by playing several different roles in one film, including dressing up as a woman – Sellers' Duchess Gloriana bearing a more than passing resemblance to Guinness's Lady Agatha D'Ascoyne from *Kind Hearts and Coronets* (1949). Yet for all its good intentions, the film didn't quite capture the spirit of the Ealing comedies, perhaps because by then those films had themselves started to date and Ealing had stopped their production. Clever marketing in America, however, meant that after seven months of careful nurturing at cinemas in central New York, word spread that this was a film with appeal. By the end of 1960, *The Mouse That Roared* had been shown in over 8,000 American cinemas, making it the most profitable film in relation to the cost of its production that Sellers ever made, with the exception of the Pink Panther series. Sellers was paid under £5,000 to

appear in *The Mouse That Roared* compared with the £7,500 he received for *I'm All Right Jack*. That didn't seem to matter. He had arrived on the international screen, which was where he had wanted to be from the start. Sellers' international recognition was then cemented with his appearance in *The Millionairess* with Sophia Loren, that same year.

Sellers decided to turn his hand to directing as well as acting, attempting both in *Mr Topaze* – an adaptation of a Marcel Pagnol play, in which an ex-schoolmaster in a French village ends up among thieves but finishes up wealthy. The production was not a success. Sellers became nervous. His own film had flopped and his other starring staple, *The Goon Show*, had come to an end.

The remedy to Sellers' woes was once again to come from Shepperton. Frank Launder and Sidney Gilliat offered him the lead role in *Only Two Can Play*, a comedy drama about a would-be adulterous Welsh librarian. The screenplay had been adapted by Bryan Forbes from a Kingsley Amis novel, *That Uncertain Feeling*. Alongside Sellers Mai Zetterling starred as his potential mistress, Virginia Maskell as his long-suffering wife and Richard Attenborough, sporting a goatee beard (which has to be seen to be believed), as a Welsh poet with whom his wife mildly flirts to try and recapture her husband's loving attention. The film was shored up by a host of other familiar comedy acting talents including John Le Mesurier, Kenneth Griffith and Graham Stark. Sellers was captivating in the role of John Lewis, primarily because he played the part down rather than up. No silly voices, no false noses, just a restrained accent and even more restrained acting, as this little man in a little town thinks of dipping his toes in murky waters only to be pulled back by conscience, uncertainty and a twist of fate. Most critics felt it was Sellers at his best, understated and very persuasive. Sellers though seemed far from convinced that the film and his performance in it was anything more than poor. He had been unhappy from the start with the casting of the pretty actress Virginia Maskell as his wife Jean. When his complaints about her, late at night over the phone to John Boulting, went unheeded, he turned on his own performance

FRANK LAUNDER

Left
John Lewis (Peter Sellers) is fed up with his lot, in Bryan Forbes adaptation of Kingsley Amis's *That Uncertain Feeling*, filmed as *Only Two Can Play*, in 1961

labelling it "a total and irredeemable disaster". Boulting and the film's director, Sidney Gilliat, disagreed. In an attempt to prove their confidence in the film and his playing of the lead role, they offered to buy Sellers out of his share of the royalties. Surprisingly, Sellers took them up on the deal, immediately selling his share for £17,500 (around £250,000 in today's money). *Only Two Can Play* was one of the biggest successes of the 1960s. The film earned Sellers a BAFTA nomination for best British actor in 1962. And Sellers share earned its new owners over £120,000 – almost seven times what they had bought it for.

Late in 1961, Bing Crosby and Bob Hope came to Shepperton to make *The Road to Hong Kong*. The film re-teamed the duo some ten years after they had finished making their famed Road series of films. This film, the seventh and last, was not a huge success, but allowed Sellers an opportunity to work with two of America's finest, and on home territory. In the film, Sellers appears uncredited as an Indian neurologist.

It was back to leading roles when Sellers was once again teamed up with Richard Attenborough to appear in the film adaptation of John Mortimer's first radio play, *The Dock Brief*, in 1962. Known also as *Trial and Error*, Sellers starred as a failed barrister who pits his wits against Attenborough's henpecked husband up on a charge of murdering his nagging wife. Once again Sellers questioned the film and his own performance, and this time his self-criticism wasn't too far off the mark. He was easily out-acted by Attenborough who looks like he's having a wonderful time as the unrepentant killer.

Sellers professional frustration was not helped by the depression and despair in his private life. A trip to America to promote *Lolita* in May 1962 did little to cheer him, even though he was hailed by American critics and producers alike. Film roles were dropping from the sky, but Sellers wanted to get back to England as quick as he could.

Back at Shepperton in late 1962, Sellers started work on another Boultings' satire, this time poking fun at the expense of the Church of England, *Heavens Above!* Sellers starred as the Reverend John Smallwood, a prison chaplain who finds himself appointed to a snobby village where he must minister as much to the emotional needs of the rich as well as the financial needs of the poor. Once again the Boultings packed their film with a raft of British comedy acting talents, including Cecil Parker, Eric Sykes, Irene Handl and a blink-and-you'll-miss-him cameo from Boultings' stalwart, Ian Carmichael. Eric Sykes recalls working with Sellers: "There are 'bread and butter' actors; then there are actors with talent which they use to great effect; then we come to a higher strata, the Peter Sellers' class, blessed with exceptional talent. The difference is in the gift that used Peter Sellers – and extracted a very high price for its services." Sykes was referring to Sellers' tendency to take a character home with him rather than leave him in the dressing room or on the sound stage or with the costume at the studios. "I was lucky enough to be in *Heavens Above!* with him.

Eric Sykes was not the first person to comment on Sellers' predilection for taking his characters home with him. The Boultings had noticed it when Sellers played Fred Kite in *I'm All Right Jack*. They watched in amazement as Sellers would walk from the sound stage to the studio canteen exactly as Kite would, talking in the same way and even eating his food in the same way. Sellers always professed that he often felt he was being taken over by a part, as if being "possessed" in some way. The Boultings believed that with all the personal anguish, self-doubt and troubled relationships Sellers experienced, this was a convenient way of not having to face up to his personal demons.

Sellers' *Heavens Above!* "happiness" was not to last, as depressions in his personal life deepened. Yet the

Above
Peter Sellers as the Reverend
John Smallwood in the Boulting
brothers' Church of England satire,
Heavens Above! (1962)

A chance phone call from Sellers to Spike Milligan proved very constructive. Off the top of his head, Milligan suggested that the final scene in which the bombs explode, implying the destruction of the world, should be accompanied by the melodious tones of former forces sweetheart Vera Lynn singing "We'll Meet Again." Another typical stroke of surreal genius from Milligan, which Kubrick was happy to run with.

more depressed he got the better his performances became, as though his only route to emotional joy and contentment was through his acting. His talents were again to be stretched by Stanley Kubrick who had been bowled over by Sellers' performance as the decadent playwright, Quilty, in *Lolita*. Now Kubrick wanted him for his next project, a nightmarish satirical comedy about the end of the world being very nigh as the US launches a nuclear attack on Russia. Sellers plays three roles in *Dr Strangelove or: How I Learned to Stop Worrying and Love the Bomb*, made at Shepperton studios in 1963. He's the President of the United States of America, an English Royal Air Force group-captain, and a US Nazi nuclear scientist. As if that wasn't enough, Kubrick had originally intended Sellers to play a fourth role – that of the commander in charge of the aircraft carrying the H-bombs to Russia. After cracking his ankle, Sellers ruled himself out of that part, requiring as it did considerable athletic movement to get around the aircraft's bomb bays on set. The part went to American actor Slim Pickens.

Kubrick claims that Sellers invented the injury because he didn't want to play the fourth role. The mystery of the ankle though was not the reason for *Dr Strangelove* being wheelchair-bound. That had more to do with Kubrick and Sellers' obsession, that powerful men carry some kind of impotence around with them.

Dr Strangelove appears to end abruptly. Its ending is not the one originally intended. Kubrick had wanted to finish the film with one almighty custard pie fight, as the behaviour of the world leaders descended even further into farce. Food was brought onto the sound stage at Shepperton and, indeed, if you watch the final scenes of the film closely, a long buffet table can be seen, with bowls and a stack of plates positioned behind George C. Scott. The food is there but never referred to nor eaten. The food fight was actually filmed. All the actors pelted each other until neither they nor the film set was recognisable. The final result was one almighty mess. Neither Kubrick, nor the actors were happy and they searched desperately for a reasonable way to end the film. A chance phone call from Sellers to Spike Milligan proved very constructive. Off the top of his head, Milligan suggested that the final scene in which the bombs explode, implying the destruction of the world, should be accompanied by the melodious tones of former forces sweetheart Vera Lynn singing "We'll Meet Again." Another typical stroke of surreal genius from Milligan, which Kubrick was happy to run with.

If Sellers had feigned injury on the set of *Dr Strangelove*, there was no mistaking a real illness when it hit most dramatically. On 7 April 1964, Peter Sellers heart stopped beating for almost two minutes. The doctors got it restarted but it stopped again a further seven times. That day Peter Sellers died. Later, he would expound at great length on the effects this "dying" had had on him. Until his final passing in July 1980, he continually searched for the reason why he had been saved, unsure whether he had suffered a miracle or a curse.

Anyone who watched the goings on during the making of *Casino Royale* at Shepperton in 1966 might well have thought poor Sellers had suffered a curse, Bond had hit the big screen, with four outings in as many years since the series started in 1962. American producer, former lawyer and talent agent Charles Feldman felt that there was big money to be made in Sellers spoofing this new genre. He had observed Sellers breathing great comic life into Woody Allen's first film, *What's New Pussycat*, in 1965. Feldman approached British novelist and screenwriter Wolf Mankowitz to work on the screenplay. When Mankowitz heard that Sellers had been cast in a major role, he balked. The two had fallen out five years earlier, during their disastrous and short-lived business partnership attempting to get Sellers' failed *Mr Topaze* off the ground. Mankowitz warned Feldman: "Do not have Sellers in this film. The man will delay everything, destroy the schedule – and you."

Feldman ignored the warnings, signed up Sellers and

Above and opposite

Stanley Kubrick directing the three faces of Peter Sellers, on the set of *Dr Strangelove* (1963)

Page 123

The poster for *Casino Royale* (1965), with five directors involved, this extraordinary production, at one point occupied every stage at Shepperton and space at two other studios employed Scottish comedy director Joe McGrath. Within weeks, Sellers and McGrath were fighting in the star's Shepperton trailer, real fisticuffs, and things weren't going to get any better.

Looking back now, the plot of *Casino Royale* shouldn't have been too complicated. The film was based on Ian Fleming's first Bond novel, which had started movie life on the small screen back in 1954. It revolves around the heads of the allied spy forces calling James Bond out of retirement to fight superpower and super-foe, SMERSH. David Niven played Sir James Bond who in turn calls on all previous carriers of the 007 title to join together to avenge the death of 'M'. A host of international stars played various relatives of Sir James, including Woody Allen as nephew Jimmy Bond and Joanna Pettet as the glamorous Mata Bond. Sellers was to play Evelyn Tremble, an expert in all matters baccarat, recruited to financially ruin SMERSH baddie Le Chiffre, to be played by Orson Welles. Sellers took an instant dislike to Welles. It may have had something to do with their differences in weight. Sellers had started his career as a chubby actor. He had shed several stone in the years that followed, partly, it is said, in his attempts to enamour himself to Sophia Loren when making *The Millionairess* (1960), and also after slavish dieting following his near-fatal heart attacks. Sellers alluded to Welles' weight and lack of personal discipline. In return the American made it quite clear that he felt acting was more than just how much space one took up. Things deteriorated rapidly. Sellers refused to appear in the same shot as Welles, which made things a little difficult for McGrath, particularly when the scene dictated a battle of wits through a duel of cards at the baccarat table between Evelyn Tremble and Le Chiffre. As McGrath recalls: "This was my first film in Panavision, the letter-box-shaped screen. You could hold a hundred yards of set in the lens. We had seven hundred extras for the gaming tables sequence – but we had no way of bringing our stars together in the same shot!"

Then Sellers decided he wanted to play the smooth-talking Tremble with a Birmingham accent. The producer himself almost had a seizure. McGrath, who

by then had had quite enough of Sellers' escapades, said he could play it however he wanted, telling Feldman he would cut out what was not usable at the edit stage. Sellers changed his mind again, deciding to play the role straight. Far too straight. There was no character coming through at all now. It was when McGrath pointed that out to Sellers in his trailer alongside the sound stages at Shepperton, that the actor threw his first punch. McGrath left the film shortly afterwards and *Casino Royale* required a further three directors during the course of its production: John Huston, Ken Hughes and Val Guest.

The film – though funny intermittently – was not a success. Columbia Pictures who had invested huge sums were even less amused. They looked to point the finger of blame. The producer Charles Feldman died not long after the film was finally released and all eyes were on Peter Sellers who, though only appearing for a small while in the film, had brought a much higher degree of chaos to the filming and an even greater amount of negative publicity as a consequence. Columbia vowed Sellers would never work for them again.

Sellers didn't work at Shepperton Studios again until 1969. In the years since *Casino Royale*, his price for making a film had fallen from its peak of $1 million a picture to just $400,000. Depression and difficulties in his private life – his four-year marriage to Britt Ekland was coming to an end – continued to dog his work and good roles were drying up.

It was the Boultings who tried to come to Sellers rescue. They had bought the rights to adapt the stage comedy *There's A Girl in My Soup* into a feature film. Goldie Hawn – who was destined for great things – was cast as the dumb blonde who visits the love-nest of an ageing playboy only to drive him so nutty after he's taken her to bed, that he decides to take her on as his wife. The Boultings wanted Sellers to play the part of the ageing lothario Robert Danvers, a character content with bachelor hood and intent on staying that way until this waif-like ditsy girl changes his life. The problem was that the Boultings' film rights deal had been made with Columbia Pictures. Mike

Frankovich, who headed the British division of Columbia Pictures, gave it to them straight: "Look at the way he loused up *Casino Royale*. Personally I think the guy is very funny. But New York would never go along with him – they're still smarting too much." The Boultings admitted that Sellers wasn't always easy to work with, but pointed out the successes that had come with his appearances in such hits as *Only Two Can Play*. Only partly re-assured, an uncertain Columbia recanted. Goldie Hawn's performance seemed to lift Sellers, who for the first time during several productions felt happier and calmer on set. The lift in spirits did not lead to a lift at the box-office; the film was not well received by audiences.

Having Sellers take on the part of the mad March Hare in *Alice's Adventures in Wonderland* (1972), may have been a touch of ironic casting. The film was made at Shepperton in 1972 and Sellers joined an all-star British cast for the screen adaptation of the famed Lewis Carroll classic, including, Michael Crawford, Dudley Moore, Ralph Richardson and Fiona Fullerton in the title role. Sellers loathed the film and did himself little favour by publicly condemning it as "lousy" before it had even been released.

As Sellers struggled to find a part that would bring him the sort of success he had earned a decade earlier, he turned once again to the Boultings to lift him out of his career malaise. They offered him no less than six roles in their next comedy *Soft Beds, Hard Battles* (1973), a comedy about life in a Paris brothel during the war. The film went into production at Shepperton in 1973 and Sellers relished all the parts. They included a French President, a British Intelligence officer, a Japanese prince and Adolf Hitler. The film was a disaster, although for a few weeks during shooting, it wasn't all bad news for Sellers. While out one evening with the Boultings, Sellers met and started a whirlwind romance with Liza Minelli who at 27, was some twenty years his junior. The couple were inseparable, whether on set for *Soft Beds, Hard Battles*, off-stage in Sellers dressing-room or away from Shepperton, where she joined him in attending the memorial service for Sir Noel

CHARLES K. FELDMAN'S

CASINO ROYALE IS *TOO MUCH...* FOR ONE JAMES BOND!

JOIN THE CASINO ROYALE FUN MOVEMENT

JAMES BOND 007

CASINO ROYALE 007

CHARLES K. FELDMAN
presents
A FAMOUS ARTISTS PRODUCTION LTD
CASINO ROYALE U
Starring
PETER SELLERS
URSULA ANDRESS
DAVID NIVEN
WOODY ALLEN
JOANNA PETTET
ORSON WELLES
DALIAH LAVI
Guest Stars
DEBORAH KERR
WILLIAM HOLDEN
CHARLES BOYER
JEAN-PAUL BELMONDO
GEORGE RAFT
JOHN HUSTON
and Co-Starring
TERENCE COOPER
BARBARA BOUCHET
with
GABRIELLA LICUDI · TRACY REED
TRACEY CRISP · KURT KASZNAR
ELAINE TAYLOR · ANGELA SCOULAR

plus a Bondwagon full of the most beautiful and talented girls you ever saw!

Produced by CHARLES K. FELDMAN and JERRY BRESLER
Directed by JOHN HUSTON,
KEN HUGHES, VAL GUEST, ROBERT PARRISH, JOE McGRATH
Screenplay by WOLF MANKOWITZ, JOHN LAW, MICHAEL SAYERS
Suggested by the Ian Fleming novel
Music Composed and Conducted by BURT BACHARACH
PANAVISION® TECHNICOLOR®
A COLUMBIA PICTURES RELEASE
Hear the CASINO ROYALE theme music played in
the film by HERB ALPERT and THE TIJUANA BRASS

Printed in England by Lonsdale & Bartholomew, Nottingham

Clouseau is generally regarded as one of the finest comedy characters in the annals of cinema history.

Coward. For a while their relationship was so intense, that the film's shooting schedule had to be hastily redrawn as Sellers spent more time with Liza and less on set. As with so many of Sellers' romantic liaisons, it was soon all over and forgotten about. And as with so many of his recent films, so was *Soft Beds, Hard Battles*.

It looked very much as if Peter Sellers' film career had finally come to a grinding halt but an old and very personal friend was to come to his rescue. A friend who Sellers hadn't been in touch with for ten years, Inspector Jacques Clouseau.

Clouseau is generally regarded as one of the finest comedy characters in the annals of cinema history. Every pratfall, every faux pas, is met with equal measures of laughter and cringing discomfort from an audience stunned by Clouseau's incompetence and Peter Sellers' mastery of the role. Sellers had first played Clouseau in *The Pink Panther*, back in 1962. However he had not been the first choice of director Blake Edwards. Famed actor and raconteur Peter Ustinov, had already been cast in the role of the hapless French policeman until pulling out just weeks before filming was due to begin at the Cinecitta Studios in Rome. Blake Edwards was very nervous. "We were desperate. I was in Europe ready to start shooting the film. I was unaware of Peter Sellers at that stage except for one film I had seen him in, *I'm All Right Jack*." On the basis of that film alone Edwards was not convinced of Sellers' suitability. The stiff, very British, slightly cockney union leader Fred Kite was nothing like the handsome but accident-prone French policeman. Edwards was reminded that Fred Kite was a character created by Sellers, as Clouseau would be if given the chance. Under pressure and short of time, the director offered the actor the role.

The Pink Panther was a massive success. The stars of the film, including David Niven and Robert Wagner, were outshone by the brilliance of Sellers' masterly creation. Clouseau was a hit. Edwards immediately went into production on a second Panther film, *A Shot in the Dark*, which was filmed at Elstree Studios in London at the end of 1963. This time, Sellers' name was at the top of the starring credits and the film is a series of hilarious set-pieces for Clouseau to bumble through.

While there was a great deal of laughter on set, off set there was tension. Sellers and Edwards had seemed to hit it off when they first met, sharing a love of physical comedy and comic heroes, especially Stan Laurel. But it wasn't long before personalities clashed as Sellers became more demanding. To a great extent Edwards had encouraged Sellers' behaviour. Scripts were not to be adhered to. "We'd take what was on the page and ad-lib around it," Edwards confessed. But Sellers wanted more and more control. "The minute Sellers came in, he started to take over." Onlookers said both men were as bad as each other. Yet the friction doesn't show on the screen and it's highly possible that these two volatile creative talents worked well together, taking each of them to higher levels of comic achievement. That didn't stop Edwards and Sellers from falling out. Such was the acrimony that Sellers withdrew from the third Panther production – his role being taken over by American actor Alan Arkin, for the film *Inspector Clouseau* in 1968. As Clouseau himself might have said, the film "bommmbed" at the box-office and with the star and director not even on speaking terms, it looked very much as if Clouseau and the Pink Panther series were finished.

By 1974 Sellers was looking for a vehicle to re-ignite his on-screen popularity. After a string of film failures – his last seven films had either not been released at all or had been financial failures – Sellers also needed to generate some money. At the same time Blake Edwards was trying to re-establish *his* own box-office clout, following films which met with only mediocre receptions in the early 1970s. An approach was made to the two men to bring the character of Clouseau back to life and back to the screen – the small screen.

The plan by Lew Grade and his company ITC – makers of such TV hits as *The Saint* and *The Persuaders* – was to produce a 26-part sitcom for television to showcase the character. Having witnessed the previous success of Sellers' earlier outings as Clouseau at the cinema, Grade was convinced that he could translate that success into a TV show that could be sold around the world – as so many of his other TV productions had been. Alas it wasn't long before Edwards and Sellers were at each others' throats once again and it soon became clear that a 26-part series, which could take up to a year to film, just wasn't going to be possible. So Grade, Edwards and Sellers agreed to make a film instead.

The Return of the Pink Panther went into production at Shepperton Studios in 1974. As well as witnessing the return of Sellers to the role of Clouseau, Edwards cleverly brought back the hit characters from *A Shot in the Dark*, including the increasingly mad Chief Inspector Dreyfus, played with insane relish by Herbert Lom, Clouseau's judo-expert valet Cato, played by Burt Kwouk, and Sellers' personal friends and Britcom familiar faces Graham Stark and David Lodge.

As each Panther film came and went, the plots grew looser. Audiences didn't seem to mind. They were there to watch Clouseau fall about while those around him fell apart. The sadistic knockabouts between Clouseau and Cato were bone-crunchingly funny, and only took second place to the French fool's verbal mispronunciations and moments of solitary destruction. Nothing and no one was safe in Clouseau's hands. For someone whose heart had taken a severe battering ten years before, Sellers was holding up exceptionally well under the physical strain of his performance – ably assisted, of course, by younger and fitter stunt men. Not surprisingly, after a decade away from the screen for Clouseau and with Edwards and Sellers putting everything they had got, into coming up with a good cinematic product, *The Return of the Pink Panther* did great box office business.

Both men agreed to start work immediately on another Clouseau outing and *The Pink Panther Strikes*

Above

Blake Edwards on set at Shepperton Studios

Opposite

Another disaster befalls Inspector Jacques Clouseau (Peter Sellers), in *The Revenge of the Pink Panther* (1977)

Left

Inspector Clouseau (Peter Sellers) makes a poor Toulouse-Lautrec, in *The Revenge of the Pink Panther* (1977)

Next page

Peter Sellers dons another inept Clouseau disguise, in *The Revenge of the Pink Panther* (1977)

THE NEWEST, PINKEST PANTHER OF ALL!

PETER SELLERS

in

BLAKE EDWARDS'

THE PINK PANTHER STRIKES AGAIN

THE ALL-NEW ADVENTURES OF THE WORLD'S MOST BUMBLING DETECTIVE

U

©U.A.C.—GEOFFREY

starring HERBERT LOM

WITH COLIN BLAKELY * LEONARD ROSSITER * LESLEY-ANNE DOWN * Animation by RICHARD WILLIAMS STUDIO

MUSIC BY HENRY MANCINI * ASSOCIATE PRODUCER TONY ADAMS * "COME TO ME" SUNG BY TOM JONES

SCREENPLAY BY FRANK WALDMAN and BLAKE EDWARDS * PRODUCED AND DIRECTED BY BLAKE EDWARDS

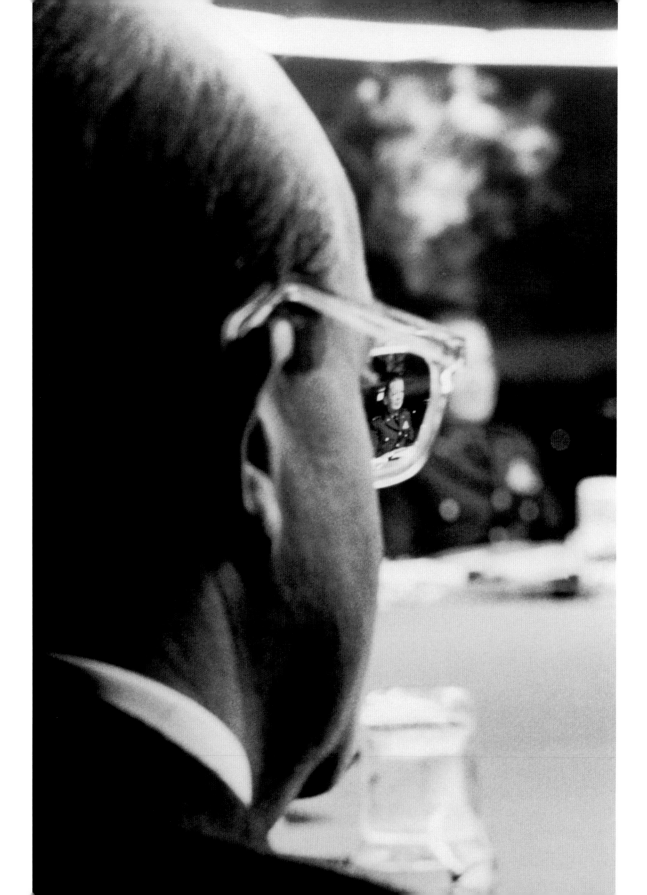

Again went into production at Shepperton in 1975. Sellers continued to tinker with the character, but the nuances now became self-indulgent and the ruses to enable Clouseau to escape from the most unlikely of situations became more tenuous and ridiculous (such as his helium-filled hunchback of Notre Dame costume carrying him up and over the rooftops of Paris). And the accent became, almost unintelligible. But the film had an in-built feel-good factor and the Christmas audiences of 1976 returned once again to the cinemas to receive their piece of Sellers' seasonal cheer.

Peter Sellers made his last film at Shepperton in 1977. Not surprisingly it was to be another Panther production, his fifth and final trip as the incompetent inspector – now promoted to Chief Inspector no less. For his part in *The Revenge of the Pink Panther*, Sellers was paid £750,000 plus ten per cent of the gross. The film's plot, what little of it there was, was even madder than before. Some of the jokes were beginning to wear very thin. Yet once again Clouseau, ably assisted by Herbert Lom, Burt Kwouk and Graham Stark, and joined by American stalwarts Robert Webber and Dyan Cannon, weaved enough magic to ensure that Sellers' last donning of the silly moustache and ill-fitting raincoat, would be a memorable and worthy addition to the long-running series.

Peter Sellers died from a heart attack while staying at the Dorchester Hotel in London, on 24 July 1980. His legacy of laughter lives on a quarter of a century later, with many of his 16 Shepperton films carrying particular affection in the eyes of both the industry and his fans. It seems therefore fitting that a film about his life, *The Life and Death of Peter Sellers* (2003), starring Geoffrey Rush, should be made, at Shepperton Studios.

Peter Sellers' Shepperton Filmography

1957
The Smallest Show on Earth
as cinema projectionist, Percy Quill

1958
Carlton-Browne of the F.O.
as Prime Minister Amphibulos

1959
I'm All Right Jack
as rebel Union leader Fred Kite,
and Sir John Kennaway

1959
The Mouse That Roared
as The Grand Duchess Gloriana XII, Prime Minister Count Rupert Mountjoy, and Tully Bascombe

1961
Only Two Can Play
as Welsh librarian John Lewis

1961
The Road to Hong Kong
as Indian Neurologist (uncredited)

1962
The Dock Brief
as barrister, Wilfred Morgenhall

1963
Heavens Above!
as vicar, The Reverend John Smallwood

1963
Dr Strangelove or:
How I Learned to Stop Worrying and Love the Bomb
as Group Captain Lionel Mandrake, President Merkin Muffley, and Dr Strangelove

1965
Casino Royale
as Evelyn Tremble

1969
There's A Girl in My Soup
as Robert Danvers

1972
Alice's Adventures in Wonderland
as The March Hare

1973
Soft Beds, Hard Battles
as General Latour, Major Robinson, Herr Schroeder, Adolf Hitler, The President, and Prince Kyoto

1974
The Return of the Pink Panther
as Inspector Jacques Clouseau

1975
The Pink Panther Strikes Again
as Inspector Jacques Clouseau

1977
Revenge of the Pink Panther
as Chief Inspector Jacques Clouseau

Pam Francis
Continuity

I started as a continuity girl in the 1950s and spent many happy years at Shepperton, and other studios, on sets with directors at the sharp end of film production.

Feature films are shot in many different pieces. Because of the expense, films are rarely shot continuously or in scene order, as you would watch them on the screen. In most cases, every scene will be shot on a particular set that has been built regardless of where that scene comes in the film. Those scenes may take place at the beginning, the middle and the end of the film. In between, there may be location work and other stage work. Yet, actors have to wear the same clothes, have the same hair style and be doing the same thing in the same place – even down to holding the same length of cigarette ends – that they had in a previous scene that may have been shot some time before. Everything has to be continuous, otherwise it does not look right on screen. If an actor goes through a door on one day and is then filmed on the other side of the door a few weeks later, you have to know if he was wearing a hat or not the first time round and be sure that you have a note of every article that the actor was wearing – what jewellery he or she had on, where hands were positioned, and so on. For example, if you shot a scene in a train carriage and the actor went to the window, you might not shoot the exterior of the carriage until three weeks later. When the actor opened the window for the interior scene, if he or she put their hands on the window sill in a particular way I had to make a note of it to ensure that the exterior shot had hands that matched the interior scene.

Today, of course, continuity is much easier using Polaroid cameras and video. But we didn't have them when I started. So I had to make a note of everything I saw. Not just what actors wore but where chairs and furniture were exactly positioned, particularly if pieces had to be moved to allow cameras through for close-ups. Was there a coffee table in shot, what was on the coffee table and so on. I needed to have instant recall down to the minutest of details. I also needed to take a note of the camera lenses, filters and all the technical details, so that when a cameraman came back to shoot a particular scene and asked "what did I shoot this on previously, what filter did I have on?", I'd be able to tell him.

I had also to time shots for a day-by-day tally of the film's length. No director wants to shoot four hours of film for what may be a 90-minute movie. So if I could give the director a very rough idea of how long it took for a carriage to come up a long drive, say 45 seconds, he could decide how much space he had to fill and how much of it he needed to use.

One of the most important things I had to do in the early days was to provide the daily continuity sheets, which tell the editor – who only had a piece of celluloid with a tiny image on it – what the shot was. He wanted to know what the take was, whether it was printed, whether it was cut – he may need to use a shot from a cut piece as a cutaway. He needed all these details to help him cut a film together.

Continuity was also helpful for new directors. A continuity girl could tell the director what shots will and will not cut together – a tracking shot into a static shot and so on. And, of course, one must never forget the importance of the direction of looks – which way were the actor's eyes facing, camera right or camera left?

GEORGE C. SCOTT

STRICT CONTINUITY DO NOT TOUCH

Above
George C Scott and Stanley Kubrick on the
set of *Dr Stranglove*

Left
Between shoots on the set of *Dr Stranglove*

In this country, but not in America, pictures have a
slate number and a scene number. Because the slate
number may be 211 but refer to scene 52, I also had to
keep a note of the slate and the scene numbers so that
the editor, who would have two sets of numbers,
would know which referred to which.

Continuity was very hard work but very good fun and
there was always a great sense of achievement when
you knew you had got it right. I often think that continuity are the forgotten heroes of film-making, playing
such an important part in making sure a film looks
and feels right. I certainly enjoyed doing that.

Horror

Freddie —
you're famous —
you're in a photograph
with... ME!!!

All that
is left of
Martin Ruthledge

thanks for maki...
me look the tallest
Roy Castle

thanks for st...
...Martin

"Working on a film with Peter Cushing was very peaceful. Peter always brought total conviction to what he did. Regardless of how unbelievable the story was."

Freddie Francis, 2004.

Mention the word horror to most cinema aficionados and the word "Hammer" immediately springs to mind. Following on from its gory success with *The Curse of Frankenstein* in 1957, Hammer films decamped to Shepperton in 1959 to make the first full-colour version of the classic scary movie *The Mummy*, starring everyone's favourite monster star, Christopher Lee, in the lead role of the misunderstood bandaged baddie. It was to be another 40 years before the original tale of *The Mummy* was resurrected and filmed once again at Shepperton with breath-taking special effects, turning its original very talky and not very scary predecessor into something more menacing and gruesome under the watchful eye of director Stephen Sommers. Within those 40 years the style of British horror films changed several times. Hammer would not be too regular a visitor to Shepperton – it was to make most of its films at its own studios in Bray. But Shepperton could once again prove – in horror as in other genres – that it would attract some very independent-minded producers intent on keeping audiences suitably frightened.

Britain hadn't made a great number of horror pictures until the late 1950s. Studios had tried to ape the success of Universal Studios' American productions in the 1930s, such as *The Ghoul* and *The Man Who Changed His Mind*, but the British versions were poor imitations of their US counterparts. This seems all the more extraordinary when one considers that it was the horror stories of the very British authors Mary Shelley, Bram Stoker and Robert Louis Stevenson that had been much adapted and copied by the American studios. To cap it all, with the arrival of sound at the end of the 1920s and the early 1930s, British talents, such as director James Whale and actors Boris Karloff, Lionel Atwill and Claude Rains, travelled across the ocean to make the US horror product sound and feel very English. Britain did have one successful horror star in the 1930s, Tod Slaughter, a quite over-the-top actor who would tour the provinces with revivals of old melodramas, many of which were then filmed. His most remembered Shepperton horror film performance was in the 1936 production of *Sweeney Todd, the Demon Barber of Fleet Street*, in which the aptly-named actor put in a truly memorable performance as the villainous, legendary throat-slitting coiffeur. Slaughter's films were less about horror and more about hamming it up, and were effectively marketed in America as being "typically British."

Hamming it up he may have been, but there was concern in some quarters that Slaughter's films and, particularly some of the more frightening entries from the Universal circuit needed to be more carefully scrutinised, before going on general release bearing an "A" certificate from the British Board of Films Censors. Until 1932, there had been just two certificates that the BBFC issued: the "U" certificate, which stood for universal and meant a film was deemed suitable for all to ages to view, and the "A" certificate, which stood for adult and meant that the film might contain material that was unsuitable for children. Young people were allowed entry to an "A" certificate film but had to be accompanied by an adult. In the wake of the early 1930s productions of both *Dracula* and *Frankenstein* – in particular, the death of a little child at the hands of Frankenstein's monster – complaints were made to the Home Office.

Page 136

The cast of *Dr Terror's House of Horrors* on set at Shepperton in 1964. From left to right: Donald Sutherland, Christopher Lee, Peter Cushing, a prop skeleton, director Freddie Francis, Alan Freeman, Neil McCallum and Roy Castle

Above

Jack Palance (left) as Ronald Wyatt with Peter Cushing (right) as Lancelot Canning, in the Amicus horror chiller *Torture Garden* (1966)

Opposite

The Day the Earth Caught Fire (1961)

"X" film. The age limit for an "X" certificate film was raised to 18 in 1970.

The coming of war brought a change in attitude towards on-screen horror. Occasionally used in propaganda films such as Basil Dearden's 1944 production of *The Halfway House*, or the 1945 Ealing chiller, *Dead of Night*, the genre was more or less laid to rest for the best part of a decade. The nation proved to have no interest in watching films with a horror content – the horrors of war had proved more than enough for the time being. If the horror film was to be left in a dusty vault for a while, the style of such films as *Dead of Night* was not to be forgotten – its collection of ghost stories would be cleverly rehashed many times over in anthology and omnibus horror films of the 1960s and 1970s.

The resurgence of horror films in Britain was thanks in no small part to Hammer Films, a small independent company founded in 1934 as Hammer Productions and named after its chairman Will Hammer, who had been a producer and performer in music hall and seaside summer shows. Will Hammer, aged 60, went back into films after the war, starting up Hammer Films in 1947. The company churned out various B movie products before having a large-scale success with two films based on the hit BBC TV sci-fi drama, *The Quatermass Xperiment* and *Quatermass 2*, in the late 1950s. With money in the bank, Hammer changed direction and switched to colour for lush gothic productions of variations on the Frankenstein, Dracula and Mummy stories. They found a new big screen hero in Peter Cushing and a glorious set of monsters and evil-doers in Christopher Lee. As Hammer settled down in its studios in Bray, Berkshire, many producers and directors were now seeking to copy its success and tap into a rich vein of bloody excitement that was attracting huge audiences.

At Shepperton there was a harking back to the days of Tod Slaughter with several historic horror films, such as *Jack the Ripper*, made at the studios in 1958, and *The Flesh and the Fiends* in 1959. The 1960 production of *The Hands of Orlac*, caused as much uproar off-stage as the scary goings-on did on celluloid. The Shepperton

These complaints were led by the National Society for the Prevention of Cruelty to Children who claimed that the BBFC was not being vigilant enough in the material it was allowing, or failing to prevent, young people from seeing. Consequently the BBFC introduced a new certificate: called "H" for horror. The aim of this new certificate was to highlight a film which may contain frightening or disturbing scenes. The certificate was meant to be advisory, but many local authorities used it as an excuse to ban all children under the age of 16. The "H" certificate was replaced by the more wide-ranging "X" certificate in 1951, which did exclude all those under 16 from entry to an

special effects team worked long and hard to invent a severed hand that could crawl without the use of wires. Tiny batteries were installed into the specially constructed finger joints on the model hand. To test their effectiveness, Ted Samuels, one of the special effects team, sneaked the hand into the Shepperton cafeteria one lunchtime and placed it next to the tray of an unsuspecting secretary who had just sat down for her lunch. The hand crawled slowly on to her plate and was convincing enough to give the poor woman a terrible shock. During the subsequent furore, Samuels quietly lifted up the hand, put it into his pocket and walked off unnoticed. The test had been a success.

By the early 1960s Shepperton's response to the increase in demand for horror films, both here and abroad, led to some interesting and clever pieces of cinema. In 1961, two very different but very important horror productions were made at Shepperton. The first was *The Day the Earth Caught Fire* by the director of Hammer's *Quatermass* hits, Val Guest. Born in 1911, Guest had started his career as an aspiring young actor in British films of the early 1930s. His acting was not a great success and after leaving for Hollywood to spend some time as a film gossip-journalist, Guest returned to Britain as a comedy writer working for some of the biggest names of the era, including The Crazy Gang, Arthur Askey and the hilarious Will Hay, for whom Guest co-wrote eight film scripts, including the 1937 classic *Oh! Mr. Porter*. Val Guest started directing films in 1942 and in the decades ahead would work with an eclectic and varied bunch of stars and talents including Frankie Howerd, Cliff Richard and, twice, with Peter Sellers – first in a naval comedy *Up the Creek*, and later, at Shepperton, as one of the many directors credited on the ill-fated Bond-spoof, *Casino Royale* (1965). In a career that lasted over 50 years, Val Guest's most admired work is *The Day the Earth Caught Fire*. Guest himself says the film "was possibly the toughest assignment I'd ever set myself." But it was a project he had set his heart on. "Every writer, every director has some pet project they've struggled over the years to get made. I had one I'd been bashing against Wardour Street walls to no avail for the best

part of seven years. It was a story I'd dreamed up called *The Day the Earth Caught Fire*, my vision of a future when mankind had done so many things to the atmosphere, then topped everything by inadvertently testing two atomic bombs at opposite ends of the globe at the same moment. All of which had altered the earth's orbit by one millionth of a degree and set us spinning slowly but surely towards the sun with disastrous climatic changes. Whereupon the government puts a security clamp on the whole incident which is eventually ferreted out by a relentless Fleet Street reporter. Since I had wanted to use the *Daily Express* as the newspaper that uncovered the story I sent a synopsis to the science editor, Chapman Pincher, asking for his comments. And he gave them. 'Good story, but a lot of balls,' he said cheerfully."

The Day the Earth Caught Fire starred Edward Judd, Janet Munro, Leo McKern and Arthur Christiansen, who was not an actor at all, but an ex-editor of the *Daily Express*. What made the film genuinely frightening at the time was that it felt like a highly plausible piece of science fiction told with great conviction through the eyes of Fleet Street's finest reporters. There were no monsters lurking around the corner, just Man destroying his own planet by his own stupidity. Shooting took eight weeks and the Shepperton sound-stage filming went without a hitch. Two of the most complicated pieces of filming could not be done at the studios but needed to be filmed on location in the centre of London. The first was for a sequence in which (due to the rising heat) swirling fogs were emanating from the Thames, engulfing south London and Battersea Park – where the shoot was taking place. With official permits in hand, Shepperton's finest crews set up their fog-making machines at the side of the Thames and started billowing out thick grey mist over the crowd of actors whose characters in the film were queuing up for water rations. All would have been well had it not been for a change in wind direction which sent some of the fog across the Thames to the Chelsea Embankment, where Her Majesty the Queen was trying to open the 1961 Royal Chelsea Flower Show in rapidly worsening visibility. Val Guest remembers 16 May 1961, very clearly indeed: "Somehow we managed

to finish shooting while our brilliant props master and assistants double-talked the police about how long it took fog machines to shut themselves off, as well as using various other delaying tactics so that when we finally wrapped up, we had managed to shoot all we needed without anyone being arrested, sent to the Tower or beheaded."

The second scene that relied heavily on careful planning was for the line in the screenplay which read: "They cross a debris-strewn Fleet Street, derelict and almost deserted." Easy to write but harder to execute. An almost military campaign was drawn up. The city police agreed to close down one of its busiest streets so long as Guest and his crew shot the scene early on a Sunday morning. No Parking signs were placed from the Law Courts to Ludgate Circus to clear the roads of parked vehicles. The scenes had to be rehearsed while traffic was still flowing and then, every 15 minutes – via a radio signal and a whistle – the police would stop the traffic at both ends of Fleet Street for precisely two minutes, during which time Guest had to get his shot, before the whistle blew and started the traffic up again for a further 15 minutes. At the start of each two-minute session, two policemen on motor-bikes would speed up each side of the street kicking down the No Parking signs, so that they were out of sight of the cameras. Two burly prop men would follow with a van in tow, shovelling rubble and dust over the signs. Guest did consider trying to shoot the scene using a back drop at Shepperton but decided that for the scene to feel convincing it had to be done in Fleet Street itself. *The Day the Earth Caught Fire* captured the imagination of both critics and audiences and won Val Guest a British Academy award for best screenplay.

The second big horror film to come out of Shepperton in 1961 was the film adaptation of John Wyndham's science fiction novel, *The Day of the Triffids*. A shower of meteors blinds almost the entire planet as intelligent plants plan to take over the world. The film itself was not exceptional and though the Triffids are menacing enough, it never really scares as perhaps it should, thanks to the lightest

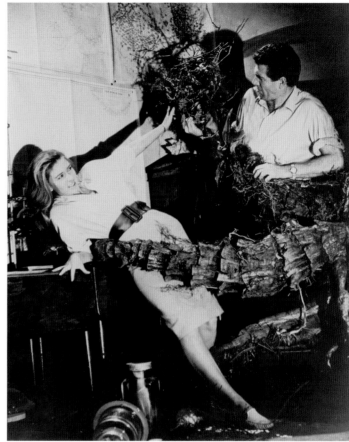

Above

The Day of the Triffids (1961)

Left

Karen Goodwin (Janette Scott) is left to the mercy of a carnivorous spore, in The *Day of the Triffids* (1961)

of directorial touches by Steve Sekely. What is interesting about the film is someone whose name is missing from the credits but without whose input the film might never have made it past the cutting rooms. Cinematographer and director Freddie Francis was brought in after location film-making in Spain had come to an end: "The stage on which we shot the interiors for *The Day of the Triffids* was "I" stage. The stage had originally been built at Walton studios and stayed there until it closed and it was then brought literally flat-packed over to Shepperton and put back up again for filming in. I wasn't involved with *The Day of the Triffids* from the outset. It was when they were pulling all the footage together and the film wasn't long enough that I was called in to shoot some extra scenes. The film was basically unshowable, so they contracted me as a director to come up with a new and expanded beginning and a new ending. Which is what I did."

Freddie Francis is as talented as he is modest. Born in 1917, he had wanted to make films as far back as he can remember. "I left school at 16. I was very interested in film. We used to have a cinema club where my friends and I would make our own 16mm movies – from then on I wanted to do it professionally. I got an apprenticeship with an elderly stills photographer for a while. My father was a bookmaker. One of the people who used to bet with him was the chief carpenter at British International Pictures. He got me a job as a clapper-boy at Elstree studios." During the war, Freddie Francis served in the Royal Army Kinematographic Unit before returning to become a camera operator at Shepperton studios. His first solo credit as director of photography was for *A Hill in Korea* in 1956. In 1960, Francis won an Oscar for his camera-work on Jack Cardiff's excellent production of *Sons and Lovers*. Within two years he was directing films, first un-credited, topping and tailing *The Day of the Triffids*, and then, also in 1961, getting his directorial debut with the Shepperton-based lighthearted romantic comedy starring George Chakiris and Janette Scott, *Two and Two Make Six*. "In those days, in order to get a film made, you had to have a completion guarantee so that people would accept you. A

lovely man called Monja Danischewsky asked me to direct *Two and Two Make Six*. I said the script needed changes and he said that was all right, to go ahead. Had I had any sense I would have refused to do it then, but having got permission out of the completion guarantors that I could direct the movie, I felt it was impossible to back out then."

Francis' early films as a director are distinguished by their stunning use of black-and-white, heightening suspense and building an air of mystery. Hardly surprising then that his talents were soon employed by Hammer Films, for whom he made three psycho-

Above
Jack Palance as Ronald Wyatt in
Torture Garden (1964)

Opposite
Director Freddie Francis

logical thrillers, almost back to back, between 1962 and 1964: *Paranoiac*, *Nightmare* and *Hysteria*. "I got in with Hammer as Tony Hinds who ran Hammer was a good friend. I started off doing one film with them and it was a lot of fun, so I did another, then another, and before I knew it, I was right into horror films." Francis' incredible work rate saw him dabbling in television as well as film – directing episodes of *The Saint* and *Man In A Suitcase* – and filming both abroad as well as in Britain. But it is perhaps for his Shepperton horror film work in the 1960s and early 1970s – particularly for Amicus Productions – that Freddie Francis is most immediately remembered.

Amicus was set up by American producers Max J Rosenberg and Milton Subotksy. They had originally filmed jazz groups and pop stars of the day, in films such as Dick Lester's *It's Trad, Dad*, in 1961. Amicus was run on a shoestring and in the early days there was little money to go round. Yet Rosenberg and Subotsky sensibly tapped into the rising popularity of the horror genre, which had flourished thanks to Hammer's output. They took full advantage of the Eady Levy – a tax break by the government which gave money back to production companies from a levy on cinema ticket prices – to produce carefully budgeted films for the booming genre. Their first horror picture was *Dr Terror's House of Horrors*, made at Shepperton in 1964. The plot revolves around a portmanteau of stories in which the central character, who turns out to be the grim reaper himself, tells the fortunes of a group of travellers on a train. The blueprint for the film had originally begun life as a handful of half hour scripts written by Milton Subotsky for an unmade television series in the late 1940s. "I had always thought that the British film *Dead of Night* was the greatest horror film ever and wanted to do something like it," Subotsky once said.

Subotsky persuaded Rosenberg to raise the £100,000 budget needed to finance the film. Rosenberg also 'borrowed' the title of the film from a compilation of German horror films he had been involved with while a distributor. Subotsky set about finding the right director for their project as he explained in an inter-

view with *Filmfax* magazine. "I had the script for *Dr Terror's House of Horrors* and was looking for a good horror director. I saw some of Freddie's work for Hammer and particularly liked his black and white films, not the colour films he made later. He did three in black and white and they were nicely done. So I thought yes, Freddie Francis will do."

After poaching one of Hammer's directors, Subotsky had no qualms in doing the same to its stars, offering lead roles to both Peter Cushing and Christopher Lee.

Above

Dr Rutherford (Patrick Magee) in a scene from the 1972 horror anthology, *Asylum*

Opposite

Torture Garden (1966)

Opposite

A captive cast – (left to right) Roy Dotrice, Richard Greene, Joan Collins, Ian Hendry and Nigel Patrick await their fate, in Freddie Francis's horror portmanteau, *Tales from the Crypt* (1973)

Following page

William Rogers (Nigel Patrick) in a scene from *Tales from the Crypt* (1973)

Both were now big names, and more importantly, big draws to cinema audiences. For *Dr Terror's House of Horrors* the pair were cast against type – Cushing donning a beard and a foreign accent, with Lee being given an opportunity to move away from the heavily made-up monster-type roles and show his dramatic range. Popular 1960s television disc jockey Alan "Fluff" Freeman, who had previously appeared in Rosenberg and Subotsky's musicals *It's Trad, Dad* and *Just for Fun*, was offered his only serious film role, and making his British film debut was Canadian actor, Donald Sutherland, who Subotsky cast after Freddie Francis had seen him in a play.

Filming *Dr Terror* was not without problems. Plans to cast musician Acker Bilk as Biff Bailey had to be abandoned when the jazz player suffered a heart attack. Freddie Francis suggested Roy Castle as his replacement. Two weeks into production, it became apparent that money was running short. Subotsky trod water, paying his crew in cash, while Max Rosenberg scurried around for the extra £5,000 needed. There were further troubles with the film's soundtrack. Musician Tubby Hayes had failed to come up with enough usable music and once again Freddie Francis had to come to the rescue, recommending Elisabeth Lutyens who had scored two of his earlier Hammer productions. Francis remembers that Subotsky came to rely on him in many productions, "Milton always wanted to be an editor. If he walked along the street and found two totally different pieces of film he would have tried to edit them together. That's what he was like. In the nicest possible way there was always a creative battle between myself and Milton. Very often the problem was that his scripts were too short for the contracted time. Sometimes I would do a timed read-through and the script may only last for around 50 minutes. On top of everything else, I had to embroider his scripts out to 90 minutes."

Dr Terror was released by Regal Film Distributors in February 1965 and was a box office success. Amicus quickly re-teamed Francis, Cushing and Lee for its next film at Shepperton, *The Skull* (1965). Between 1965 and 1970 Freddie Francis directed an average of two

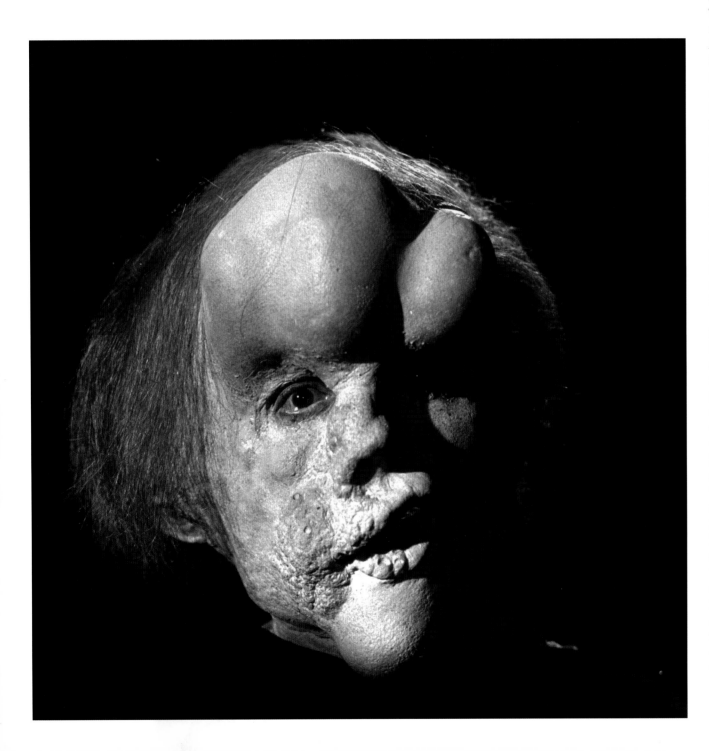

"In an age of horror movies this is a film which takes the material of horror and translates it into loving kindness."

films a year for Amicus and Hammer, including *The Psychopath* (1965), *Torture Garden* (1967) and, the most successful of Hammer horror films, *Dracula Has Risen From His Grave* (1968). By 1970, Francis was directing horror films away from the Amicus and Hammer stables, though still at Shepperton, but with only mixed success. Probably the most notable was *The Creeping Flesh* in 1972. Peter Cushing and Christopher Lee were reunited once again as good versus evil, in this suitably scary story of a Victorian scientist discovering that water causes the recompositon of living tissue on the skeleton of a huge Neanderthal man. Francis continued to make horror films at Shepperton for the next few years with star casts brought in to bolster often ropey material. There was the crude shocker *Craze* (1973) along with two better portmanteau productions, *Asylum* (1972) and *Tales from the Crypt* (1972). Among the casts for these films were such notable names as Jack Palance, Diana Dors, Britt Ekland, Joan Collins and Ralph Richardson.

In the mid-1970s, after making two horror films for his son Kevin's company Tyburn, Freddie Francis decided he'd had enough of the horror genre: "I decided I didn't really want to do any more horror films. I was sick of them. For a little while everything dried up. It seemed that horror was all people wanted me for." Fed up with being pigeon-holed and with the phone not ringing as much as it had been, Francis decided to return to cinematography. He was offered *The Elephant Man* to shoot at Shepperton in 1980. The story of a Victorian pauper who is severely deformed by a rare illness and who is rescued from a fairground freak show by a doctor who introduces him to fashionable society, was curious, shocking and true. Starring Anthony Hopkins and John Hurt, the film was to be the first mainstream production directed by the often surreal David Lynch. Freddie Francis is a little humble as to why he was asked to shoot the film. "The script for *The Elephant Man* originally implied that it was a horror film, which is one of the reasons I may have been offered it." Francis does himself an injustice. There were few cinematog-

raphers at the time who could have brought the level of feeling and expertise to the job, which translated into a very moving piece of cinema. As critic Dilys Powell wrote: "In an age of horror movies this is a film which takes the material of horror and translates it into loving kindness." Paul Taylor in *Time Out* heaped further praise on *The Elephant Man*: "If there's a wrong note in this unique movie – in performance, production, design, cinematography or anywhere else – I must have missed it." Freddie Francis has happy memories of working on the film: "*The Elephant Man* was David Lynch's first big movie. We became very good friends. He didn't give me instructions. We worked as a team. There was mutual respect. We filmed in black and white because Mel Brooks was giving David his break and I think he wanted to keep the budgets down. As it happens, I

think it was the right decision." *The Elephant Man* was nominated for eight Oscars® and won three British Academy awards.

Freddie Francis returned to Shepperton to make one last horror film in 1984, *The Doctor and the Devils*, a sorely underrated piece of British cinema. Starring Timothy Dalton, Julian Sands and Twiggy, it tells the story of an eighteenth century surgeon in Edinburgh who pays for bodies for use as specimens without enquiring as to where they came from. To some, this was just another rehash of *The Flesh and the Fiends* which had been made at the studios almost 30 years previously. Yet the scale of the sets and the production values were so high that 15 years later one of America's biggest directors would show them off as an example of film-making at its best. British film producer David

Opposite

The disfigured John Merrick as played by an unrecognisable John Hurt in *The Elephant Man* (1980)

Above

John Hurt as Merrick, in David Lynch's mainstream directional debut, *The Elephant Man*, beautifully shot in black and white by veteran cinematographer, Freddie Francis in 1980

Parfitt, who started out in the business as an actor and who appeared in *The Doctor and the Devils*, recalls a trip to America in 2001: "As a favour to Miramax I worked as a consultant on their film *Gangs of New York*. They were looking for someone to oversee the budget – it was their biggest ever production and they were nervous. It was an awkward job, because it looked like I was the Miramax spy, so I was never going to be popular with the director, Martin Scorsese, or any of the creative team because I was there, as they saw it, to cap their spending. Early on, Martin had been showing films to his crew that had inspired him and on the screening list I noticed *The Doctor and the Devils*. I mentioned that many years previously I had appeared in the film. There were hoots of laughter when I came on screen. The inspirational thing is that he's a great fan of Freddie Francis and his work and the use that

Freddie made of studio sets, particularly the massive street set at Shepperton for *The Doctor and the Devils*. Martin Scorsese screened the film to his own production designer to show some of the things he wanted to achieve in *Gangs of New York*." Scorsese was so impressed with Francis's work that he employed him as director of photography on *Cape Fear* in 1991.

If it seemed for some years as if the only people making horror films at Shepperton were Freddie Francis and Amicus Productions, that may not have been far from the truth. Their work dominated the smaller sound stages for many years in the 1960s and early 1970s. But other horror productions were also made at the studios and while *Dr Terror's House of Horrors* was shooting on "I" stage, famed horror director Roger Corman was also at the studios, with

Vincent Price, making a highly regarded version of the Edgar Allan Poe suspense story *The Tomb of Ligeia*, in "E", "F", and "G" block.

Everyone's favourite king-size spotted pepper pots, the Daleks, were wheeled into Shepperton for two cinema outings, filmed back-to-back, following the huge success of *Doctor Who* on BBC TV. Small screen doctor, William Hartnell, was not deemed a big enough star for the lead role in the widescreen versions. Instead, Peter Cushing was drafted in to play the eccentric time-traveller in *Doctor Who and the Daleks*, and *Daleks: Invasion Earth 2150AD*, both made in 1965. The films saw our planet's inhabitants threatened with enslavement by the evil Daleks that destroyed everything and everyone who got in their way. Both films were thought suitable for universal

Right

The tormented Creature
(Robert De Niro) in *Mary Shelley's*
Frankenstein (1993)

Opposite

Patricia Velasquez is Anck-Su-
Namun, in *The Mummy* (1998)

viewing and the British Board of Films Censors granted each a "U" certificate – proving that regardless of what the censor thinks may or may not be scary, there will always be a generation of viewers who, on hearing the word "exterminate," will run for cover behind the settee.

Horror productions at Shepperton tapered off through the 70s as viewing tastes changed, and only a handful of shockers were made over the next 20 years. Laurence Olivier returned to Shepperton in 1978 for an unintentionally camp and theatrical version of *Dracula*, in which the part of the infamous vampire was played by American actor Frank Langella. *The Hunger*, director Tony Scott's stylish but not greatly lauded tale of a couple of ageless vampires desperate for blood, was made in 1981. While Freddie Francis was working on *The Doctor and the Devils* at Shepperton in 1984, director Franc

Roddam was working on a remake of *The Bride of Frankenstein* (1935), entitled *The Bride* (1984), starring pop-icon Sting and Jennifer Beals. Ten years later Kenneth Branagh took horror film-making to a whole new level with his version of *Mary Shelley's Frankenstein*. His budget of $44 million was many times more than had ever been spent on any horror film in the studios' history, a record to be broken in 1998 by Stephen Sommers' *The Mummy*, who brought a delightfully tongue-in-cheek rendering of the story of an Egyptian priest, buried alive, who returns to wreak havoc 2,000 years later. Stages at Shepperton were taken for *The Mummy* and its sequel, *The Mummy Returns*, two year later. Both films are great fun with stars Brendan Fraser, Rachel Weisz and John Hannah playing most of the film for laughs, which helped assuage the slightly more gruesome moments as twenty-first century technology and digital effects created genuinely scary screen moments. Both films did huge box office, making them

the sixth and fifth respectively highest grossing horror films of all time.

Ironically, in a time when the BBFC has reviewed its certification of earlier horror films and re-classified them as more suitable for general viewing – for example, *Dr Terror's House of Horrors*, formerly suitable for an adult audience, is now classified as a "PG" ("a PG film should not disturb a child aged around eight or older") – the 1998 version of *The Mummy* was re-classified up a category on its video and DVD release from a "12" certificate to a "15", to allow for an extra seven seconds of footage to be added which had been excised from the cinema version. Does this reflect genuine concern from the censor or just sales hype by the distributors? Whichever it is, one thing is certain, almost half a century after Britain got the formula right for frightening its audiences with style, horror still sells.

Peter Cushing as Grimsdyke, returns from the grave, in the ghoulish anthology *Tales from the Crypt* (1973)

Opposite

An unrecognisable Jack Palance, in Freddie Francis's *Craze* (1973)

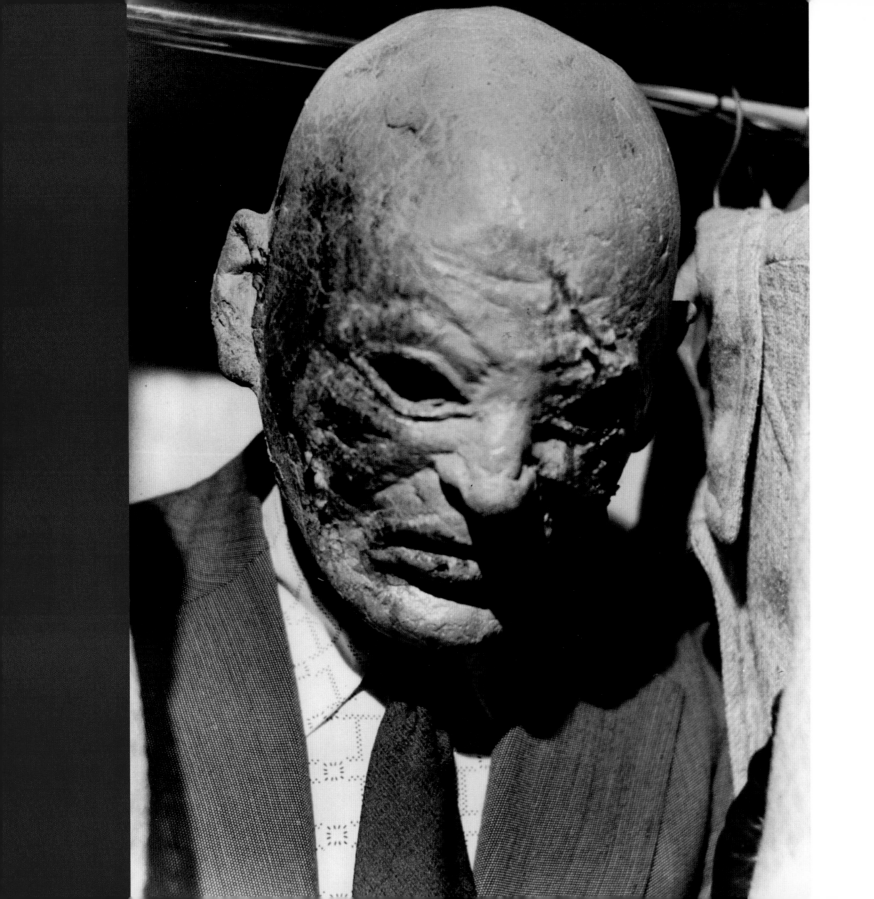

Terry Sharratt
Boom Operator

I started my life in the film industry in 1952. I was fifteen-years-old and had just come out of hospital after spending two years in a sanatorium for TB. The doctor told me that I could start work but it would have to be a very light occupation. I was sent to a special labour exchange in Oxford Street, London that dealt with the disabled and people like myself. The first interview I had was with a company called Romulus Films who were looking for an office runner. I was lucky enough to get the job and began a career in films that lasted fifty years.

At the time Romulus were shooting *The African Queen* on location in Africa and at Shepperton. My main duties were to collect boxes of special cigars from a shop in Mayfair and post them to John Huston in the Congo. I did this once a week. The cigars were Huston's favourite and he couldn't work without them. I reminded John Huston of this many years later when we were shooting *The Man Who Would be King* (1975) in Morocco, with Sean Connery and Michael Caine. By now I was a boom operator.

My first job on the shooting stage at Shepperton was on a film called *The Extra Day* (1956), directed by William Fairchild and starring the American actor Richard Basehart. It was Beryl Reid's first film. The clapper boy was called up to do his National Service and I was given his job. I was completely useless, partly because no one told me what to do. It was at this time that I met Mike Roberts and Peter MacDonald who became two of the best camera operators in the business, with Peter eventually becoming a director in Hollywood and recently directing the second unit on Harry Potter. Both tried to help me become a clapper loader but unfortunately without much success. Peter Price, the second assistant on *The Extra Day*, suggested I join the sound department as a trainee boom operator. Here I would be able to learn what actually happens on the set without inflicting damage on the production.

A boom operator is the guy who holds a very long pole with a microphone dangling on the end. Most people, especially electricians, will tell you that anyone could do the job. What few people understand is that the boom operator has to learn all the dialogue, just like the actors. Today's microphones are very directional and must be pointed in the direction of the artist who is speaking and be ready to swing to another artist before he or she speaks. Being late swinging over is known as off-mike and would sound like switching the volume on a radio up and down. The other thing a boom operator needs to understand is the lens size on the camera – if it is wide, medium or close in the shot. In my early days you could be fired for getting the mike in shot. The other thing a boom operator must not do is to get a mike shadow in picture; you have to learn to skip around the lighting. The sound from the microphone is fed back to the sound mixer who will set the levels on the sound console.

After periods at Ealing and MGM Elstree I left to work on *Lawrence of Arabia* (1962) in Jordan with David Lean. From that time onwards I became a freelance boom operator working with some of the great directors, including Billy Wilder, Otto Preminger, John Sturges, Nic Roeg, Stanley Kubrick, Ken Russell, Lewis Gilbert and many others.

It is well known that most directors have no time for the sound department; the director Anthony Mann once said to me that "sound people are a necessary evil." Terence Young who directed the first Bond film told me exactly the same thing while working on *The Jigsaw Man* (1985). "I would rather re-record the picture than have sound men on my set." he said. He told me not to take this personally, but he hated all of us! Being on the set all day, up front, he made my life hell.

Camera crews can do no wrong in the eyes of the directors or producers. I have been on shoots where they forgot to put film in the camera. "Oh we will have to go again," was the usual response, but woe betide the poor boom operator who gets a mike or its shadow in the picture; the whole crew look at him as if he is completely mad. Some of the directors would fire you on the spot.

The one thing that my list of directors above had in common was that they were all real film-makers. They did not sit on the set surrounded by banks of monitors with dozens of people watching them and giving their advice and opinions on the best way to shoot the scene. These films are made by committee. The greats would sit in their chair, tell the focus puller what lens to use, the grip how much track to lay and operator which way to point the camera. I have worked on films where a scene is covered from every angle, wide shot, medium shot, over the shoulders, close ups all round and then the editor would make a picture. I cannot tell you how many times I have worked on a film where this proved to be the case.

Billy Wilder never attended "the rushes" where you view the day's filming. I worked with him and Jack Lemmon (the nicest, kindest actor I ever met in my fifty years in the industry) on *Avanti* (1972) in Rome and Billy said he always liked to print the "first take" if

he could. It was all in his head, no fuss no hassle, and Billy would boast that he never did a shot he didn't use.

At Shepperton I worked on *Force Ten From Navarone* (1978) starring Harrison Ford and Robert Shaw with location shooting in Yugoslavia, Plymouth and Jersey. We finished the picture on the lovely island of Jersey as both Robert Shaw and Guy Hamilton, the director, were tax exiles. Both had run out of allocated working days in the UK without paying tax. Guy Hamilton would fly in daily from Paris to work at Shepperton, which was handy for the crew as he would bring back duty free cigarettes. I also worked on *SOS Titanic* (1979), which we shot on the big silent stage at Shepperton. I was lucky; this film was one of only two made at Shepperton in 1979.

I will always remember *The Keep* (1983), directed by Michael Mann, because I made more money on this film than on any other. It was made in the days when we were paid by the hour and not by the dreaded "all in deal." Michael Mann was a director who never knew when to stop, which meant we earned lots of lovely overtime. Funnily, it is also the only film where we had a meeting to complain about making too much money when we just wanted to go home! Another Shepperton based film was *The Man Who Fell to Earth* (1976), directed by Nic Roeg and starring David Bowie. I didn't know much about pop music and had to ask my kids who Bowie was.

We shot several scenes of *The Elephant Man* (1980) at Shepperton and I remember what John Hurt endured while making the film. The make-up used to take several hours to apply and we had to work every other day to give Hurt's facial skin a chance to recover. This was David Lynch's second movie and the film that launched his successful career.

I always thought Shepperton a very professional studio which made some of the best British pictures. Many studios have now gone but Shepperton remains, still making great pictures.

Mind Games

Harvey Stephens is Damien in
Richard Donner's *The Omen* (1975)

The things that really frighten us are those things that make us think we're losing our mind

David Seltzer – Writer, *The Omen*

Every good Horror film needs a monster – something or someone that the audience can focus on, to help us understand the chaos that we are witnessing being inflicted on those poor souls on the big screen. Some categories of monster are scarier than others and we deal with them all in different ways emotionally. There is the horror of nature which, even after thousands of years of evolution, Man seems to fail to understand. Films abound where humankind must pay the price for meddling with the universe: from *Jaws* (1975) to *Armageddon* (1998) or *The Swarm* (1975) to *Earthquake* (1974), Man discovers his biggest enemy is himself.

There is supernatural horror – far safer because it can't easily be understood and, therefore, we can't blame ourselves for what's going on. Cinema audiences have always found supernatural monsters enjoyable to watch, knowing that whatever bloodletting may be taking place in front of their eyes, the horror will stay very much within the safe confines of the nearest multiplex. Vampires and possessed creatures know their place.

Perhaps the most troubling monsters are the psychological demons. What is scarier than the horror of a disturbed mind. Death and chaos in the real world that is caused by real and apparently normal people is very troubling. When the wrong-doers seem to be getting away with their crimes, it becomes even harder to watch, as our natural instinct and belief that ultimately good will always win over evil is left in tatters. That's what appears to happen in *The Omen*, which was made at Shepperton studios in 1975. The lead characters meet grisly deaths apparently at the behest of a small boy who, by the end of the film, most audiences believe is the son of the devil. Director of the film, Richard Donner, says, "Did evil win over good? That's your choice. I always looked at *The Omen* not as a horror film but, in my mind, as a mystery suspense thriller."

The Omen was one of many films from Shepperton which have pushed our understanding and fears about human nature to the limit and exploited our fears and phobias even further. As *The Times* said of the film in 1976: "A cut above the rest in that it has an ingenious premise, a teasingly labyrinthine development, a neat sting in the tail, and enough confidence in its own absurdities to carry them off."

By the end of the film, most of the cast had been dispatched, their characters killed with style and panache. Gregory Peck as Ambassador Robert Thorn is shot by the police in a church as he prepares to plunge a knife into his child's heart. Lee Remick as Katherine Thorn first falls from a balcony onto a wooden floor and when that doesn't finish her off is tossed out of a hospital window and comes crashing through the roof of an ambulance. Patrick Troughton's crazed Father Brennan is impaled by a lightning conductor in a church graveyard while David Warner, as the journalist Jennings who is piecing the whole story together, is decapitated by a sheet of glass falling from a lorry in front of a horrified crowd. For the mid-1970s this was scary stuff and for a film with a very tight budget, Richard Donner and his special effects team had to work that much harder to make the horror convincing. The decapitation was originally supposed to take place by plate glass falling from the top of a building. But special effects man John Richardson

Below

Lee Remick and Gregory Peck
facing evil in Richard Donner's,
The Omen (1975)

Opposite

A catalogue of murder and
mayhem forces Senator Robert
Thorn (Gregory Peck) to extreme
measures in *The Omen*

The Omen took less than three months to film and cost just
$2.8 million – well below the average American film budget
of the time, which cost at least $4 million.

just couldn't get it to work. Then he came up with the idea of making the sheet of glass come straight off the back of a van. Donner had little money to make the film and knew he was likely to have just one attempt at getting the scene in the can. He ensured that there were six or seven cameras rolling – Donner himself was shooting on one of them – to capture every moment from every angle. Donner recalls editing the infamous scene that anyone who has seen *The Omen* still talks about. "Audiences are conditioned to look away when something bad is going to happen. If you count for them you know they're going to look up after 'three' when the bad thing should be over. That's how we cut the decapitation scene originally. We then went back to re-cut it. Instead of counting to three, we counted to five, so when the audience came up from their count of three, after having seen the head come off, they thought it was gone. But of course it was still there rolling around, and the screams were compounded. I remember driving home with David Warner's 'head' in my car one day. David wouldn't even look at it. He just couldn't."

The Omen took less than three months to film and cost just $2.8 million – well below the average American film budget of the time, which cost at least $4 million. Yet the film fired the public's imagination and was a huge commercial success, taking some $60 million at the US box office alone. It's extraordinary then that the picture had been turned down by almost every American studio, including Fox, who must later have been more than satisfied that they changed their mind. Some of the film's success may be attributed to the well-publicized stories of filming difficulties and frightening coincidences that occurred during production. Gregory Peck's plane flying from Los Angeles to London, was hit by lightning. Just a few days later, *The Omen* screenplay writer, David Seltzer, was on the same flight from America when his plane was also hit by lightning. Director Richard Donner

was getting out of a car to go into a house after shooting one day when a car coming the other way slammed into him.

The camera crew spent some considerable time filming at the old Windsor Safari Park in Berkshire. After a few days shooting a sequence in the lions den – for a scene which never made it to the final cut – they left to film in the baboon's compound. As they did so, some of the lions attacked a guard in his booth and killed him. Two even more horrific incidents happened shortly after. Richard Donner recounts one of them: "We chartered an airplane. We had no money. We were going to shoot with it on the ground at a small airport. We got a call from the owners who told us that they had a full charter that day and said that if we let them charter the plane out on the day we needed it, they'd let us have it later for nothing. So we said 'go ahead and use it.' The day they used it, the plane took off and hit a flock of birds. The engines quit and the plane crashed at the end of the runway and veered into a stream, hitting a car on the way and killing the people inside the car, who were the wife and two children of the pilot. It's a true story. And it could have happened to us."

And a devastating accident was to befall John Richardson, *The Omen*'s special effects man, who had created the notorious decapitation scene. Filming in Belgium on another project, he and his girlfriend were involved in a head-on collision with another vehicle. The girlfriend was beheaded. When Richardson woke up at the scene of the accident he saw a road-sign which read, Liege 666 kms.

The Omen still continues to frighten audiences some three decades after it was first made, and though the film spawned three sequels, none was as highly regarded as the original. Writer David Seltzer enjoyed working on *The Omen* and attributes some of its

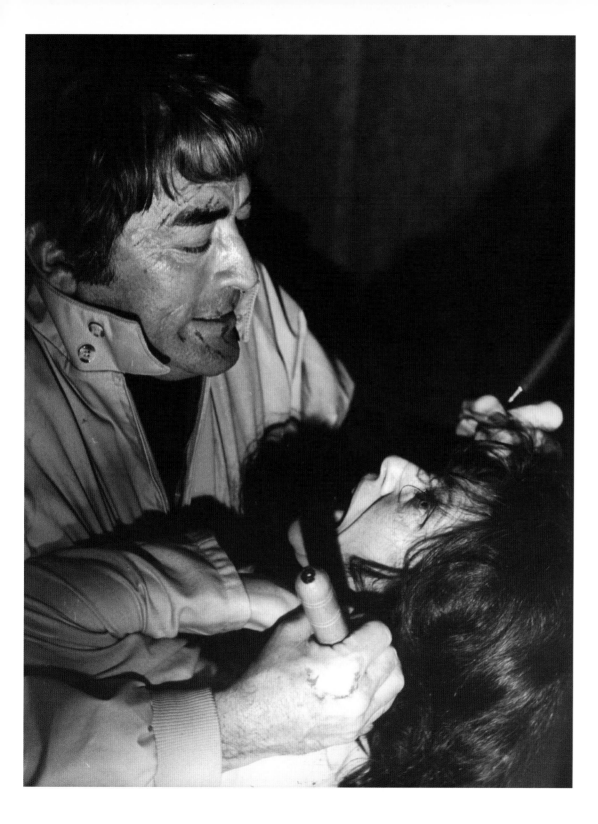

success to the expertise afforded to cast and crew by Shepperton Studios. "I set *The Omen* in Britain because I tended to write scripts set in places I wanted to visit. In London, at that time, they took production design far more seriously than we did in America. I wrote stage directions that were fulfilled to the letter. In the graveyard scene, I talked about rats scurrying from one end to the other and when I went on to the sound stage at Shepperton, they were training rats to scurry around. I talked of the priest's room being covered in sheets of paper from the Bible and sure enough that was there too, literally page by page."

Ten years before *The Omen*, Polish director Roman Polanski produced a stylish psychological thriller, *Cul de Sac* (1965). Filmed on a Northumbrian island as well as at Shepperton Studios, the film tells the story of two gangsters arriving at an old castle whose reclusive owner is trying to keep his young voluptuous wife hidden from the outside world. The film is generally regarded as being overlong and more perplexing than entertaining. One critic described it as. "A voyeur's wallow in schizophrenia and murder to no point beyond sensation – but one could not deny the talent at work." This somewhat macabre thriller seems equally as macabre in its making. The part of the highly-sexed wife was played by French actress Francoise Dorleac who arrived on Holy Island, Northumbria, with 20 suitcases and a chihuahua that she had illegally smuggled into Britain in her handbag. The reclusive castle owner, George, was played by Donald Pleasance. Polanski said that, despite Pleasance's obvious outstanding acting capabilities, he was constantly trying to upstage everybody, always seeking to hog the camera and finding increasingly ingenious ways of doing so. Lionel Stander, the gruff-voiced American actor made famous in later years as the "butler" in the US hit crime show *Hart to Hart*, was accused by the cast and crew of becoming in real life, Richard, the gangster character, that he was playing.

At the time of its production *Cul de Sac* had one of the longest continuous scenes in cinema history. While Pleasance and Stander have a heart-to-heart

Right
Billie Whitelaw plays Damien's
nanny in *The Omen* (1975)

discussion on the beach, Dorleac, as Teresa, takes off her dressing gown and walks into the sea. The scene lasts almost seven and a half minutes and became increasingly difficult to shoot as retake after retake saw the French actress having to spend five minutes at a time in freezing icy waters. Stander had his own reasons to complain. In a scene where the on-the-run gangster is hunting for food in the kitchen, Polanski insisted on 16 takes until he was satisfied that he had what he needed. Each take required Stander to down a pint of milk. That was a lot of milk. *Cul de Sac* was released in November 1966 and though it met with mixed reviews – frequently from those who couldn't quite understand what the film was about – it won the Golden Bear award for best film at the Berlin Film Festival in 1967.

In 1972, Frederick Forsyth's novel *The Day of the Jackal*, in which the British and French police combine to prevent a professional assassin's attempt on the life of Charles de Gaulle, was excellently translated to the big screen. The film remains compelling viewing even now, thanks to the hauntingly convincing portrayal of the cool and calm killer known simply as The Jackal, played by Edward Fox. Fox was cast in the role after director Fred Zinnemann was impressed by his performance as Hugh Trimingham opposite Alan Bates and Julie Christie in *The Go-Between* in 1971. Another reason Zinnemann chose Fox for The Jackal was that he was looking for a relatively unknown face to play the lead, so that audiences would be not be diverted from being carried along by the suspense in the story. At the time, it was rumoured that Michael Caine had wanted to play the role of The Jackal. Perhaps if Zinnemann had realised that the film would disappoint at the box office, he may have changed his mind about putting a star name into the lead role. Though no one doubts that what makes the film so plausible, believable and therefore ultimately frightening, is the key central performance of Fox, which is never less than real. Indeed, for a while, the audience – if they didn't know better from history – would be excused for imagining that the cool calculating killer could pull off one of the murders of the century, while frustrating the police of two countries

Left
Ringo Starr as the Pope and
Roger Daltrey as Liszt in Ken
Russell's biographical
fantasy *Lisztomania* (1974)

Opposite, top left
On the set of *Cul De Sac*

Opposite, top right
Donald Pleasance in Roman
Polanksi's *Cul De Sac* (1965)

Opposite, bottom
Roman Polanski's *Cul de Sac*
(1965)

that have little or no idea who this man is and where
he can be found until the dying seconds of the film.

With hits of varying degrees of success under his belt,
such as *The Devils* (1971), *The Music Lovers* (1970), *Mahler*
(1974) and *Tommy* (1975), director Ken Russell went to
Shepperton to make what many regard as his most
excessive and controversial film – a biographical
fantasy of the life of Liszt, portraying the composer as
a modern day pop performer. The lead role of Liszt, in
Lisztomania, was taken by the pop idol from The Who,
Roger Daltrey, with fellow musicians and actors such
as Paul Nicholas playing Wagner and Ringo Starr as
the Pope. It wasn't just the dialogue that seemed to
put critics off, for example, "Piss off, Brahms!" What
surprised many was not the excess of the movie –
excess was something that they had come to expect
from Ken Russell – but the seemingly poor production values. Russell was renowned for expensive look-

MICHAEL DEELEY and BARRY SPIKINGS present
for LION INTERNATIONAL FILMS

DAVID BOWIE

in Nicolas Roeg's film

THE MAN WHO FELL TO EARTH

Also starring RIP TORN · CANDY CLARK · BUCK HENRY · Produced by MICHAEL DEELEY and BARRY SPIKINGS · Directed by NICOLAS ROEG
Screenplay by PAUL MAYERSBERG from the novel by WALTER TEVIS · Executive Producer SI LITVINOFF · Musical Director JOHN PHILLIPS
Services by MAYFAIR PRODUCTIONS · DAVID BOWIE records and tapes on RCA · BRITISH LION INTERNATIONAL

ing sets and expensive looking films, and *Lisztomania* seemed to have neither. For once the critics were in agreement. *Sight and Sound* declared: "This gaudy compendium of camp, second-hand Freud and third-rate pastiche is like a bad song without end." Critic Patrick Snyder was even harsher: "Oscar Wilde once said 'Each man kills the thing he loves', and the remark perfectly suits Ken Russell's film treatments of classic composers... he has bludgeoned into pulp some of the finest music civilization has produced."

While Ken Russell was making *Lisztomania* at one end of Shepperton, at the other work was underway on an altogether different piece of cinema, an intellectual science-fiction film, *The Man Who Fell To Earth*. Directed with his usual style by Nicholas Roeg, the film tells the story of a visitor from outer space who comes to colonize Earth, where he finds his powers are destroyed and he becomes an alcoholic cripple. The lead role was taken by cult pop star yet cinematic newcomer David Bowie whose character, on arrival at our planet, becomes increasingly wealthy by his intergalactic inventions but soon becomes corrupted by Earth's vices. *The Man Who Fell to Earth* is obscure and expects its audiences to think at many different levels. It's cleverly written and beautifully photographed but it is never an easy film. *The Illustrated London News* said of the film: "Once you have pierced through its glittering veneer, you find only another glittering veneer underneath." *The Times* wrote: "You feel finally that all that has been achieved has been to impose an aura of mystery and enigma where essentially there is none; to turn a simple tale into the sort of accumulation of sensations that has become fashionable." This new age fairytale has gained quite a cult following since it was made. Director Nicholas Roeg has always been pleased with the film. "I enjoyed the content. An alien living in a strange world. It's not just sci-fi. David had tremendously good thoughts about the piece. He trusted me. It wasn't an overnight success but it built up. I wouldn't want to do anything that's inaccessible."

Following on from the success of *The Omen*, and seeing his cinematic career on the up once again, veteran American actor Gregory Peck returned to Shepperton

in 1977 to star in a suspenseful fantasy thriller, *The Boys from Brazil*. Peck played Dr Josef Mengele in the film of Ira Levin's ingenious novel, about the cloning of Adolf Hitler through DNA and body tissue, intended to breathe new life into the Third Reich. The film was ahead of its time, and what remains haunting after each new viewing is that the ideas it threw up in the late 1970s can now be matched by the technology which has evolved since *The Boys from Brazil* was made. At the time, the film was a high quality thriller with cast to match. Now, its plot with an added dose of twenty-first century reality, allows an audience a glimpse at the potentially harrowing consequences of cloning a madman's DNA. Peck was joined in the film by James Mason playing fellow Nazi, Eduard Seibert, and Laurence Olivier as a Nazi hunter modelled on the famous Simon Wiesenthal. Ironically, Olivier had only taken on the part to fight accusations of anti-

Above

Gregory Peck as Dr Josef Mengele in *The Boys from Brazil* (1977)

semitism, that followed his playing of a vicious Nazi from Paraguay who drills Dustin Hoffman's teeth in *The Marathon Man* (1976) the year before. For both roles, that of a Nazi and then a Nazi hunter, Olivier was nominated for an Oscar®. While *The Boys from Brazil* was being made, the real Josef Mengele was still alive and living in exile in Sao Paolo, Brazil. He died shortly after the film's release.

One of the unexpected box office successes of the early 1980s was the adult supernatural fantasy *The Company of Wolves*, directed by Neil Jordan. This dark story of a girl who dreams of werewolves was made at Shepperton in 1983 and starred Angela Lansbury as the Grandmother, David Warner as Father and Sarah Patterson as Rosaleen. The dark variations on the theme of *Little Red Riding Hood* are beautifully

explored via clever make-up and stylish filming, and the sequences of dreams within dreams give the psychological aspects of the film that much more frisson and resonance. It is perhaps a thinking man's Hammer horror film, or as one critic exclaimed: "A horror film as literate as it is visionary, it's great fun."

"If you want a vision of the future, Winston, imagine a boot stamping on a human face forever." O'Brien's words to Winston Smith, in *1984*, remain as haunting as when they were first spoken by Richard Burton in the film version of George Orwell's famous novel. Made at Shepperton in the year of its title, its cinematic release was planned to coincide with that much-fated year, so that we could all sit back and ask how real was Orwell's second world war vision of the

Opposite and left
The Company of Wolves (1983)

Above
On the set of *The Company of Wolves* (1983)

future which had finally arrived? There had been a film version faithful to the book in 1955, but then, the year of the title was still some three decades away. Making *1984* for 1984 required a little more from a story that was supposed to be prophetic – about Big Brother taking over the world and Doublethink becoming the norm. The film managed a few twists to Orwell's original nightmare and the lead roles are excellently played by Burton, as the personification of Big Brother and John Hurt as a very little cog in a very big wheel of government-run life who, following brain-washing, comes to love the world he lives in. Filming for *1984* took place at both Shepperton and at various locations across London, including Alexandra Palace. The Palace had been gutted by a fire in 1980 and the roofless shell provided the necessary structure required to film the rallies in Victory Square. Though Richard Burton was the fourth choice for the lead in the film, it's now hard to imagine anyone else playing the role of O'Brien. Sadly, the actor died shortly after filming had been completed. Quentin Crisp said that *1984* was: "A tale of unrelieved bleakness told with relentless accuracy to Mr. Orwell's novel, to which it is a kind of homage."

Taking its name from a 1960s hit British pop song, *The Crying Game* was made at Shepperton in 1991 and was released the following year. This complex tale of an IRA gunman who befriends a black British soldier and the troubles that ensue following the soldier's death, after a hostage-taking and the gunman falling in love with the dead soldier's lover, is never less than a brilliant study of identity and gender. Indeed, such was the power of the film with its beguiling blend of political thriller and romantic drama, that *The Crying Game* won an Oscar® for best screenplay by the film's writer and director Neil Jordan. The strength of the film – which was shot in Ireland, around London and at Shepperton – emanates from the acting of the leads including Stephen Rea as the confused terrorist, Miranda Richardson as Jude, and Jaye Davidson as Dil – a role which Stanley Kubrick had warned Jordan was probably uncastable. It was also Kubrick who advised Jordan to change the name of the film from

Opposite
Miranda Richardson as Jude, in *The Crying Game* (1991)

Left
Stephen Rea as IRA terrorist on the run Fergus, in *The Crying Game* (1991)

Below
Forest Whitaker as British soldier Jody, in *The Crying Game* (1991)

Page 177
Richard Burton and John Hurt in a scene from Michael Radford's *1984*

its original title, *The Soldier's Wife*, because Kubrick believed that films with military or religious connections in their titles put people off from going to see them. Jordan had previously witnessed such failure with his religiously entitled films, *The Miracle* (1991) and *We're No Angels* (1989). As with many small budget films, turned down by all the studios at the outset, the production almost ran out of funds before it was completed, but it was saved by producer Stephen Woolley who borrowed money against a cinema he owned in London to help keep the production afloat. Time magazine summed up the essence of the film: "Every so often a 'little' film hits the collective heart. *The Crying Game* is one of these, because it shows that a man is never so naked as when he reveals his secret self." As well as winning the Oscar® for best screenplay, the film also garnered another five Oscar® nominations.

Miranda Richardson was back at Shepperton in 1992 filming in Louis Malle's, *Damage*. She played the wife of a Conservative minister, played by Jeremy Irons, whose life is destroyed when he falls obsessively in love with his son's girlfriend, played by Juliette Binoche. The film is an erotic tale penned by the famous playwright, David Hare, and deals with the mental torment caused by love... or is it lust? As Anna Barton (Binoche) utters in the film: "Damaged people are dangerous. They know they can survive." Alas, the film, known as *Fatale* outside England, did not survive quite as well. Miranda Richardson won an Oscar® nomination and a British academy award for her portrayal of Ingrid Fleming, but the film never quite received the critical plaudits some thought it deserved. *Variety* called it: "A cold, brittle film about raging traumatic emotions," while the *Observer* was more generous: "A carefully controlled picture about uncontrollable passion, in which precise camera movements and unobtrusive editing subtly complement the immaculate acting." What almost everyone who saw the film agreed was that it left the audience, if not mentally traumatized, then certainly emotionally drained.

Left and below

Member of Parliament Stephen Fleming, (Jeremy Irons) continues his affair with Anna Barton (Juliette Binoche), in Louis Malle's erotic drama, *Damage* (1992)

Opposite

Juliette Binoche plays Anna Barton, the object of an MP's lust, in *Damage* (1992)

man who represents the law, the man who is a virgin – and I thought that if we fitted up someone with all those attachments and qualities then we had the ideal sacrifice. In order to put it into the shock ending, I used the age-old trick of flipping everything on its back and showing the truth to be diametrically opposed to what it is, so that in this case the hunter becomes the hunted." In other words, no happy ending for Edward Woodward as Sergeant Howie who finds the young girl, her disappearance merely concocted to entice him to the island, where he is ritually burnt to death in the wicker man as a pagan sacrifice.

The Wicker Man was filmed in the winter of 1972 in Dumfries and Galloway. From the word "action" there were problems as Ingrid Pitt, who appeared as the librarian recalls: "The film faced a nightmare all through its making, its post-production, its travels to get distribution. Ever since the film got started in script form, it felt like there was a dark cloud hanging over it."

Much of the problem with the film coincided with problems that were taking place back at Shepperton, which was going through a troublesome time. Earlier in 1972, the studios had again changed hands – taken over from British Lion by financier John Bentley. The name of the new overseeing company was Lion International. Immediately there were suspicions that Bentley – a renowned asset-stripper – was looking at ways of disposing of the studios. Shepperton was said to be losing £12,000 a week and Bentley, it appeared, wanted a quick sell-off. However, sensing the heat and wanting to proceed with caution, Bentley did seek to encourage film production at the studios as Peter Snell, producer of *The Wicker Man* recounts: "Everybody was nervous that Bentley was going to get rid of Shepperton, which is one of the great studios in England. So he beseeched me to get something into production as soon as possible to put everyone's mind at rest that he was going to make films." Ironically, after a parlous year at the studios in 1971 – one of the reasons that prompted the sell-off – some eighteen productions were made at Shepperton in 1972. This

One of the most emotionally draining films ever made is *The Wicker Man*. The star of many films that keep us all awake at night, Christopher Lee, has often said that *The Wicker Man* is the best film he's ever made. Fans of the classic horror film may well think he is right. *The Wicker Man* tells of a devout Christian policeman who is sent to a Scottish island, where paganism is rife, to investigate the disappearance of a young girl, and finds his own life at risk. The screenplay was written by Anthony Shaffer whose script lifted the tale to something well above the average shocker it could have been. Shaffer recalls trying to do something different with the story. "It seemed that I ought to try and dress it up in a way that provided something in the shock detective story – like *Sleuth*. I started with a checklist of who would make an ideal human sacrifice. There was the king for the day, the

assuaged some of the fears that a closure of the studios for development was imminent. Though the problems for many films, including *The Wicker Man*, were not to end there.

The Wicker Man continued production, oblivious to much of the politics being played out hundreds of miles away at the studios. Director Robin Hardy and his cast and crew braved the wintry elements to come up with a first class horror-thriller that culminated in the burning of an actual wicker man on the south west coast of Scotland. Edward Woodward, who had to read his lines from huge cue cards on the cliff top, remembers filming the final scenes. "It was me in there up to the very last stages of the burning wicker man and that was rather scary." Rumours circulated that real animals would be burnt alive during filming, inflaming the passions of animal activists who protested loudly and vigorously. Petitions were drawn up with animal rights people howling all over the place. I put out an inflammatory little notice that only cuddly woolly animals were going to be burnt and nothing else." Of course, none were, and the controversy soon died down. Rumours still abound as to the reason why a body double was used in the naked dancing scene of the character Willow, played in the film by Britt Ekland. Some claim it followed protests by Britt's new husband, Rod Stewart, and others say that it was because Britt Ekland was pregnant at the time.

Right
Edward Woodward (left) and
Christopher Lee (centre), as
Sergeant Neil Howie and Lord
Summerisle, with director Robin
Hardy, on location for cult horror
The Wicker Man (1972)

Below
Sergeant Neil Howie (Edward
Woodward) is further disturbed
by the unusual goings-on on the
island of Summerisle, in the classic cult horror film, *The Wicker
Man* (1972)

Opposite
On the set of *The Wicker Man*

Back at Shepperton, Robin Hardy got to work with his editor to cut the film together. An original 102-minute version was presented to the new board at Shepperton who immediately ordered the film to be cut and cut again. It appeared that no one wanted the film to be a success. The director was shocked. "The new management sliced the film up like salami. I was very disappointed because the film had been gutted." *The Wicker Man* ended up with a running time of only 86 minutes, so that it could be released by Lion International merely as a supporting feature at the cinemas. The original full length negative along with the out-takes and deleted scenes, were supposed to have been stored safely in a vault at Shepperton. But an order went out to clear the vaults of all old and useless material. Somehow the original negative for the film ended up with all the useless trimmings and dumped as landfill for the construction of a new motorway at that time, the M3 near Shepperton. This prevented Robin Hardy from ever being able to piece together his original cut of the film.

When Ingrid Pitt said there was a cloud hanging over the film from start to finish, it seems that she knew what she was talking about. Nevertheless, and probably partly as a consequence of the way the film was treated, *The Wicker Man* has achieved a cult status which it thoroughly deserves.

It's fair to say that *The Wicker Man*, along with all the other films in this chapter, leave the viewer asking the same question: could any of that really happen and if it happened to me, what would I do in such a nightmare scenario? Everyone will, no doubt, have a different answer to these questions, which is quite possibly what the makers of the films would have wanted. Keep your audience thinking and just a little nervous that what they are seeing could happen to anyone and they'll come back for more, if only to be assured that if something is going to happen, it's going to happen to someone else first.

Above

Britt Ekland is Willow MacGregor,
in *The Wicker Man* (1972)

BRITISH BOARD
OF FILM CENSORS

3, SOHO SQUARE LONDON W.1.

President

The Rt. Hon. The Lord Harlech K.C.M.G.

PRESIDENT *Harlech*

SECRETARY *Stephen Murphy*

BRITISH BOARD OF FILM CENSORS BRITISH BOARD OF FILM CENSORS BRITISH BOARD OF FILM CENSORS BRITISH BOARD OF FILM CENSORS BRITISH BOARD OF FILM CENSORS BRITISH BOARD OF FILM CENSORS BRITISH BOARD OF FILM CENSORS BRITISH BOARD OF FILM CENSORS BRITISH BOARD OF FILM CENSORS BRITISH BOARD OF FILM CENSORS BRITISH BOARD OF FILM CENSORS BRITISH BOARD OF FILM CENSORS BRITISH BOARD OF FILM CENSORS BRITISH BOARD OF FILM CENSORS BRITISH BOARD OF FILM CENSORS BRITISH BOARD OF FILM CENSORS BRITISH BOARD OF FILM

THE WICKER MAN

THIS FILM HAS BEEN PASSED

Dave Godfrey
Studio Manager

I came to Shepperton Studios in 1985, shortly after John and Benny Lee, the owners of Lee Lighting Ltd, purchased the site. I didn't have the perfect CV, being an aircraft technician by trade and more used to keeping 747s aloft! It was soon apparent that my qualifications were just right; studio management is as much about plate spinning and juggling, as it is about the more recognised managerial skills, so ironically, I still keep things in the air.

In the first month, I had to learn a new and colourful vocabulary. Everything in the film industry has a nickname and I made copious notes on the difference between Blondes and Redheads, that there was nothing sweet about Honeywagons, where I could find a Pancake, what to do with a Pig's Ear and how to tell a Windbag from Skypan. I also met Robert Redford, Meryl Streep, David Bowie and Patsy Kensit and learned the art of cleaning inspections, toilet checks and eighteen-hour days.

Over the years I have been privileged to be involved with somewhere in the region of 200 feature films and major television projects. I still remember the pride I felt when Sydney Pollack's *Out of Africa* (1985) was the runaway success at the 1985 Oscars, winning seven of its eleven nominations. It was the first feature film I had been involved with and a fantastic introduction to my new world.

I've since seen dreams become reality on many more projects and still feel the same sense of pride in the final product that I did nearly twenty years ago. People say that when the excitement wears off, it's time to move on! My own view is that once it's in your blood, it is almost impossible to move on.

As we move forwards into a new and exciting era of development and improvement, firmly established as a key player and centre of excellence on the world stage, I still find this business of smoke and mirrors just as exciting as ever; it's now in my blood, and I've listed plate spinning and juggling skills as prerequisites for all new staff.

For those who are interested:

Blondes and Redheads are small film lights
Honeywagons are mobile toilets
A Pancake is a wooden plinth that you use to raise props
A Pigs Ear is a scaffolding fitter that looks like... you guessed it!
A Windbag is a framed canvas backing
A Skypan is an uplighter for illuminating a backcloth from ground level.

Above
Director Sydney Pollack, with Meryl Streep and
Robert Redford, on the set of *Out of Africa* (1985)

Left
Dave Godfrey on the roof at Shepperton

Gary Stone
Group Sales Manager

I joined Lee International in Kensal Road in 1976 straight from school. I was a temporary assistant runner initially and used to set off at 6am to get 60 sausage rolls from the Greasy Spoon to feed the crews. In 1977 the company bought Wembley (the old LWT studios) and I progressed through the ranks until in 1984 I was made studio manager, one of my proudest moments. In 1989 Wembley was sold and I came to Shepperton.

My first position at Shepperton was Commercial Manager. It was a new environment for me and a difficult time as the banks had an increasing control and the close teamwork I was used to was more difficult. However it broadened my experience and I knew this was the career I wanted. In 1998 Shepperton merged with Pinewood and I was appointed Group Sales Manager.

The key part of my job is building up contacts and going out to meet people and negotiate deals. I am charged with bringing in new business but I generally stay involved when the new customer comes into the Studios and try to ensure that any queries or issues are effectively dealt with. It is a bit like running a hotel.

What is special about my job is the opportunity to meet lots of different people. I remember being bowled over when I met Katherine Hepburn and George Cukor right at the start of my career and knowing that I wanted to be part of the film business. But it is the range of people whom I meet which really enthuses me. The fun is bumping into Phyllis in the canteen one moment and then Lord Braborne the next. I love the opportunity to mix with everyone and they all have special qualities.

I am often asked which stars have made the most impact on me. It is a hard question but I particularly remember greats like Charlton Heston, James Mason, Maggie Smith and Peter Ustinov. I had the privilege to meet Barbara Streisand when she was filming *Yentl*. Her PA brought a piano into the office and I agreed to try it out. I am an enthusiastic pianist but struggle to read music. She came in as I was just playing a small section of the *Yentl* soundtrack which I had picked up by ear when I was in the cutting room. I was caught totally unaware by her arrival and awaited her reaction with trepidation. To my amazement she stood by the piano and started to sing as I continued to play. I will never forget the power of her voice. It was like playing with an orchestra. Unforgettable.

Once I had a very small part in *Quadrophenia* (1979). I had some temporary black dye mixed into my hair and it stayed in my hair for three months.

I know I have been lucky to work in a place where every day is different and you never know what is around the corner. The film industry provides an

invigorating environment and I feel very positive about Shepperton's future. The merger gives us a lot more flexibility in meeting customers' needs and I take pride in working with my colleagues to provide the facilities and environment in which talented film-makers can continue to thrive.

Above
Gary Stone

Epics

"The easiest kind of picture to make badly."

Charlton Heston on the making of an Epic.

Charlton Heston knew what he was talking about when he described an 'epic' as "the easiest kind of picture to make badly." Having appeared in several epics in the 1950s and 1960s, Heston was well aware just how easy it could be for a lavish spectacle with a huge budget to become more of a legendary event as it flops than the historical and lavish story that the film was trying to portray. Epics are big extravagant affairs of the silver screen; a handsome lead hero often parading round in little more than a loin cloth and open toe sandals, taking on the corrupt leadership of a nation or freeing a people oppressed by immoral government. Heston had his fair share of acting plaudits for his roles in epics, indeed for a while it seemed that he would become typecast in these medieval or biblical parts, in such films as: *The Ten Commandments* in 1956, *El Cid* in 1961, *The Agony and the Ecstasy* in 1965 and, of course, as the Oscar®-winning lead in *Ben Hur* in 1959.

Heston joined British acting greats, Laurence Olivier and Ralph Richardson, at Shepperton for *Khartoum*, in 1965 one of the Studios' first epics. The big-budget film tells the story of General Gordon's last stand against Sudanese warriors, as the British Empire takes a hit. The film boasted high production values and good lead acting. Heston played General Gordon and Olivier, the Mahdi, who has Gordon killed. Olivier, never one to be out shone, threw himself into his role with great gusto as always. Looking for a "voice" for his character – as he always did – Olivier wrote to Michael Relph, long-time associate of the film's director, Basil Dearden, asking "if they were able to be obtained, please send me the tapes of the Mahdi made by any Peter Sellers type from the Sudanese Legation…" Olivier wasn't joking. He wanted to get the part right and had been working on the voice and characterisation of the Mahdi five weeks before filming began. It was a busy time for Olivier. His scenes for the film were being shot between performances of *Othello* at the Queen's Theatre, as part of a National Theatre season. Just weeks before, he had been shooting a film version of the play at Shepperton. But if Olivier was finding the journeys between the Studios and the West End of London tiring, he certainly wasn't showing it. Bedecked in tribal costume, his performance as the Mahdi by day was as powerful as that of *Othello* by night. "I shall take Khartoum in blood, and the streets will run in blood, and the Nile will taste of blood for one hundred miles, and every Egyptian will die; every child, woman, man, Sudanese too, who opposes the will of my Lord Mohammed will die…" It was powerful stuff, particularly when delivered by an acting force as strong as Laurence Olivier. Yet *Khartoum* was not ranked a classic, with most critics thinking it bland. As *Sight and Sound* declared: "Beautifully photographed, lavishly mounted, intelligently acted, but ultimately dull."

Gone are the days when an epic was only called an epic if it portrayed an event of ancient history. Following World War II the term "epic" also came to be used for any long, expensive film that featured a large cast and contained plenty of action. One of the first of these types of epic to be made at Shepperton was *The Guns of Navarone* in 1960. This classic wartime adventure, based on the novel by Alistair MacLean, was set in 1943. A team of saboteurs is gathered together and sent on a mission to destroy two giant guns strategically placed on a Turkish island. The cast was impressive: Gregory Peck, David Niven, Stanley Baker, Anthony Quinn, Anthony Quayle and Richard Harris. The Shepperton sets were equally as impressive, though with the studios working at full capacity at the time it was always likely that something was going to give. And it did. The night before the first day's shooting was due to take place on the massive gun-cave set – built on the studio lot near "H" stage – a bad thunderstorm hit the area. The torrential downpour that accompanied the storm, brought down the set. The next week, by day and by night, Shepperton's expert teams of carpenters, electricians, riggers and plasterers, rebuilt it, while director J. Lee Thompson and his cast waited patiently to start shooting. David Niven thought that the break could not have come at a better time "*The Guns of Navarone* was a long and physically very arduous picture culminating with five weeks in England in November, simulating a storm at sea by working nine freezing hours a day in a huge tank of filthy water." For Niven and co-star Gregory Peck, it wasn't to end there. Together, they had two weeks of exhausting night filming at

GREGORY PECK
Mallory

Once the greatest mountain climber in the world, he knew the job was impossible—but he had no choice, for two thousand lives were at stake.

DAVID NIVEN
Miller

The misfit, but a genius with high explosives. After every obstacle was cleared, everything would depend on him.

ANTHONY QUINN
Andrea

The Greek giant, killer without mercy, who hated only two things in life— Germans and Keith Mallory.

STANLEY BAKER
Brown

The Butcher of Barcelona. He had been killing longer than any of them, since 1937 in Spain. He was about ready to quit—though he hardly knew it himself.

ANTHONY QUAYLE
Franklin

One of the war lovers, he was unable to understand why none of the others shared his enjoyment of danger.

JAMES DARREN
Pappadimos

The baby-faced killer from Navarone. They sent him to America for an education, and he got the wrong kind. War gave him a licence to murder.

Above

Publicity material produced for *The Guns of Navarone* (1960)

Opposite

A daring commando raid is planned and executed against the Nazis, in *The Guns of Navarone* (1960) (right to left); James Darren, Stanley Baker, David Niven, Gregory Peck, Anthony Quinn and Anthony Quayle

Shepperton, literally from dusk to dawn, to shoot the finale of the picture – the blowing up of the guns. Niven, whose character was the "genius with explosives", had to be on set the whole time. With just three days of filming left on this multi-million dollar action picture, Niven picked up an infection via a cut lip and ended up in Guy's Hospital, London, with septicemia. The picture ground to a halt. Emergency meetings were held by the film's makers, and studio heads flew in from America to work out what could be done to save their investment. Under pressure and against doctor's orders, Niven, pumped full of anti-biotics,

went back to work. He completed his three days filming and promptly suffered a relapse that lasted almost two months.

The Guns of Navarone was well-received. The epic blockbuster earned five Oscar® nominations and won the Golden Globe award for best drama motion picture. A less successful "sequel," *Force Ten from Navarone*, starring Robert Shaw, Edward Fox and Harrison Ford, was made at Shepperton in 1977.

When Richard Burton was offered the lead role in the

Above

Peter O'Toole as King Henry II
in *Becket* (1963)

Right

A twelfth century medieval
cathedral – actually a set built at
Shepperton for the 1963
historical drama *Becket*

The cast of *Becket* was impeccable; Burton joined by Peter O'Toole, John Gielgud and Martita Hunt. The sets for the film were breathtaking – the most famous being the replica interior of Canterbury cathedral, which was painstakingly reproduced on Shepperton's "H" stage.

1964 Shepperton-based production of *Becket*, he is said to have exclaimed to Elizabeth Taylor: "What! After all the scandal you want me to play a saint? Are you crazy?" *Becket* was to be the film version of Jean Anouilh's bitter stage comedy about Henry II's relationship with his Saxon friend, which turns sour and leads to Thomas à Becket's assassination by Henry's knights. When Burton heard that the producer, Hal Wallis, wanted him for the film, the actor automatically assumed that he would play the part of the bawdy and lusty monarch King Henry II. Wallis and Elizabeth Taylor persuaded him otherwise.

The cast of *Becket* was impeccable; Burton was joined by Peter O'Toole, John Gielgud and Martita Hunt. The sets for the film were breathtaking – the most famous being the replica interior of Canterbury Cathedral, which was painstakingly reproduced on Shepperton's "H" stage. Set designer and art director Maurice Carter, who was nominated for an Oscar® for his work on *Becket*, remembers the effort that went into building the sets and the clashes he often had with the producer. "I was building Tudor sets, a period when ceilings rarely exceeded eight or nine feet high, so the sets obviously needed ceilings to be seen. You couldn't shoot the length of a palace room without having a ceiling. But producer Hal Wallis insisted on no ceilings because he reckoned it slowed up shooting as they would have to be lit with reflectors and so on. He had to give way to me in the end. I couldn't build a set that went up ten or twenty feet high. It just looked absurd but the battles continued, set by set by set."

While the production design team battled with their producer, the actors appeared to be getting on famously. Burton and O'Toole struck up a unique friendship. Physically the two could not have looked more different, yet they had very similar minds and

each tried to out-act the other and in doing so lifted their own performances higher. Both would later be nominated for an acting Oscar®, though neither would win. Away from filming and when Elizabeth Taylor came to visit Burton, O'Toole would take the couple out for lunch at one of the many pubs that adorned Shepperton village, including the King's Head where the landlord greeted Burton with the immortal line: "Now is the winter of our discontent made glorious summer by this leg of pork." Trips to the pub in the first weeks of shooting Becket were not infrequent. Burton often recounted the story of how an actor in his private life can be influenced by the character he is portraying on screen or stage and that, during *Becket*, he only drank heavily with O'Toole when they were shooting the early scenes of Thomas and Henry in their debauched youth. Once Becket becomes Archbishop of Canterbury, Burton reformed, stayed in at night and sat quietly reading. That good behaviour lasted just ten days, after which Burton felt he had come to grips with the role and at which point he rejoined O'Toole where the pair had left off, less than a fortnight earlier.

Becket was a good film, though not a brilliant one. The acting was magnificent as were the sets and costumes, but the production dragged, losing some of its theatrical magic on widescreen. One critic dubbed it: "Handsome, respectable and boring." Nevertheless the film was nominated for nine Oscars®, picking up one, and winning two British Academy awards.

It has often been stated that Charlton Heston desperately wanted the role of Sir Thomas More in the next epic to be filmed at Shepperton, Columbia Pictures' 1965 production of *A Man for All Seasons*. The role went to Paul Scofield who was in great acting company alongside Wendy Hiller, Susannah York, Robert Shaw

Above

The assassination of Thomas à Becket. A scene from *Becket* (1963)

Above

A scene from the making of
Becket (1963)

Opposite

Burton and O'Toole on horseback
during production of *Becket*
(1963)

Page 204

Robert Shaw (left) plays
Henry VIII, with Paul Scofield
(right) as Sir Thomas More,
in the historical drama *A Man for
All Seasons* (1966)

Page 205

Orson Welles is Cardinal Wolsey,
in *A Man for All Seasons* (1966)

and Orson Welles. Directed by Fred Zinnemann, the film version of Robert Bolt's 1960 play tells the story of Sir Thomas More opposing Henry VIII's divorce, winning the argument, yet paying the ultimate price for his moralising. Once again, the studio set designers and costumiers pulled out the stops, ensuring that at all levels – whether acting, direction, sets, locations or costumes – the film was to be a success; which it was, both financially and critically, picking up five Oscars® and five British Academy Awards. As one critic proclaimed: "A beautiful and satisfying film, the ultimate demonstration, perhaps, of how a fine stage play can be transcended and, with integrity and inspiration, turned into a great motion picture." More than twenty-five years after he made the film, Fred Zinnemann was still waxing lyrically about his time working on the epic. "One of the happiest experiences of my professional life was the making of *A Man for All Seasons* at Shepperton Studios. The crews and departments were top class and no request was too much trouble. It was a wonderful way of making a movie. There is still a glow when I think of the lovely time we had."

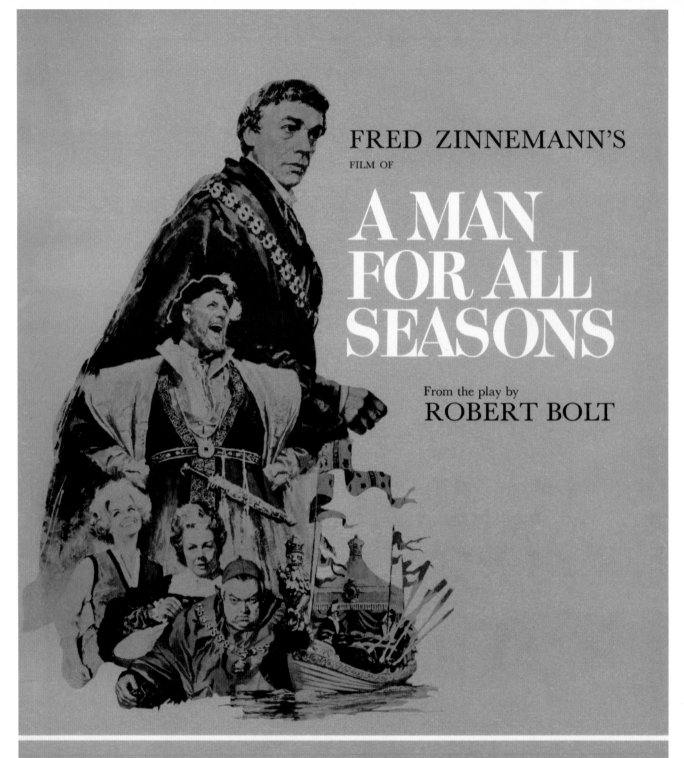

FRED ZINNEMANN'S FILM OF

A MAN FOR ALL SEASONS

From the play by ROBERT BOLT

COLUMBIA PICTURES Presents FRED ZINNEMANN'S FILM OF "A MAN FOR ALL SEASONS" From the play by ROBERT BOLT
CO-STARRING WENDY HILLER · LEO McKERN · ROBERT SHAW · ORSON WELLES · SUSANNAH YORK
and PAUL SCOFIELD as Thomas More
with NIGEL DAVENPORT · JOHN HURT and CORIN REDGRAVE · Music by GEORGES DELERUE · Executive Producer WILLIAM N. GRAF · Screenplay by ROBERT BOLT · Produced and Directed by FRED ZINNEMANN · TECHNICOLOR®

"It was apparent from the very first day on the set at Shepperton studios that we were working on a winner. The money being spent on the project was tangible. To wander round the outdoor sets was to be taken back in time. The recreation of early Victorian London was authentic down to the tiniest detail. There were even real loaves of bread in the baker's shop windows."

Above

Child actor Mark Lester, on location for *Oliver!* (1967)

Right

One of the Victorian street sets built at Shepperton for *Oliver!* in 1967

Producers and brothers John and James Woolf, who had been responsible for cinematic hits such as *The African Queen*, *Moulin Rouge* and *The L-Shaped Room*, turned their attention in the mid-1960s to the filming of a big and lavish musical. Over the past few years from Shepperton's stages had sprung some classics of British cinema; now it was time to show that as well as good period epics, the Brits could still put together a table-thumping, award-winning, sing-song. John Woolf had cannily bought the 'matching' rights to Lionel Bart's musical *Oliver!* when the show was originally staged. Those rights meant that if anyone made an offer to film the musical, Woolf had the legal right and opportunity to match that offer and make the film himself. In the early summer of 1964, while in Cannes, at a screening of his company's latest film, *The Pumpkin Eater*, Woolf received a telegram informing him that an offer had been made to film *Oliver!* Woolf immediately matched the offer. Yet, Lionel Bart refused permission, claiming that while Woolf's company, Romulus, may well have matched the financial side of the offer, it had not matched the quality of the star name lined up for one of the main roles – the original bid had included the assurance that Peter Sellers would appear in the role of Fagin. Romulus dismissed the claim as nonsense and argued that they could cast whomever they wanted for any of the roles, so long as they matched the monetary bid, which they had done. The case ended up in court and after three days of legal argument, Woolf and his company finally won the right to make the film.

Sadly, James Woolf, who had been sent to America to try and sign Julie Andrews for the film, died suddenly from a heart attack. There was to be a further setback when, just weeks before shooting was to start, the film found itself without a director. Lewis Gilbert was all set to take the helm on the production but he had a contract with Paramount that required him to make a film in Japan. John Woolf recalls the difficulty: "I was without a director four or five weeks before we were due to start shooting. I suddenly thought of Carol Reed, because of that marvellous film he had made with the little boy, *The Fallen Idol*. I signed him, albeit having some difficulty with Columbia over it. I brought over Johnny Green, the celebrated music director, and Onna White, the well-known Canadian choreographer, to supervise the musical numbers." Woolf also turned to Shepperton's expert designers and builders to create one of the most memorable outdoor sets of Victorian London ever produced at a British studio. Harry Secombe, who was cast to play Mr. Bumble in the film, was taken aback by the scale of the set: "It was apparent from the very first day on the set at Shepperton Studios that we were working on a winner. The money being spent on the project was tangible. To wander round the outdoor sets was to be taken back in time. The recreation of early Victorian London was authentic down to the tiniest detail. There were even real loaves of bread in the baker's shop windows."

Carol Reed's direction inspired both actors and crew alike. He was never heard to raise his voice in anger and would at the beginning of shooting each morning sit down with the cast involved in the scenes for that day. He talked through the action, reminding them of the scene which immediately preceded the one they were to film – which might have been recorded some time before. This especially put the young actors at ease and made for a happy filming environment. The first scenes to be filmed were the ones in the workhouse where Oliver is goaded by the other boys to ask for more. Harry Secombe, as Bumble, had to grab child actor Mark Lester, as Oliver, firmly by the ear and march him off to the Governors, as all around sang "Oliver, Oliver, never before has a boy wanted more..." Secombe tugged gingerly at the boy's lobe, not wanting to hurt him. Reed called cut and pulled Secombe over to one corner: "No, no,

Above and left

Oliver! (1967) won an Oscar® for art direction – the Victorian sets created at Shepperton Studios, impress audiences and the American Academy alike

Top left

Oliver Reed (Bill Sykes) and Shani Wallis (Nancy), in *Oliver!* (1967)

Harry," he said, "you really must seize hold of his ear as roughly as you can." Secombe protested that the boy was such a little lad. "Never mind that," Reed insisted, "do it harder next time." Harry Secombe recounts what happened next: "We waited until the cameras and lights were ready for another take, and off we went again. When we got to the same piece of action, I really put everything I had into grabbing Mark's ear. To my horror it came away in my hand. The prop man had fitted a false plastic ear on the boy. I had been set up." That atmosphere of fun persisted throughout the production, which was also blessed with fine weather during much of the filming on the backlot at Shepperton, helping to ensure the film came in on time and within budget. *Oliver!* was nominated for 11 Oscars® in 1968. It won five, including best picture and a special award for choreography. One critic declared: "Only time will tell if it is a great film but it is certainly a great experience." Almost 40 years after it was made, most people would say that it is still very much both.

Richard Burton returned to Shepperton to make another period epic in 1968. *Anne of the Thousand Days* made by *Becket* producer, Hal Wallis, and flamboyantly told the story of Henry VIII's divorce and subsequent marriage to Anne Boleyn, played by the well-cast and young actress, Genevieve Bujold. The period interiors were once again stunningly reproduced on the sound stages of Shepperton, the costumes were equally as regal – winning their designer, Margaret Furse, an Oscar® for her work. The costumes gained more notoriety the following year, when Pinewood film producer Peter Rogers hired the suit worn by Burton as Henry VIII, for Sid James, who was appearing in Rogers' latest bawdy comedy outing, *Carry On Henry* (1970). For Burton, *Anne of the Thousand Days* was another opportunity to prove to the world he was a serious actor to be reckoned with. So intent was he on getting the part right, that the patriotic Welshman even turned down an invitation to attend the investiture of Charles the new Prince of Wales at Caernarvon Castle. Burton prerecorded a television narration for the ceremony, but filming took precedence on the day itself and Burton

Anne of the Thousand Days

Sadly, as with *Becket* and *The Spy Who Came in from the Cold*, Burton would receive another Oscar® nomination for best actor, but would lose out yet again, this time to John Wayne in *True Grit*

was absent for the ceremony – though he did fly the Welsh flag and display the Red Dragon on his car and Shepperton dressing-room door. Sadly, as with *Becket* and *The Spy Who Came in from the Cold* (1965), Burton would receive another Oscar® nomination for best actor, but would lose out yet again, this time to John Wayne in *True Grit* (1969).

CROMWELL

Director Ken Hughes' underrated *Cromwell* was produced at Shepperton in 1969. Boasting a solid cast of acting greats, including Richard Harris in the lead role, Alec Guinness as Charles I, Robert Morley as the Earl of Manchester and Dorothy Tutin as Queen Henrietta Maria, the film charted the rise of Cromwell to power, the execution of Charles I and the Civil War. *Cromwell* was accused of being disappointingly dull by some, while others pointed to the high production values and convincing battle scenes. Dorothy Tutin remembers the film and its director with much affection. "I found Queen Henrietta fascinating as a woman – I had to read about her because she really isn't written up very much in the script. But Ken was meticulous about the historical accuracy and perspective of the film and he really knew his stuff. I thought it was a good script and of course Ken was able to use a transcript of the trial scene, which is wonderful, it's famous. That business about the Divine Right of Kings and Parliament suddenly having the strength and courage to say no. It was extraordinarily dramatic and beautifully incorporated, I thought."

Almost 30 years since he had last made a film at Shepperton, acclaimed director David Lean returned to the studios in 1984 to make *A Passage to India*

Above

Publicity image for *Mary Queen of Scots* (1971)

Opposite

Alec Guinness as Professor Godbole, with director David Lean, on location for *A Passage to India* (1984)

Shepperton's output of lavish costume pictures dwindled in the 1970s as viewing tastes changed. The films were also becoming increasingly expensive to produce and it became more difficult to recoup substantial financial outlay. Picture company heads were less keen to take risks on multi-million pound productions unless they could be guaranteed a success. The days of the epic, at least as they had become known, were disappearing. The 1971 production, *Mary Queen of Scots*, didn't appear to do a great deal to help their cause. Two of the country's greatest actresses, Vanessa Redgrave and Glenda Jackson proved they were worthy of the roles of Mary Stuart and Elizabeth I. The Tudor drama was brought to the screen with all the expertise and eye for detail that Shepperton productions had become renowned for, but somehow the critics didn't take to the film, complaining that even with liberties being taken over historical facts, *Mary Queen of Scots* never comes to life. As *The New Yorker* described it: "Without a better script, Hercules couldn't lift this story off the ground." The film received a nod from the Motion Picture Academy when it nominated the film for two Oscars®, one for Miss Redgrave and the other for John Barry for the film's score, yet it won neither and quite tellingly received no major nomination nor award from our own country's British Academy for its ceremony in 1971.

Richard Attenborough produced the next two epic films to come out of Shepperton, his 1971 biopic of the early years of Churchill, *Young Winston*, and ten years later his multi-award-winning portrait of the life of *Gandhi* (1981).

Almost 30 years since he had last made a film at Shepperton, acclaimed director David Lean returned to the studios in 1984 to make *A Passage to India*, which he also wrote and edited. The film, which tells the story of an English girl in India who accuses a native doctor of rape, starred Peggy Ashcroft, James Fox, Alec Guinness, Victor Banerjee and Judy Davis. Of the nine films made at Shepperton that year, it is widely acknowledged that *A Passage to India* was the most prestigious. Sadly the relationship between David Lean and Alec Guinness had deteriorated somewhat since their days working together on *The Bridge on the River Kwai*, *Lawrence of Arabia* (1962) and *Doctor Zhivago* (1965), and had become virtually unrecognizable compared with the happier times they had spent on *Great Expectations* and *Oliver Twist* in the late 1940s. During the filming of *A Passage to India*, the men spoke very little. Guinness was frustrated by what he saw as being a far smaller role in the film than he had expected. That role was cut further by Lean during editing. The men did not speak again.

A Passage to India was well received and highly regarded. At 75, David Lean had shown that he had lost none of his skills for bringing masterly and visually exciting epics to the big screen. The film was nominated for 11 Oscars®, winning two. It was to be Lean's last film before his death in 1991.

In 1985, there were just two major films made at Shepperton, one being the musical *Absolute Beginners*, the other a scenic epic, *Out of Africa*. Directed by accomplished film-maker Sydney Pollack *Out of Africa* beautifully portrays the story of a Danish woman who arrives in Africa in 1914 for a marriage of convenience with a German baron, who has no interest in her. The cast was as lavish as the scenery that Pollack so tastefully brought to life on celluloid, with Meryl Streep, Klaus Maria Brandauer and Robert Redford on good form, ensuring that the film, although long, never bores. As *Sight and Sound* declared: "The film purrs pleasantly along like one of its own big cats." The film won seven Oscars® including best picture and best direction for Pollack, and two BAFTAs, for photography and screenplay.

Through the 1980s and 1990s, Shepperton continued to produce some big films. Many may not have been epics in the true sense of the word – that of being "a genre of film in which historical or legendary events provide a background for heroism and lavish spectacle" – but they were pretty close. Besides, with the term epic now applied to any longish and expensive film with a large cast and plenty of stunningly-shot action scenes and set pieces to tell a story from the past, many more titles potentially qualified to be named an epic. These included Kevin Costner's *Robin Hood: Prince of Thieves*, made at Shepperton in 1990, Kenneth Branagh's monumental interpretations of Shakespearean plays made throughout that decade, Franco Zeffirelli's *Hamlet* in 1990, and Richard Attenborough's 1991 biopic on the life of famed filmmaker and actor, *Chaplin*.

The first epic musical to be made at Shepperton since *Oliver!* back in the late 1960s, was *Evita* in 1996. Written by Oliver Stone and Alan Parker, who also directed it, this cinema version of the stage musical starred pop-idol Madonna as Eva Duarte, who rises from the obscurity of poverty to become the wife of the President of Argentina. The majority of the film's shooting took place in Argentina and Hungary but a variety of sets had to be built at Shepperton, as there was doubt until the last minute as to whether or not Argentina's President Menem would allow filming at his palace, the Casa Rosada. In the event, filming did get the go ahead and a relieved Alan Parker, cast and crew shot the all important Casa Rosada scenes in early March 1996. After filming in Buenos Aires, the production moved to Budapest for six weeks before returning to wrap-up shooting at Shepperton. Though the film wouldn't premiere until December, Parker produced a ten-minute preview for the Cannes Film Festival in June – only a few weeks after filming on *Evita* had come to an end.

Evita received a mixed reception from the critics on its release. *The Times Literary Supplement* declared: "No effort or expense has been spared in transforming the stage musical into a Hollywood spectacular. As such, the film is, as the hype would have it, a triumph. The problems start, however, as soon as one has lost interest in the sumptuous clothes, virtuoso tango-dancing and necrophiliac display. There is very little dramatic tension." Audiences were far kinder and the film proved a box office hit. *Evita* won three Golden Globe awards – including one for Madonna – and picked up an Oscar® for best song. Not quite on par with the success of its Shepperton predecessor, *Oliver!*, but a great achievement nonetheless. Its popularity has ensured it a place in the top 10 musical films of all time.

Over the past decade, cinema attendances in the UK have been consistently rising – with the exception of 2003 when sequel fatigue and a long hot summer caused a blip in the figures – and most recently stand at around 160 million visits a year. In the 1980s that figure had been as low as 40 million. The running time of films has also been increasing, with many productions now well over two and often heading towards three hours in length. Comfortable cinemas, continuing advances in audio and visual technology and the advent of affordable home cinema, and particularly the success of DVD, has ensured an almost insatiable appetite for big movies.

The first epic – in the traditional sense of the word – to have come out of the Shepperton stable in the new millennium, was *Troy*. The film began shooting at the Studio in April 2003 before moving on to Malta, where the city of Troy was constructed. After filming in Malta and 10 weeks in Baja, the production returned to Shepperton's stages where most of the film's interiors were built. *Troy* was based on Homer's *The Iliad* and *The Odyssey* and recounts with much style and effect, the triumphs and tragedies of the Trojan wars. The cast list was as long and impressive as the film and included Brad Pitt, Orlando Bloom, Sean Bean, Peter O'Toole and a two-minute cameo appearance by Julie Christie. The film, directed by Wolfgang Peterson, was one of the big box office successes of 2004, and with a running time of 162 minutes is further proof that epics can be as popular today as they were half a century ago.

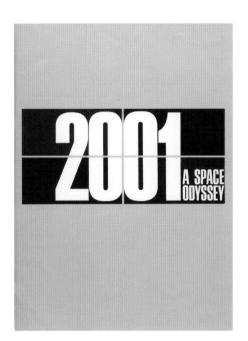

Another Oscar® and Bafta winner, Stanley Kubrick's,
2001 A Space Odyssey remains an important and thought-
provoking film. Above all it is an outstanding visual
experience made at a cost of $10.5m in 1968. Douglas
Trumbull won the Oscar® for Special Effects.

Right
Shepperton Studios were used to create the scene where the astronauts discover the monolith on the moon. *2001: A Space Odyssey* (1968)

Mark Sanger
Visual Effects Editor

My first day on a film set was the result of a friend in the industry taking me door-to-door around Pinewood, introducing me to everybody he knew, and explaining what a great asset I'd be as an employee. Amazingly a special effects company actually believed him and the next day I found myself on the studio back lot, trying to look competent as a wind machine operator and pretending I understood how the thing worked.

I wasn't fooling anyone and the special effects work soon dried up, but the contacts I'd made got me new jobs in different departments. I didn't impress in any of these either as one day a concerned production manager asked, "Mark, what do you really want to do?" Taking my opportunity, I told her that I had always wanted to get into editing. A month later I was back at home counting the pennies (the end of a film means the end of the salary), when the phone rang and it was my production manager friend calling to say that she needed an editorial trainee on the new Bond film. It was the first rung of the ladder and the break I needed.

A common misconception is that film editing occurs at the end, when the shooting crew have finished. On the contrary, we often start before they do. The editor assembles the material as it arrives and the cut gradually evolves as more material is shot. Somebody once famously said that film-making is a war. We don't call it 'shooting' a film for nothing. A single days shoot can cost hundreds of thousands of pounds so "breaking ranks" is not an option. A crew works in a military fashion with a strict chain of command and I'm sure some potentially great filmmakers have probably been lost to other careers when they found they couldn't fit into the regime. Equally those who do pass muster, don't necessarily need any talent. I fit into the latter category.

Right
The glamour of location filming.
Mark outside his no star caravan
in Cabo San Lucas, Baja, California.

Opposite
Mark Sanger at the mixing desk.

Each day produces a number of camera 'set ups', each with its own set of takes. The entire day can often be spent covering three lines of dialogue from the same actor, from different angles. There is a tremendous amount of work involved to ensure the collaboration of all departments for the few short seconds that pass by between the words, 'action' and 'cut'. The next day the best of the shoot has been printed and editorial get to work with the fruits of the crew's labour.

Whether they are epics like *Troy* or *The Mummy* or smaller, character-driven pieces like *Possession* (2000), or *Felicia's Journey* (1998), I still find screening the 'dailies' is always exciting. Gone are the lighting stands and the smell of wet paint. Suddenly the crew may forget yesterday's stressful shoot as they watch the illusion of cinema begin before them. This is what makes working in editing so satisfying.

A visual effects editor acts as a liaison between the VFX supervisor, editor and director. Until the advent of digital technology a lot of what we do now was handled optically. In very basic terms, different 'elements' were shot separately and then later combined onto a fresh piece of negative, creating a composite. To make this work, each element was 'matted' from the other. So a hole is created on the background element for the foreground to fit into. Without this the two images would appear semi-transparent. Some of the most elaborate and beautiful visual effects have been produced this way, but it is a physical process, involving multiple exposures on the same piece of negative, so there is more risk of dirt damage and less control over matching the colours.

With schedules as they are today, there is less time for error, so though we still treat shots the same way, the matting and compositing is now done in the computer. We don't "output" back to film until the shot is complete. This gives us the peace of mind to know that what we're sending for printing already works. The technology evolves significantly from one film to the next so we never stop learning (not if we want to get another job!).

Part of my job is to ensure that each visual effects shot is assembled from that day's best dailies. Then it's time to make rough composites in the Avid, our computer-based editing tool. Once these are approved by the director, we digitally scan each frame of negative from each element. These 'scans' are given to the VFX facilities for them to correct all my mistakes and make it all look beautiful. They then return these; I cut them into the edit, take credit for their work and bask in the glory of their combined talents.

Nowadays complex visual effects sequences are planned months ahead of shooting with pre-visualisation or "pre-vis", a computer-animated version of what

the director intends to shoot. They are often mini works of art, containing precise detail right down to the exact camera moves and lens information. The shooting crew then shoot to match the pre-vis and then we replace the edited pre-vis with the live action shots. I then sit down with the director and editor, discuss the ramifications of these changes, suggest alternatives and work to get the directors exactly what they need.

I am lucky enough now to be able to jump between two jobs; one as a first assistant editor and the other as visual effects editor. In an industry with so many crews available and relatively few jobs on offer, a lot of us jump between different roles on different films. Typically the first assistant editor manages editorial, ensuring all the shot material is available for the editor and director and that nothing disrupts what can often be a manic schedule. The first assistant editor can often act as a buffer, ensuring all logistical problems are dealt with properly and that the creative work is not interrupted unnecessarily.

The very nature of film editing means that occasionally chaos erupts in the assistants' rooms. A good day is when this happens but the cut remains up-to-date, the director is pleased with his sequence and he and the editor go home unaware of the disruption.

During my short time in the industry, I've been privileged to work with some great people on high (and low) profile films, many of them based at Shepperton. It's very gratifying to quiz American directors about their favourite film because, more often than not, you can inform them that it was made at Shepperton, which has produced so many classics.

Army1_before

Army1_after

Army2_before

Army2_after

Cinema crop

Cinema crop

Visual Effects Supervisor Nick Davis
Visual Effects Supervisor for MPC Chas Jarrett

The following pictures, courtesy of the Moving Picture Company, show how three shots were constructed for Warner Bros' 2004 film *Troy*, directed by Wolfgang Petersen.

Computer Generated Imagery

(Army1_before / Army1_after)

Here the Trojan and Greek armies collide and the camera move was designed to swoop down into the clash.

As the majority of soldiers could be added using computer-generated characters, only four hundred extras were required, just for the part of the shot when we are closest to them.

As well as the three other camera crews who were simultaneously filming alternate angles, MPC had to also digitally remove the orange 'tracking' markers that were placed to assist them in building a 3D terrain to match the real one and ensure the digital armies appear to be running on the same plane as their real counterparts; the cable shadows on the ground, the white crew catering tents in the top right of frame and a barely visible twentieth century light-house on the highest background peak.

Once this was done they digitally added the walls of Troy and the remaining thousands of soldiers.

(Army2_before / Army2_after & Army3_before / Army3_after both show the same shot later in the camera move.)

Aspect ratio

One of the early decisions a director must make, long before shooting begins, is what aspect ratio the picture should be on the big screen. It will play a crucial role in the way that the film is photographed.

There are many aspect ratios to choose from but in the case of *Troy* it was decided to present it with a ratio of 2.35:1 (or 2.35 times wide as it is high). This is often used on action or epic films where the rectangular shape can add extra power to panoramic shots.

As we shoot on the same sized frame of film regardless of the aspect ratio size, 2.35 can be photographed in one of two ways. An anamorphic lens can be used to squeeze the picture on either side, much like looking at yourself in an elongated mirror. Another lens is then used on the projector in cinemas to 'un-squeeze' the image again. Alternatively, we shoot a square image with no squeeze and project it with 'masked' top and bottom sections in the cinema.
This is very practical on visual effects films because it means we have a much larger canvas to work from.

Blue Screen Composite

Shooting actors against a consistent colour that does not appear elsewhere in the frame allows digital compositors to 'lift' out the colour, create mattes and then add in other backgrounds. In these shots, MPC created a highly-detailed digital model of the city of Troy.

Images courtesy of The Moving Picture Company

Great
Scotts

"Film-making is a vocation, not a job."

Sir Ridley Scott – Director

Although many of Ridley and Tony Scott's films have been made elsewhere, their involvement with Shepperton runs deep. Not only has there been a significant financial interest but a very personal interest as well. Indeed, there is good reason and much proof for stating, that the Scotts are generally regarded as being the last of four different sets of brothers in the Studios' history to save Shepperton from closure.

Ridley Scott was born in 1937 and Tony in 1944, sons of Elizabeth and Frank Scott – a successful businessman in the run up to World War II. The young Scotts lived in the north east of England. Ridley Scott showed little aptitude at school for anything but art. While his classmates aspired to become lawyers and teachers, Scott set his heart on attending art school and becoming a stage designer. His trips to the cinema were frequent, as he recalls: "I was more enthusiastic about film than the average teenager. My access to the cinema was, at that point, whatever was showing at the local cinema where I would try and see everything."

Scott took his first tentative steps towards a career in film in 1954, at the West Hartlepool College of Art. He spent four years there, honing his already adept skills of sketching and painting. He discovered a passion for music and literature and a future in the arts seemed assured. National Service almost put a stop to his progress in 1958 when he was called up. Ironically, his father, who had served with the War Office at the end of World War II, talked Scott out of signing up to join the Marines for a two year stint. The offer of a scholarship from the Royal College of Art in London sealed his decision not to enlist. He moved to London and started at the RCA in the autumn of 1958. Cinema remained in his blood. "In those days, the late 50s, my Mecca was the NFT where I saw all types of alternative cinema that wasn't Hollywood. My essential cinema fodder had been until that stage whatever came out of Hollywood, particularly John Wayne. I was a Western fanatic. The biggest question for me at the time was how do I get into it?"

Scott was overwhelmed by what the new age of cinema appeared to be offering audiences at the end of the 1950s and beginning of the 1960s. The French had their new wave and Britain had followed with its gritty and realistic kitchen-sink dramas which made stars of Richard Burton, Richard Harris, Alan Bates, Tom Courtenay, Albert Finney and others. Scott knew he wanted to be part of this world but also knew that as an art student he was unlikely to get to where he now knew he wanted to go.

He applied to join the BBC in 1961 and was offered a job in the scenic design department – a position which was held open for him for 12 months, while he took advantage of a travelling scholarship in design which took him to work in New York with top advertising agency Bob Drew Associates.

Right
One of the many powerful war scenes from Ridley Scott's multi-award winning film, *Gladiator* (1998)

The following two years at the BBC proved invaluable. Scott was involved in a host of famous shows of the time, designing sets and learning to work within tight time constraints and even tighter budgets. Yet he soon became frustrated and started moonlighting for advertising agencies, designing sets for commercials – allowing him to spread his artistic wings while topping up his meagre BBC salary. His bosses could see Scott's frustration and sent him on a director's course, which he has often since described as "marvellous." Soon he was being offered episodes of the long-running BBC police drama *Softly, Softly* – the sequel to *Z-Cars* – to direct. The shows were transmitted live and each director had three weeks to prepare an episode. Scott found the whole experience nerve-wracking but picked up the skills quickly.

Scott's BBC career came to an end before it had really started, an intentional move he felt he had to take. "I had gone into the BBC as a designer and started working with directors immediately. Yes, I got my shows as a director. But then advertising caught up with me. It was a financial decision. I worked out what I could be paid as a director of commercials, as opposed to a director of BBC programmes, and there was no contest. I knew advertising was the way to go. I wanted to be freelance and independent which was a kind of dangerous thing to do when you had two kids and a mortgage. Even my mother had a go at me for giving up all my art school training to go and do film!"

At just 27, Scott's visual flair kept him much in demand in a world of advertising that was ever changing. Out of fashion were the cheesy soap-flake adverts with two-dimensional characters and even flatter scripts. As television became the norm across the country, a whole new approach to selling products on screen was taking place. In print media too there was a sea change, as quality papers started to produce weekly colour supplements. Big retailers had big money to spend to ensure their products were the ones that people wanted to buy.

Within a year of leaving the BBC in 1965, Scott set up Ridley Scott Associates, a commercials production company which proceeded to make literally thousands of ads in the years ahead. Among the most famous, and still fondly remembered, are RSA's award-winning commercials for Strongbow Cider, Levi Jeans and Hovis Bread.

Tony Scott, meanwhile, had recently graduated from the Royal College of Art Film School. While there and as part of his studies, the budding director had produced two half-hour films financed by the British Film Institute (bfi). He concluded his course with one final piece of work. "I had an hour long film to make. It was financed by Albert Finney and the British Film Institute – Albert had just made a load of money from *Tom Jones* (1963) and didn't want to give it to the tax man, so he gave it to me instead. My film was called *Loving Memory* – a black and white artsy-fartsy piece." Tony wanted to move straight into film production but Ridley invited his brother to join him, a move which Tony initially wasn't keen on making. Ridley was insistent: "I'm older than my brother and by the time he had left college, my company was six years old and was a good place to be working in. I told him to come and join me and not to go. I promised him that one way or another we'd get to make movies. Which was the goal in those days." What the brothers both knew was that to get the chance to make movies they were going to have to get some money behind them first. RSA was certainly helping them to do that.

While RSA had its main offices in Central London, Ridley Scott chose to use two studios for the filming of his commercials. "My first connection with Shepperton was with advertising. Not so much as an art director but as a director of commercials. I tended to use both Isleworth and Shepperton Studios in the 1960s. Rarely Pinewood. Pinewood in those days was not commercial friendly. In fact it was really the presence and success of these other studios that made Pinewood pay attention and realize that business is business and whether you're renting a stage to a Bond film or to a company making commericals, it makes no difference. That's what the studios' business is about."

If there was a perceived snobbery in the British film industry that shooting commercials was not like "the real thing," that attitude extended to Shepperton too. If anything, Shepperton's producers, with their reputation for independent film-making, looked even further down their collective noses at what was coming to a sound stage near them. Ridley Scott says that snobbery has always been around. "Yes, there was a great deal of snobbery and not just in Britain. There was certainly an attitude towards advertising as being "not quite film." In fact, what was really happening was that people like Dick Lester were coming in from an advertising type of arena and adopting commercials' techniques for films like *A Hard Day's Night* (1964). Slowly, the whole language of film-making and communication started to change. It became about educating the audience to actually get what was going on, faster. Now of course, we've paid the price – the audience attention level of concentration is only a matter of seconds, which is why we get very jumpy busy, films."

The British film industry took a tumble in the 1970s. Studios such as Shepperton inevitably became more financially reliant on the rental of its stages to advertising companies who, it seemed – in direct contrast to film producers – had endless amounts to spend on big commercials campaigns across a host of mediums, now taking in cinema, as well as television and the printing press. And the fewer films that were being made at Shepperton, the more commercials RSA seemed to be producing. Financially, both RSA and the Scotts were becoming increasingly stable. With that stability resurfaced the desire – which had never been far away – to turn their hands to film-making proper.

For Ridley Scott, now fast approaching 40, the final straw was broken when fellow commercials' guru Alan Parker, broke into film. Parker had teamed up with David Puttnam and his company Enigma, to find the finance for *Bugsy Malone* in 1976. The musical about gang wars in America during prohibition, in which all the parts were played by children, was an instant success. Parker had put up around £80,000 –

"We had to be a bit closed-shop about the project. I just followed what Steven Spielberg had done with Close Encounters – he didn't want anyone to find out what the spaceship looked like. We had big lock-ups at Shepperton including a sound stage which very few people were allowed to go into at any time."

Above and left
Filming on the Shepperton set of
Alien (1978)

Scott had been careful not to tell the actors the details of that particular gut-busting scene in advance of its filming. Only John Hurt knew how it was going to play.

Above

Ridley Scott on the set of *Alien*
at Shepperton Studios

half of everything he had – towards the cost of the film. Puttnam, as producer, found the backing to fund the rest of the £1 million plus production. Ridley Scott, via RSA, had now built up some considerable wealth himself and approached Puttnam to ask if he could achieve a similar deal for a film project Scott was trying to get off the ground. Puttnam agreed, set about organising the finances, and by the autumn of 1976 Scott was making *The Duellists* – the story of two Hussar officers in the early nineteenth century, who spend 16 years challenging each other to duels before they finally agree to call a truce. To many who saw the film, it either didn't make a lot of sense, or they just couldn't see the point of the tale. Yet critics and audiences alike all agreed that the film looked visually stunning. *The Duellists* received a screening at the 1977 Cannes Film Festival where it was awarded the Special Jury Prize. That was the encouragement that Scott needed; he had now turned 40 and had achieved what he had wanted to do for most of his life – he was now a bona fide film director.

It was while in Hollywood in the summer of 1977, that Ridley Scott and David Puttnam found themselves at a cinema watching a film which had just been released to great reviews. Even the industry of which they were a part, was murmuring that *Star Wars* was "pretty good." Scott loved the film so much that he went to see it again and then a third time in the same week. He found *Star Wars* a visual dream. Not since Stanley Kubrick's *2001: A Space Odyssey* had he been so moved by a science fiction motion picture. "I'd come to science fiction gradually. When I saw Kubrick's *2001*, I remember thinking how goddam real it felt." Then *Star Wars* arrived. Scott realised that these were the types of film that people wanted to see. He immediately dismissed his own further ideas for the art house productions that he had wanted to make. Fatefully, back in London, Scott had been sent a script. "I was actually fifth in line for a project called *Alien*, by

Dan O'Bannon and Ronald Shushett. Producer David Giler had seen *The Duellists* at Cannes and thought I may be the right person to make this piece of science fiction – try and follow that, I can't! Anyway, he sent me the script. I loved it. Within 22 hours I was at a meeting in Hollywood. We all decided it was going to be a $4 million movie. The producers said they wanted me to audition for it, so I spent the best part of the next month in a house in Hampstead storyboarding the entire film."

Scott was used to storyboarding. That experience, along with an immediate innate vision for the film, spurred his creativity and within the month he was back with the same producers talking them through his ideas. Except now the budget was going to have to double to over $8 million, but that didn't seem to matter. They were impressed with what they had seen. By February 1978, Ridley Scott was confirmed as the director of *Alien*.

Immediately, sound stages and lock-ups were booked at Shepperton and placed under the heaviest security. Very few people were allowed in without the express permission of the director himself or of his favoured band of top art and set designers. Ridley Scott admits that security was tight. "We had to be a bit closed-shop about the project. I just followed what Steven Spielberg had done with *Close Encounters* – he didn't want anyone to find out what the spaceship looked like. We had big lock-ups at Shepperton including a sound stage which very few people were allowed to go into at any time." Shooting at the studios was scheduled from July to October 1978. The result was to be spectacular.

Alien is a hugely successful science fiction horror film, which tells the unnerving story of the crew of a spaceship pitted against a frightening life-form which enters their vessel and attempts to destroy them. The appeal of the film undoubtedly rests on the series of nail-biting and nasty surprises that Ridley Scott executes brilliantly, via late-1970s cutting edge special effects – the most remembered is the "birth" of an embryonic alien which erupts from John Hurt's stom-

ach. Scott had been careful not to tell the actors the details of that particular gut-busting scene in advance of its filming. Only John Hurt knew how it was going to play. The actors arrived on set at Shepperton to discover the crew wearing raincoats, which should have given them an idea that something bad was going to happen. Scott wanted genuine alarm from the actors and knew he only had one chance to get it. He started four hand-held cameras rolling with all the effects pre-set to go, and off John Hurt went. As Sigourney Weaver recollects: "They never rehearsed it. John Hurt started screaming and because he's such a

Above

Sigourney Weaver testing the flame thrower in the grounds of Shepperton

Tony Scott's first feature was to be *The Hunger* which he made at Shepperton in 1982. The film tells the story of a couple of vampire lovers desperate for blood

good actor, all I could think of was 'what's happening,' not to John, but to Kane."

The alien was designed by surrealist artist H R Giger and "brought to life" by Carlo Rambaldi, who just a few years later would produce everyone's favourite visitor from outer space, *ET*, for Steven Spielberg.

Originally, the film was due to end with Ripley (played by Sigourney Weaver) closing the spaceship door on the alien. Ridley Scott though had other plans. "I suddenly thought wouldn't it be great if there's a fourth act with Ripley inside the shuttle and that's where the bastard is!" The additional 17-minute sequence at the end of the film, sustained only by Ripley muttering to herself and the sounds of the ship about to blow, added another five per cent, or $400,000, to the budget.

Alien was released in America on 25 May 1979. By 2000, the film had grossed $225 million across the world. The film also won an Oscar® for best visual effects. Ironically, despite feeling frustrated by having too little to do in the film, and the producers concern that it was slow to get going, *Alien* was a smash hit, an outcome which Ridley Scott never doubted: "I wasn't surprised by the success of the film. I knew I had it as I was doing it – even as the sets were forming we knew we had something really good. You get it in your gut. By the time I made *Alien* I had done around 2,000 commercials plus *The Duellists* (1977). I had run through more celluloid than most feature directors have done in their lifetime. I knew all the beats."

The success of *Alien* meant Ridley Scott would now spend more time away from England, and although RSA would continue to make advertisements at Shepperton, it was to be another 17 years before he would return to the studios to produce a feature.

For Tony Scott the 1970s had also been extremely busy. His career was following a similar pattern to that of his older brother. Tony had joined Ridley Scott Associates with one arm tied behind his back. But the advice his brother gave him about learning production skills – as well as making money – in commercials, had proved to be right. It also brought Tony to Shepperton. "I loved doing commercials. I hardly looked back for ten years. I went shooting all over the world, though I shot whatever I could on stage at Shepperton. It became my home. It was the first studio I ever filmed in and so became my favourite."

As with his brother, Tony Scott perceived an undercurrent of snobbery in the film industry's attitude to the men from the advertising agencies. "England took longer to get over the stigma that commercial directors were somehow selling their souls. They looked down at us. The States came to terms with it sooner. Ridley, Alan Parker and Hugh Hudson broke through into films coming out of advertising and they then got their rightful recognition through groundbreaking movies. The next generation included Adrian Lyne and myself. American producers were once again looking for something different from what their feature directors had been doing in the 1980s. They

gave Adrian Lyne *Flashdance* (1983) to make, which is good rock and roll and made a lot of money. Then I did *Top Gun* (1986), which is good flash, made a lot of money, and is good rock and roll! No one could accuse us of not knowing what we were doing. I used to shoot 100 days a year for commercials, so I got to understand my craft the hard way. Talking with actors, shooting on top of mountains or under the water. Believe me, by the time I came to make a feature I was well versed in every situation that anyone could drop me into."

Tony Scott's first feature was to be *The Hunger*, which he made at Shepperton in 1982. The film tells the story of a couple of vampire lovers desperate for blood. Starring Catherine Deneuve, Susan Sarandon and David Bowie, Tony Scott attempted to revitalise the Dracula mythology, adding in copious amounts of sex, rock and roll, and spectacular photography. While making the film Tony Scott was aware that Shepperton also needed revitalising. The studio had been in decline for some time and little appeared to have been done to make it attractive to film-makers.

Tony Scott recalls: "Making *The Hunger* at Shepperton was like an army of occupation. I took a stage and I had to bring everything in because they didn't have the facilities that they have today. Nowadays, Shepperton matches any of the studios in the States but it wasn't like that then. The production offices were covered in grubby old shag pile carpets that were covered in old Chinese food. The heating didn't work. It needed a paint job. The roofs were leaking. The studios hadn't been maintained. The Americans of course are used to their creature comforts and the studios didn't appear to have an understanding of American sensibilities. Some producers said they would never come back again and that always stuck in my mind. It upset me. Shepperton was my home."

More upsetting for Tony Scott were the reviews for *The Hunger*. The film was not well received. *The Observer* described it as "one of the most incoherent and foolish pictures of recent months." Scott was hurt by the criticism: "I never read another press article after *The Hunger*. I got so slammed. The film was accused of putting in too much style over substance. It's an easy shot from critics who just wanted to have a dig about us guys who came out of advertising."

The 80s and early 90s, brought the film careers of Ridley and Tony Scott both successes and failures, though more of the former than the latter. Ridley's best work of that period includes *Blade Runner*, and *Thelma & Louise* (1991); for Tony it was, *Top Gun*, *The Last Boy Scout* (1991) and *Crimson Tide* (1995).

Location work saw the brothers filming round the world and although RSA was still making commercials at Shepperton throughout this time, it wasn't until the mid-1990s that the Scotts would be back – this time to forge a much closer tie with the studios than the simple hiring of a couple of sound stages. In 1995, Shepperton was suddenly put up for sale. The Scotts decided to buy the studios. Tony insists they had no choice. "When we saw Shepperton go up for sale in the market place, it was like someone was trying to sell our home. Ridley and I were very attached to it. So we decided to jump in, take it over

and try and put it back on its feet. Yes, it was a gamble. We knew that we had to get the films in that would support the Studios' overheads. But we had one major advantage: directors like the idea of a director-run studio. We provided for their needs because we know what they are, we know what the problems are and we could fix them, because we've been there and done it ourselves."

Ridley Scott agrees. Buying Shepperton Studios may have been impulsive, but he's always been that kind of guy. "I always ride everything by the seat of my pants. I follow my intuition. When you're doing commercials as quickly as I was, you have to work on your first idea, on impulse, you can't fiddle about. When someone asks me what's the most important thing about being a director I tell them, making decisions. Just make a decision. Making a decision is better than not making one. That applied to buying Shepperton. If we hadn't acted quickly, who knows what might have become of it?"

The impulsive brothers purchased the site for around £12 million and invested many millions more in the Studios over the coming seven years. Their efforts were applauded by many in the industry and the big films started to return, both American and British. The Scotts themselves, in between juggling their new roles as managing directors at Shepperton, brought their own productions to the studios, proving to sceptics that this buy-out had not been some real estate deal, but was genuinely an attempt to raise Shepperton's profile and put it right back up there among the top studios in the world.

Ridley's first post-purchase production to include a base at his studios was *White Squall* (1996), an average rites-of-passage drama with above average excitement. A boat sailing in the Caribbean, crewed by teenagers and a seemingly less-than-competent captain, runs into trouble. The film starred Jeff Bridges, Caroline Goodall and John Savage. The idea had been developed by Ridley Scott before the Shepperton buy-out, and was based on a true story of a sailing tragedy involving the deaths of six pupils and a teacher from

The film had its fair share of production problems – from the questionable behaviour of the lead actor Russell Crowe through to huge storms in Malta and the untimely death of Oliver Reed before filming of his final scenes was complete.

Above

Gladiator director Ridley Scott with Oliver Reed, who died before filming of his role as Proximo had been completed. Reed was posthumously nominated for a British Academy Award in the best supporting actor category

Opposite

Russell Crowe as Maximus Decimus Meridius in *Gladiator* (1998)

one of America's top schools back in 1961. Location photography extended as far as the Cape of Good Hope in Africa, with most of the dramatic and complicated storm scenes having to be recreated at the Mediterranean Studios in Malta, often chosen by directors who have difficult water scenes to shoot. *White Squall* was not a huge success. Costing some $36 million to make, it only grossed around $40 million worldwide, a great deal lower than one would have expected for such a high-profile film.

If Ridley Scott felt he'd been blown off course, he didn't show it. He threw himself into his next project *G I Jane*, which starred Demi Moore in the lead role of a female intelligence officer, who attempts to become the first woman to join the elite Navy SEALS in the face of much hostility from the men around her. The film was shot mainly in Florida, including location work at a genuine military training institution, Camp Blanding. The film was described as "a very entertaining get-tough fantasy with political and feminist underpinnings," and the two female leads – Demi Moore joined by Anne Bancroft as the Senator who nominates Moore's character for the training programme, expecting her to fail – were just the sort of tough women that Ridley Scott liked to portray. After *G I Jane*, he appeared in no great hurry to get to work on another big budget movie. He used his company, Scott Free, to produce, rather than direct, a couple of projects while he waited for the right screenplay to come along. He got to work on developing ideas for other directors, including a science fiction vehicle for Arnold Schwarzenegger, *I Am Legend*, which Warners pulled when they got nervous over the $100 million budget.

At around this time, the executive producer and joint head of DreamWorks Pictures walked into Ridley Scott's office with producer Douglas Wick, and showed him a painting called *Pollice Verso* – or Thumbs Down – by the nineteenth century artist Jean-Leon Gerome. It shows a Roman gladiator standing in the centre of the Coliseum looking upwards towards his emperor who has his arm extended and thumb outstretched, ready to signal the gladiator to kill his

opponent. Ridley Scott was mesmerized by the powerful image and knew he had to make *Gladiator*.

For Scott, *Gladiator*, was going to be a fine tightrope to walk. He admired the period costume dramas of the past but felt he had almost to re-invent the genre so as to keep the atmosphere and excitement high, but avoid a film that would feel out of fashion the moment it was released. Scott focussed on the political dimensions to the story – the way leaders across time have used entertainment as a means to distract an often downtrodden society. The story was akin to David and Goliath – if a man can rise out of the carnage of the arena to become a genuine champion of the people, then maybe there is a chance he will be strong enough to overthrow a tyrannical leader.

The film had its fair share of production problems – from the reportedly questionable behaviour of the lead actor Russell Crowe, through to huge storms in Malta and the untimely death of Oliver Reed before filming of his final scenes was complete. Nevertheless, Scott kept the show on the road and wherever he was filming, be it Morocco or a field adjacent to the M23 motorway, there was one thing he knew he could rely on – the craftsmen from Shepperton Studios coming up with the goods. Ridley Scott is indebted to their work. "Imagine making a Roman film. You can't just go out and rent that material, you've got to make it. Armour, swords, chariots, food, furniture, tables, tents, the whole bloody lot. We shot the whole German front fight scene at the beginning of the film in Tilford, Surrey. And everything was made at or serviced from Shepperton. We made every plaster cast and column at Shepperton and shipped it to Malta. All the detail was pre-determined at Shepperton. Believe me, that's a great plaster-cast and fibre-glass room we've got there."

Scott also took 100 British technicians to join the 200 local Maltese tradesman, who took 19 weeks to build the Coliseum set in Malta.

Gladiator is a stunning piece of cinema and for that Ridley Scott was rewarded at both the box office and awards ceremonies. In the six months following its release in May 2000, the film – which cost $100 million to make – took more than $620 million at cinemas across the world and garnered 12 Oscar® nominations. The film won five Oscars®, including best picture, and four British Academy Awards, including best film.

After his own box office successes with *The Crimson Tide* and *Enemy of the State* (1998), Tony Scott returned once again to the world of espionage with his 2001 slick thriller, *Spy Game*. Acting legend Robert Redford stars as a veteran CIA agent who finds himself, on his last day at the agency, ignoring orders to go out and save the life of his protegee, played by Brad Pitt, who faces death in a Chinese prison. *Spy Game* was the first film that Tony Scott had made at Shepperton in 20 years, and he was glad to be back. "Whenever I get the opportunity I try to find my way back home. I was in Europe filming *Spy Game*, so I thought 'Great, I'll come back to Shepperton.' I filmed about a third of the film at the studios. We built some huge sets there. We've got some of the best craftsmen and artisans in the world so if I'm filming close by, why would I want to go anywhere else?"

Ridley and Tony Scott continue to make films worldwide. Today, they shoot more on location and less in studios than ever before. Ridley insists that the evolution of computer-generated imagery is not all it's cracked up to be, the cost of CGI often outstripping the cost of going out and doing it for real. Which is what they both do. The merger of Shepperton Studios with Pinewood, eventually saw the brothers sell their share in the company in the summer of 2004. Both are now content that the future of Shepperton Studios, which has been their second home for over forty years, finally seems secured. Tony Scott hopes he'll soon be back again making a film there. "I'd love to make more films at Shepperton but I make most

Right
Tony Scott

Shepperton Studios

films on location in the main. I will be back though and hopefully soon."

For Ridley Scott there is relief that the Shepperton he and his brother took over in 1995 has gone through something of a rebirth. He hopes people will take the British film industry seriously again, and at the same time give a little more respect to those people who work tirelessly to bring projects to the screen. "People don't realise the hours we keep in this business. We arrive on set at 6.30 in the morning and I get to bed at 11 at night having come straight from the editing rooms. In the film industry, whatever level you're at, for the most part, if you're serious, you work like a dog. And I don't give a damn whether the studio is decrepit, as long as I've got a good camera there, a good script, I know what I'm doing and I'm enjoying myself.

"Thankfully, Shepperton's shabby days have now gone. They reflected all the other bad habits we had in those days. You'd have a bottle of wine at lunchtime and smoke 40 cigarettes a day and all other things that were part and parcel of the romantic idea of being a film-maker. In fact we were still working like stink. There's always been this suspicion that film-makers just have a good time, drink champagne, call 'Cut' and 'Action' and go off and have lots of parties. We don't. We work hard. We work harder than most other industries on a daily basis.'

Right
Ridley Scott

Neil Corbould
Special Effects

The movie business has been a part of my life since a very early age. My uncle, Colin Chilvers, used to take me into to Shepperton and Pinewood when I was off school and that is when I fell in love with special effects and the movie business.

One of the first movies that I worked on at Shepperton was in the late 70s. The movie was called *Saturn 3* (1980), staring Kirk Douglas, Farrah Fawcett and Harvey Keitel. It was amazing to be part of a movie with such great Hollywood legends. Some of my duties, apart from making the tea and getting the breakfast rolls, was running the steam pipes under the set, as I was the smallest of the crew and could get under the confined set and also to help carry Hector the robot around from stage to stage. Hector was about seven feet tall and was mounted on an actors shoulders. A breastplate was mounted on the front of him to hide him. So it was very claustrophobic but a lot of fun.

Since then I have worked on many movies in Shepperton including, *SOS Titanic* (1979), *The Keep* (1982), *Muppet Treasure Island* (1995), two Macgyver movies and more recently *The Mummy Returns* (2000), *Gladiator* and *Black Hawk Down* (2001).

Muppet Treasure Island was a fun movie to work on. Nick Allder was the special effects supervisor on the movie and I was his floor supervisor. I grew up with the *Muppets' TV show* and to work with Kermit and Miss Piggy was a dream come true. It's amazing when the puppeteers start the performance. They bring the Muppets alive and before you know it you are having a conversation about everyday life with Kermit and then they start talking amongst themselves about silly things like what they want for lunch, and "oh no not another take, what was wrong with the last one", you stop thinking about the Muppeteer and just focus on the Muppet as a person. It was an incredible experience.

When I started *The Mummy Returns*, the Shepperton management put me into their new workshop facilities in the Orson Welles building, which was great. Finally a studio had designed a workshop facility that had all the necessary requirements for a modern special effects workshop; plenty of 3 phase power, over head beams that could support weight, offices and a canteen adjoining the workshop, good access to the workshop for loading and unloading trucks, it was a pleasure to work in them.

I chose Shepperton to set up my workshop facilities for the prosthetic side of my company, working on projects such as *Black Hawk Down*, *Beyond Borders* (2003), *Cold Mountain* (2003), *Alexander* (2004), *King Arthur* (2004), and the *Kingdom of Heaven* (2004). Shepperton was the perfect base to work from with all the facilities that are available there. I even built the two full size Black Hawk mock-up helicopters there for Ridley Scott's movie and then shipped them out to Morocco.

The Corbould Family has been a part of Shepperton Studios since the mid 70s with my older brothers Chris, Ian and Paul and my sister Gail and father Cliff being involved with movies, television and commercials throughout this period. It seems like there is always a Corbould in Shepperton. It is a big part of our history and we are proud to be a part of Shepperton Studios' history as well.

Opposite

John Nelson, Neil Corbould, Tim Burke and Rob Harvey receive the Special Effects Oscars® for *Gladiator*

Attenborough

Co-producers of *The Angry Silence*, Bryan Forbes (left) and Richard Attenborough (right), with the film's female lead Pier Angeli, receiving an award for the film – which Forbes also wrote and Attenborough starred in – at the 1960 Berlin International Film Festival

It wasn't until I read the book on the life of Gandhi that I suddenly wanted to direct – but I didn't want to direct anything else. It was Johnny Mills and Len Deighton who said: "Dick. If you really want to direct, here's something wonderful for you."

Lord Attenborough recounting how he came to direct his first film, *Oh! What a Lovely War* (1969).

When it comes to the survival of the British film industry in general and to the dedication of independent film production in particular, few names can be so closely linked with Shepperton Studios as that of Richard Attenborough. His career as first an actor, then producer and director, and then a lead spokesman for the film industry in this country, has spanned the entire second half of the twentieth century. In all that time Attenborough has refused to sell out. If he felt his career wasn't going in the direction it should, he never compromised, but instead took a close look at what was disappointing him and then made moves to change. He has never taken the easy route that fame offers – grabbing the money and running. Instead, his beliefs have led his heart and he has stuck firmly by them. Attenborough made *Gandhi* in 1981, but the struggle to bring the production to the screen had taken two decades and he had never given up hope. And for Attenborough the British studio that most sums up what an independent film producer stands for, is Shepperton. "Shepperton was created by and has always been manned with the expertise of film-makers. You were not dealing with accountants or lawyers but people who genuinely understood what an independent film producer wanted. The facilities, the attitudes, the priorities that were important to you, were there. It was and still is a welcoming place. For a film, we would take over whole blocks at the studio.

One's wardrobe, make up, dressing rooms, props department were all in that block. A production became an entity with a family atmosphere – which was so very important – and that encouraged me and others to keep going back."

Richard Attenborough was born in 1923. Acting was in the blood from the beginning. "I always wanted to be an actor. I never wanted to be a director. While I was at RADA, famous American agent, Al Parker, saw me in a play called *Our Wilderness*. He suggested to Noel Coward that I should test for *In Which We Serve* (1942). That role got me going in the film industry – though I had only really ever wanted to appear on the stage."

Attenborough's big theatrical break came when he appeared as Pinkie Brown in the stage adaptation of Graham Greene's *Brighton Rock*, at the Garrick Theatre in 1943. He then joined the air force and was seconded to the RAF Film Unit which was based at Pinewood Studios in Buckinghamshire. The unit lived at the studios, with dressing rooms turned into sleeping accommodation for the servicemen. He appeared in a film made there in 1944 called *Journey Together*. The production was a Second World War documentary drama which also starred a young Jack Watling and Edward G Robinson, who waived his fee to appear as an instructor training pilots to fly Lancaster bombers. The film was written and directed by Flight Lieutenant John Boulting. Attenborough and Boulting became good friends, a relationship that was to bring out some of the best of both of them on the big screen. Attenborough repeated his stage role of Pinkie Brown in the highly respected Boulting brothers' 1947 film version of *Brighton Rock*. The men were to work together again in some of the most popular British films to be made at Shepperton in the 1950s.

"Peter Sellers was wonderful to work with because he was a genius. He had the most extraordinary gift to paint his characters with absolute reality – they were always just a bit over the top but they always had absolute truth within them."

During the 1940s and 1950s, Attenborough appeared in over 30 films, but as the tally of spivs and below deck naval officer roles increased, his enthusiasm for such parts quickly waned. He didn't feel at all stretched as an actor. His frustration was partly assuaged by the Boultings who brought him onboard into their repertory group of actors who starred in their 1950s satires, such as *Privates Progress* in 1955 and *I'm All Right Jack* in 1958. In the latter, Attenborough worked alongside Peter Sellers. The two were to star in two further Shepperton outings, *Only Two Can Play* in 1961 and *The Dock Brief*, the following year. He recalls their times together with affection. "I remember doing several pictures with Peter Sellers. I had become great friends originally with the Boultings, because John had been my commanding officer in the RAF film unit at Pinewood, and it was they that introduced me to Peter. Until then, I had only heard his work on the radio.

"Peter Sellers was wonderful to work with because he was a genius. He had the most extraordinary gift to paint his characters with absolute reality – they were always just a bit over the top but they always had absolute truth within them. He wasn't reliable that I will say. He didn't appear exactly dead on time for shooting. But in terms of his work he was wonderful. The real problem was that he broke you up. On *The Dock Brief* there were times I couldn't continue. It was the same for all the cast and crew. The king of the show was Sellers because he had this realistic comedic capability which was extraordinary."

By 1959, Attenborough decided he had had enough of the parts he was being offered. He formed a production company, Beaver Films with Bryan Forbes, who as an actor and writer, shared Attenborough's career frustrations. Their first production was to be one of the most important films ever to be made in Britain.

The Angry Silence, made at Shepperton in 1959, told the story of a strike-breaker who is sent to Coventry by his work mates and driven almost to the point of death by their behaviour towards him. Attenborough wasn't out to bash the unions. "I was passionately opposed to the fascistic control of the trade unions. I was and always have been a passionate Labour man since 1945, but I felt that the wrong elements in trade unions were being fostered which lead to this true story of men finding themselves being treated in this way. That is why we made the film." The film was almost not made at all. British Lion ordered Attenborough to slash the already paltry budget of £142,000 to nearer £100,000. This he did by getting the cast and crew to appear for as near to nothing as he could get away with. It meant losing the film's star, and Attenborough taking over the lead role, as he recalls. "I wasn't supposed to play in it. But British Lion wouldn't give us enough money to make the film. Kenneth More was going to play the lead in *The Angry Silence*. Then he got a wonderful "paid" offer elsewhere and so, he told us that he couldn't play in our film for nothing. It was just a short while before we were due to start filming. There was nothing for it, I had to play the lead. I was very happy producing and acting at the same time."

As a producer, Attenborough knew that the buck stopped with him and all eyes at British Lion would be fixed on how successful he could make *The Angry Silence,* even under the most stringent of financial restrictions. Attenborough was faced with a major problem. At that time, there was no major film distribution in Wales. Most Welsh audiences would go and see a film at their local miners halls. If you couldn't get your film to play at miners halls across the country, a film could potentially lose up to a quarter of its UK sales. A film such as *The Angry Silence* couldn't afford to lose that type of ticket income. The story line was unlikely to welcome itself to the miners, who were all members of unions. There was nothing else for it, Attenborough would have to go to Wales to explain that his film was not attacking unions in general but certain types of activity by certain types of members. Attenborough admits that he found the

Above
Richard Attenborough (right) as Sydney de Vere Cox, in conversation with director John Boulting (left), on the set of *I'm All Right Jack* (1959)

Right
Richard Attenborough (left) and Bryan Forbes (right) with veteran television broadcaster Alan Whicker (2nd left) during the making of *The Angry Silence* (1959)

Attenborough remembers going to see the show. "I'd seen the play at the Criterion and laughed so much... it was brilliant. I don't know why they asked me to play in the film but they insisted. It was totally different for me."

whole process quite troubling at the start. "I travelled to Aberdare in Wales and asked to meet the miners union executive to explain why I had made the film and what it was about. They didn't tell me they were going to play the film to all the local miners immediately afterwards. When I arrived, I got to meet the executive in advance of the screening then I climbed onto the hall stage and told the audience why I'd made the film. There was stony silence. I left the stage and they put on the film. At the end there was still stony silence. I got back onto the stage and they started to applaud. They all stood up and yelled their approval. It was very emotional. After that, they made me an honorary member of the union."

Even though money had been tight on the film, Attenborough had found the experience of producing his first film an energizing one. He credits much of the success of his work at Shepperton at that time to the way that the Studios were run: "The great thing about Shepperton in those days was its general manager, Andy Worker. He epitomized the opportunities at Shepperton for independent production. Pinewood was essentially Rank and if you weren't part of Rank you felt, when you were there, that you were almost an interloper. At Shepperton, John and Roy Boulting, and Frank Launder with Sidney Gilliat, had taken over the studios via British Lion. They had formed an independent film-makers society. So when you turned up at Shepperton with a production, you knew that the production was king and that the studios were at your command." Attenborough returned to produce Bryan Forbes' hit film, *The L-Shaped Room*, at the studios just a short while later in 1961.

Richard Attenborough first wanted to make a film about the life of Mahatma Gandhi back in the early 1960s after being approached by Indian diplomat Motilal Kothari to work on the project. Away abroad, Attenborough read Gandhi's biography and immediately agreed to the film. Directors such as Michael Powell and David Lean had already been said to have turned the idea down – its sheer scale was said to be unworkable. Attenborough, who hadn't even directed

His success at directing *Oh! What A Lovely War* in 1969, showed that Attenborough was more than suited to directing a large-scale production and he was chosen by American producer and screen writer Carl Foreman to direct *Young Winston*

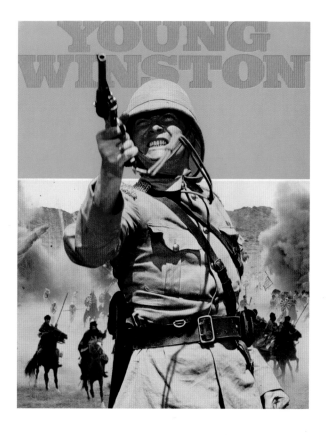

a film at that time, couldn't wait to give it a try: "I remember phoning from Switzerland on one of those old slot machine phones screaming down the phone, that I had never directed a film but would give up anything to direct it. But then they told me that no one had the money to make it. It took us 20 years to get the money together. It took forever." He didn't remain idle for the next two decades and continued to work in film, with one eye always on the look out for financial opportunities to get *Gandhi* made.

Attenborough got his first chance to direct after being approached by friend John Mills, nervously agreeing to make the film version of Joan Littlewood's stage production of the First World War musical satire, *Oh! What A Lovely War*. The screenwriter for the film was novelist Len Deighton, who was said to be so unhappy with the film that he asked to have his name removed from the credits. Yet the film with its star cast including Dirk Bogarde, John Gielgud, Kenneth More, Ralph Richardson and Laurence Olivier, was very well received and won Attenborough considerable critical acclaim.

Richard Attenborough returned to Shepperton as an actor in the role of Inspector Truscott, in Joe Orton's *Loot* (1969). The play – a farce about a crook who uses his mother's coffin, to transport the proceeds of a robbery – was a huge success in London's West End in the late 1960s. Attenborough remembers going to see the show. "I'd seen the play at the Criterion and laughed so much ... it was brilliant. I don't know why they asked me to play in the film but they insisted. It was totally different for me." It most certainly was. While the film version may not have been as great a success as its stage play counterpart, most critics agreed that the most memorable moments from the

film came from Attenborough as the suitably creepy and kinky detective.

His success at directing *Oh! What A Lovely War* in 1969, showed that Attenborough was more than suited to directing a large-scale production. He was chosen by American producer and screenwriter Carl Foreman to direct *Young Winston* – the account of the early years of Churchill – at Shepperton, in 1971. From the start there were troubles with the production. J Lee Thompson who had made *The Guns of Navarone* at Shepperton with Foreman, once said of him: "I think I was the only director who ever made a second film for Foreman. He was an excellent producer and excellent, if lazy, writer but he did interfere with writers as well as being obsessive about credits." Thompson's criticism of Foreman appeared to be mirrored in the producer's behaviour towards Attenborough while making *Young Winston*, which Attenborough found increasingly frustrating. "I knew what I wanted to do with the film. I disagreed with Carl the producer and writer. But he was giving me a big break with *Young Winston*. I'd only done *Oh! What A Lovely War*. Originally he had asked me to play the part of Randolph as well as direct. I said that I thought the job of directing the film was enough for me. So I cast Robert Shaw in the role instead. During shooting, Carl wanted to use a television technique of people talking directly into the camera. I was unhappy with that. I felt it was a trick that interrupted the reality of the narrative. So we shot it both ways, mine and his. He won though. *Young Winston* was not a totally happy movie, Carl treated me with great respect, but he would disagree on various issues. The picture then didn't have the same joy for me as a number of others did." Ironically, most critics agreed that the film looked good but that the script was quite stodgy and yet it was Carl Foreman who was nominated for an Oscar for his

Left

Richard Attenborough (left) as Inspector Truscott with Milo O'Shea (right) as Mr McLeavy, in the film version of Joe Orton's mordant comedy play, *Loot* (1969)

For all the frustrations, Attenborough's experience of working on *Young Winston* brought other pleasures, primarily the "joy" of working with actors such as Anne Bancroft, Robert Shaw and a young but nonetheless intense and exciting actor, Anthony Hopkins. Attenborough chose to work several times again with Hopkins, finding each occasion more exciting than the time before.

Above

Richard Attenborough and Anthony Hopkins preparing for their next scene, in *Shadowlands* (1993)

Right

Ben Kingsley as Mahatma Gandhi and Candice Bergen as Margaret Bourke-White, in Richard Attenborough's *Gandhi* (1981)

script, while Attenborough received no nomination for his directing.

Everyone in showbusiness has their heroes and Richard Attenborough was no exception. So when he was offered the chance to act opposite John Wayne he jumped at the part. The film was *Brannigan*, made at Shepperton in 1974, with John Wayne in town from the States to pick up a crook and take him home. Attenborough played the Scotland Yard detective, whose job it is to ensure that *Brannigan* plays everything by the book. It had all the ingredients of a classic western but transported to the heart of London – pub brawls and all. Attenborough thoroughly enjoyed himself: "I adored the Duke. I would have done almost anything to appear in a film with him. He was a huge and enchanting man. Politically, he was way to the right of Ghengis Khan, but as an actor he was god-like to me. Now, I'm quite short and Duke's very big. We had this fight scene that we staged on a set of a London pub. The scene worked by me having to lay him out with a punch. The only way we could get it to work was by building a ramp so that as I walk across the pub – and nobody realises it – I'm walking up a ramp, so that by the time I got to him I could reach his chin to deliver the knock out punch. Great fun."

In the late 1970s, after so many years of hope and cajoling, Attenborough finally looked set to realise his dream of making a film about the former Indian leader Mahatma Gandhi. The budget for the type of film that was to be produced could not be described as high – less than £10 million – yet tying down the final monies was proving difficult. Attenborough and his actress wife Sheila Sim, who owned a share of the rights to Britain's longest-running stage play, The *Mousetrap*, sold those rights to help fund the production. Yet Hollywood was still not forthcoming. Everyone seemed to like the idea of a film about *Gandhi*, but few wanted to put their hands into their corporate pockets to pay for the film's making. Richard Attenborough still recalls, with a sense of irony, his meeting with Twentieth Century Fox. "I told them about the story of the life of Gandhi and

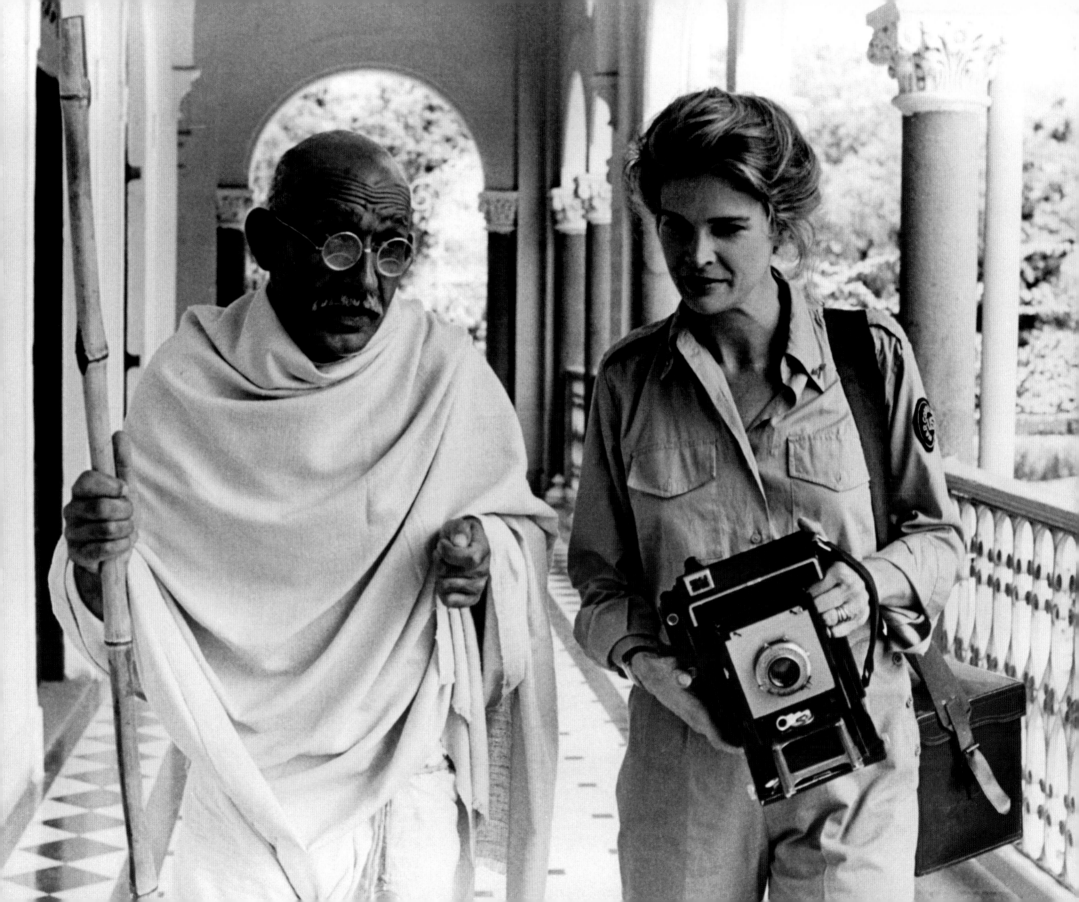

how dramatic it was and how great it would be. One of the big bosses said to me, 'Dickie, we've done a lot of pictures together over the years and I'm very touched that you've brought this to us, but who do you think is interested in a little brown man dressed in a sheet carrying a bean pole.' I literally gave up. But then I met Jake Ebbetts. Jake read the script in one night. He said it was the greatest subject he'd read about and he set about raising the money from private individuals, trade unions, city investors – but not a penny from the film industry. Then he wrote to Prime Minister Indira Gandhi, Nehru's daughter, who gave authority to the National Film Development Corporation to allow us the use of facilities such as laboratories, the army, locations, labour and so on."

Gandhi went into pre-production at Shepperton Studios during 1980 with filming taking place, between 26 November 1980 and 10 May 1981, mainly in India. Both Alec Guinness and Anthony Hopkins were considered for the lead role, the part finally going to cinematic newcomer Ben Kingsley, on a recommendation to Attenborough by his son Michael. The cast of the film was suitably star-studded and included; John Mills, John Gielgud, Edward Fox, Martin Sheen, Candice Bergen – to whom Attenborough had first offered her role back in 1966 – and Trevor Howard, whose cameo as Judge Broomfield was shot at Shepperton in just two days. Attenborough's crew was made up of the finest that Shepperton had to offer, from its camera, sound and art departments. With shooting underway the financial pressures on the production continued. The last third of the film was to be financed by the Hinduja brothers. But with just days to go until their money was due to be handed over, Attenborough received a telex explaining that unfortunately they had to withdraw from the project. Attenborough was devastated. "I hadn't got sixpence. I couldn't pay the crew at the end of the week and certainly didn't have the money to get them back to England. Eventually, one of our backers, Pearson, came up with the money. They sent one of their men over to discuss the situation and view the rushes. At the very same time former Labour

Prime Minister, Jim Callaghan, decided he wanted to come and watch us filming. So there I was in this huge hotel dining room with the guy from Pearson's talking to my line producer, Terry Clegg, at one end and me entertaining Jim Callaghan at the other end of the room, pretending everything was fine when we didn't really know if we were going to get the money or not. Thankfully, we did and we were able to continue filming."

Several hundred thousand extras appeared in *Gandhi*'s funeral scene. Around 200,000 of these were volunteers who had come far and wide, many by foot, following notices which Attenborough's team had dropped into villages and towns – some up to fifty miles away. The sequence was filmed on 31 January 1981, the 33rd anniversary of the funeral of Gandhi. There were eleven separate camera crews used to shoot the funeral, and they used some 20,000 feet of film between them. The final scene lasting just over two minutes on the screen. Getting all the extras ready took military planning. Just one red jacket or pullover in a crowd of thousands of people would have stuck out and ruined the shot. All the extras had to pass through gates where, if they weren't already wearing white, their clothes would be swapped, in order that everyone was dressed correctly for the occasion and, more importantly, for the camera.

Once the film was made, *Gandhi* still didn't have a distributor and Attenborough turned to the legendary doyen to Hollywood agents, Marty Baum, to help sell his film. "Marty came to London. I showed him the film at Shepperton. When it finished – after three hours – he said it was one of the greatest films he had ever seen in his life. He said we'd sweep the Oscars®. He promised that every head of a studio in

> Attenborough turned to the legendary doyen to Hollywood agents, Marty Baum, to help sell his film: "Marty came to London. I showed him the film at Shepperton. When it finished – after three hours – he said it was one of the greatest films he had ever seen in his life.

America would see the film. And they did. Ultimately, every single company in LA bid for the film – many who had previously turned me down. The final battle took place between Columbia and Paramount and in the end we got a huge sum of money for it from Columbia."

Gandhi swept the board at awards ceremonies across the world, winning eight Oscars® and five British Academy awards in 1982. Attenborough was delighted. "People say Oscars® are a pain and all fixed. Not true. We had no idea. *Gandhi* struggled to get made, it had run out of money, had no distributor whatsoever – we didn't know if the film would be shown. So if people say movies are all commercial, I'll say yes of course they are, and thank goodness that they are."

The runaway success of *Gandhi*, both critically and financially, allowed Attenborough to film another epic biographical drama, *Cry Freedom*, in 1986. Telling the story of the doomed South African civil rights leader, Steve Biko, *Cry Freedom* was filmed in Mombassa, Kenya, as well as Zimbabwe and at Shepperton Studios. As ever, Attenborough achieved strong performances from his lead actors including Kevin Kline as Donald Woods, a South African journalist who has to flee the country after investigating the death of his black friend in custody, and an Oscar®-nominated role for Denzel Washington as Steve Biko.

Although most of the filming was undertaken on location, Richard Attenborough still continued to use Shepperton as the base for his films. Most of *Gandhi*

was shot in India, with the majority of *Cry Freedom* shot in Zimbabwe.

In 1991, Attenborough chose Shepperton again for the pre-production of his next movie biopic, *Chaplin*, about the life of the famous film-maker and silent comedy film star. The director recalls: "We filmed most of *Chaplin* in America and most of the British stuff was shot on location in the east end of London where Charles Chaplin grew up. We used Shepperton for interiors. It wasn't really a studios movie for over here, since most of Chaplin's life was spent in America. It made more sense to film it there."

For Attenborough, *Chaplin* brought more pleasures than just that of making another Oscar®-nominated film. It brought him back together with Bryan Forbes,

ters in the film were factual. Indeed actress Geraldine Chaplin played her own real-life grandmother. The only truly fictional character was that of George Hayden, a publisher to whom Chaplin, in later life, recalls his history. Hayden was played by Anthony Hopkins, who over the years had become one of Richard Attenborough's favourite screen actors. Indeed, out of the eight films that Attenborough had directed to that date, Hopkins had appeared in four of them. Their fifth, and so far, final outing together, was to be in 1993, when Hopkins took on the role of CS Lewis, in the romantic biographical drama, *Shadowlands*. The film recounts the life and unsuccessful love of the emotionally repressed Oxford don and writer of children's books. The film is beautiful to look at as well as to listen to. The acting of Anthony Hopkins and Debra Winger as the American woman that CS Lewis marries and then grows to love before she learns she has terminal cancer, is a tearjerker with exceptional depth of feeling. Attenborough believes that is due, in no small part, to Hopkins' performance. "I think Tony is the film actor of his generation. He has a skill and understanding of cinema even though he emanated from theatre. He has a concentration and resultant fire in the belly which is magical on the screen. Tony hates rehearsals though – you didn't really get a rehearsal out of him – because he believes that if you have to keep rehearsing lines they lose part of their spontaneity. On the set of *Shadowlands*, I used to read Tony's lines with Debra Winger and then Tony would come in, do a technical rehearsal and then I'd shoot it."

the two having first worked in partnership some 30 years earlier on *The Angry Silence* at Shepperton. "It was great getting back with Forbesey. He was my real partner. We'd begun with *The Angry Silence*. He's such a wonderful screenwriter. It was great to be working with him again on *Chaplin*." The role of Chaplin was taken on by Robert Downey Jnr, his superbly entertaining portrayal winning him an Oscar® nomination and the British Academy award for best actor in 1992. Some critics commented that, *Chaplin* could have done with a longer treatment, having to incorporate as it did such a long and momentous life. Ironically, Attenborough's original cut of the film was nearly four hours but it was trimmed back to 145 minutes. Most of the charac-

Attenborough donned his director's hat once again to make the 1996 biographical drama of *In Love and War*, the life of writer Ernest Hemingway during the First World War. Attenborough chose Shepperton as the base for the film, although much of the story was filmed in and around the Italian village of Vittorio Veneto. For the battle scenes, many of the extras playing the soldiers were airmen from the nearby Aviano Air Base. The role of Hemingway was taken by Chris O'Donnell, and the nurse who takes care of him when he is injured in combat, Agnes Von Kurowsky, was played by Sandra Bullock. The film was not regarded as

Right
Richard Attenborough and close friend, John Mills

Page 264
On the set of *Shadowlands* (1993)

Page 265
On the set of *Cry Freedom* (1986)

one of Attenborough's best, some critics claiming the lack of chemistry between the leads as the reason the film doesn't quite hit the mark. *Variety* declared: "It doesn't get under the skin of its protagonists, leaving the viewer unmoved and passably interested at best."

Certainly during his long and illustrious career, Richard Attenborough has become renowned for doing what *Variety* claimed *In Love and War* did not – he has, on more than one occasion got under the skin of his protagonists. As film historian Neil Sinyard so accurately surmised: "He has always been something of a Brutus of the British Establishment: loyal and loving, but not averse to sticking the knife in when it takes a step too far in the direction of authoritarianism." It was that very Establishment that recognised Richard Attenborough's contribution to British cinema when he was knighted in 1976. Sir Richard Attenborough became Lord Attenborough when he was elevated to the peerage in 1993. As well as film production, Lord Attenborough has chaired many cultural and charitable bodies, including Channel Four Television and the British Film Institute. He has been married to actress Sheila Sim since 1945 and they moved to their Richmond home in 1949 – Shepperton Studios not just close to his heart, but his home too.

Now in his 80s, there is no sign that this much-acclaimed and admired film-maker, producer, actor and ambassador for the industry is ready to hang his boots up quite yet. As for the future, will there be more films at Shepperton? "I wouldn't go anywhere else to make a film. If I had the choice to shoot anywhere in the UK, I would have no hesitation in coming back to Shepperton every time. I feel at home at Shepperton. I feel welcome at Shepperton. I never doubt the capability of the facility. And, on top of everything else, it's just twenty minutes from home!"

Robin O'Donoghue
Head of Post Production

Well it seems a long time ago now but in my latter years at college I had a great love of photography and, although I had planned to go into banking, my heart wasn't in it. A good friend of our family, one time head of sound at Ealing Studios, mentioned there could be the possibility of joining the Rank Film Laboratory at Denham as a trainee. I jumped at the chance.

After two years at Denham I joined Twickenham Film Studios as a sound loader, the guy who loads the Sound Optical Camera for the final process of recording the soundtrack to a photographic medium. At Twickenham I had a wonderful apprenticeship, working in all aspects of the recording process from location assisting to the recording of forty piece orchestras, disc cutting, Foley/ADR work and dubbing.

During this period I had three job opportunities; clapper loader attached to a freelance camera crew,

production department runner and, the one I chose, second assistant mixer on the dubbing stage at Twickenham Film Studios. It was during this period, from 1965 through to the 80s, that I had the opportunity to work with some of the greatest directors of the time: Richard Lester, Joseph Losey, Sidney Lumet, Tony Richardson, Richard Attenborough, John Schlesinger, Ridley Scott, Carl Foreman and later Kenneth Branagh, Terry Gilliam, Neil Jordan and Jon Amiel along with many others, who really taught me my craft along with the taste and judgment in mixing.

I mentioned Ridley Scott and it was he who invited me to join Shepperton when the Scotts purchased the studio in 1994. Up to that time Shepperton had become very run down, with no real post-production facilities. It was a shadow of the studio it was in its heyday. The asset stripping of the 60s had sold off the back lot and the remaining studio had become an industrial estate for any business which required

space. There was a revival in its fortunes for a while under the Lee Brothers but once again financial difficulties caused the demise of their brave plan; only under the Scotts did the dream start to come alive.

One of the first things the Scotts wanted to achieve was a leading post-production facility, one to rival anything around. The first project was to reclaim the original premiere mixing stage which, in the intervening years, had been turned into a preview theater. Theatre Four, as it is known, was completely refurbished and a Harrison fully automated mixing console installed, along with the newly employed talents of Ray Merrin and Graham Daniel. *White Squall*, *GI Jane*, the first two *Harry Potters* along with many others were mixed in Theatre Four.

A little while later I joined to head up the Korda Theatre, a new mixing theatre built in what had been the Old Power House. The Korda was designed by Norris Spencer with acoustics by Andy Monroe and it was here I installed another Harrison and the first Akai hard disc recorders, along with, 35mm film play-off and record machines. Although I knew the days of 35mm sound were numbered my first couple of bookings were being sound edited on 35mm so I needed to have that capability. Very soon afterwards sound editing became purely electronic. Projects mixed in the Korda over the last few years have been numerous: *Notting Hill* (2002), *Shakespeare in Love* (1998), *Gosford Park* (2001), *Love Actually* (2002), *Troy* and *Alien vs Predator* (2003).

Theatre One, another excellent re-recording theatre from the original studio days, had been consistently busy in the intervening years and for a long time was owned by Delta Sound, one of the on-site independent companies. Delta was much respected as a TV mixing facility and the first post-production outfit to use digital sound editing and recording equipment. The Lees brought Delta back under studio control and with the Scotts investment and input became Theatre One. The theatre was refurbished with another Harrison console and, with the mixing talents of Mike Dowson and Mark Taylor, successfully mixed films such as *Elizabeth* and the much applauded *Band of Brothers*.

The Korda is now eight years old and has stood up well to the advances in technology; only in 2004, I changed the desk to Euphonix, a console designed for the twenty-first century with the capabilities of controlling over six hundred tracks. The Akais have also come to an end and are being replaced by a computer-based record/playback system, Pyramix. Film has now really finished and only used right at the very end to check the final sound and image, before the labs bulk print thousands of copies to send around the world.

A mixer from fifty years ago would still recognise the

Above

A scene from *Notting Hill* (2002) mixed in the Korda Studio

Above

A scene from *Elizabeth* (1997) mixed in Theatre One at Shepperton

principles of dubbing mixing, or as it is more commonly called "re-recording mixer." It is still how loud or soft and what equalisation to apply, but there have been huge changes in the quantity of tracks, complexity of the process and the time taken.

Dubbing mixing has changed from some of the early films I worked on to the present day. The soundtrack for films of the 60s was prepared on 35mm magnetic sprocketed tape. The sound would be made up of, say, 10 nine hundred foot reels each lasting ten minutes. The soundtrack supplied to the mixing theatre would consist, on average, of six dialogue tracks, twenty effects tracks, eight foley tracks and three music tracks, so for one reel of action there would be thirty-seven reels of magnetic tape, a lot to carry up and

down the stairs from the cutting room to the projection box. These tracks would be premixed down to a manageable amount so they could all be run together on the 35mm playoff machines to achieve a final balance. The six dialogues would be equalized, compressed, balanced and re-recorded onto one roll of 35mm. The twenty effects tracks would be premixed in a manner which still gives final control over the ultimate balance between items like wind, rain, gunshots, cars and so on; this would reduce the effects tracks down to five rolls of 35mm. The foleys would be premixed onto one roll and the music run in live; the amount of tracks on the final mix would be made up of ten rolls of magnetic tape, not thirty seven. Premixing time was usually two weeks; final mixing one week,

followed by delivery items such as foreign versions and trailer material.

Sound re-recording and editing today is all based around computer technology, with the track-laying usually done in Protools, often reaching the realms of over one hundred and fifty tracks or more. There are no longer any tins of film to move around, only one or two 250Gb hard drives, the size of a biscuit tin. Mixing as I said is still ostensibly the same process except that all films are now mixed in 5.1 Dolby and directors expect complete flexibility, often changing because you can, major ingredients of the track lay and picture edit during the mixing process.

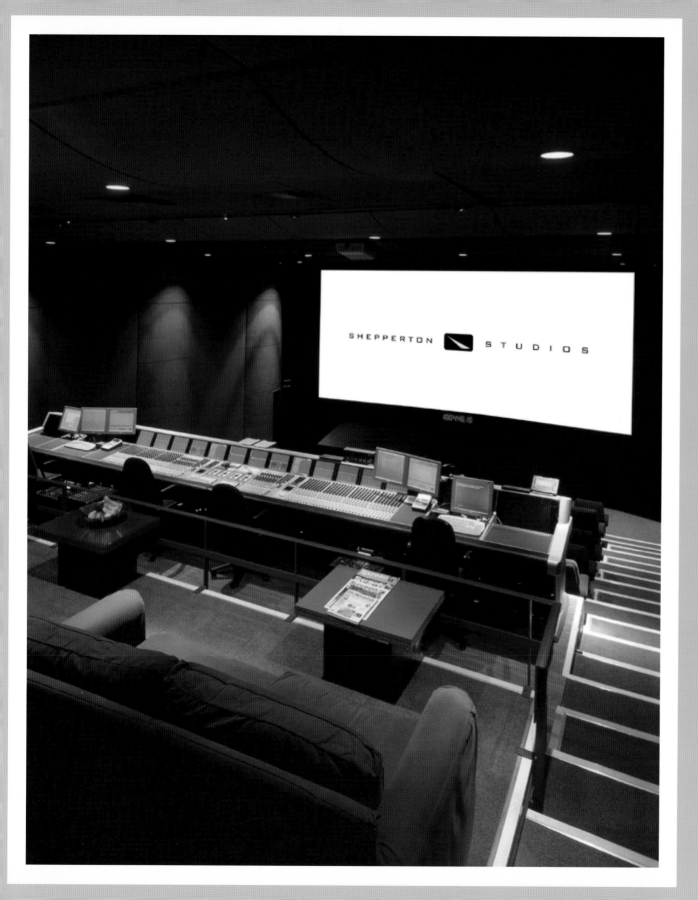

Whether soundtracks are any better today is open to discussion. Many think they are too loud and cinemas regularly run them several decibels lower because of complaints. The truth is that we now have the capability to recreate realism, never possible in the distant past of the mono optical track. In my opinion a well thought out and prepared track lay along with technically perfect location recorded dialogue and a sensitively balanced final mix goes a long way to enhance the whole cinematic experience.

Post-production and sound mixing at Shepperton were always something to be proud of, and it is good to see today that Shepperton is back at the forefront of technological developments and still producing acclaimed soundtracks.

269   Post Production

Branagh

"We have a very British idea about how things should be done. It's not just what we achieve, but the way in which we do it. Nothing twee or precious, but things need to be done justly, and honourably."

Kenneth Branagh launching the Renaissance Theatre Company in 1987.

In 1984, Kenneth Branagh, just 23, became the youngest actor to play the title role in *Henry V* with the Royal Shakespeare Company. Critics dubbed Branagh's performance "the most exciting Stratford debut for years." From that moment, the Belfast-born actor would find himself inevitably compared to the best actor of the previous generation, Laurence Olivier. The comparisons frustrated Branagh. Not all were kind. *The Times* once wrote: "Branagh seems as remote from Laurence Olivier as... Sandra Bernhard is from Sarah Bernhardt." As Branagh moved from the RSC to co-found his own group, the Renaissance Theatre Company in 1987, the move into the role of actor-manager continued to fuel the comparisons. Yet few were wholly accurate. Laurence Olivier was a matinee idol some time before he was acknowledged as a great classical actor and theatrical manager, and after he had failed to make a lasting impression in Hollywood. Kenneth Branagh became an actor-manager at a much earlier age and before he had wholly established himself as a classical actor.

It was early in 1989, that Branagh and Renaissance co-founder David Parfitt embarked on filming *Henry V*. They intentionally chose not to watch Olivier's 1944 version, as Parfitt explains: "My first job as a producer at Shepperton was on *Henry V*. We had talked first about a production of *Hamlet*, but Mel Gibson's *Hamlet* (1990) was just ahead of us, so we changed course. There were many in the industry who said that there was the Olivier version which nobody could match, and that we should stay well clear of it. But Ken's approach to *Henry V* was a modern interpretation. We weren't trying to match Olivier. That was the 1940s. Now it was the late 1980s. It was post-Falklands and a different world. No one in theatre says 'Olivier played *Richard III* so no one else can do it.' Each generation has its star productions."

I remember Prince Charles coming to Shepperton to visit the set of *Henry V*. I had been chosen to be his guide for the day. We worked out in advance precisely where he would arrive, where he'd be taken, what he'd see on the stages and the backlot. I walked the route in advance with the studios' management. When I came to take him round on the day itself, everything on that route had been painted.

Henry V tells of the young King of England invading France to claim his right to a kingdom and to the daughter of the King of France, and of the war that ensues as Henry's embattled troops meet the French forces on the field of Agincourt.

Getting their first production off the ground was hard work. To raise the $8 million budget for the film there were seemingly endless lunches with city stockbrokers, sometimes three-a-day, with Branagh arriving in time for dessert to put across his persuasive pitch. Shepperton helped too. There was an "unofficial" policy to encourage film-makers by giving them offices at the studio at either a peppercorn rent or no rent at all, in the expectation that if things went well and a production was commissioned, the company would bring the film on the site. That assistance was of great benefit to David Parfitt and lead producer Bruce Sharman as they attempted to bring *Henry V* together. The producers utilised the Shepperton stages and grounds to the full. Parfitt knew that this was the only way to make the film. "All but one scene was filmed in or around Shepperton. It was so important. It gave us much more control. We wanted to stage the piece without it being too stagey – to keep the structure of the play intact within a film." Branagh meanwhile, who was also directing the film, focussed his attention on the actors. An impressive array of stars including Derek Jacobi, Alec McCowen, Ian Holm and Judi Dench, were allowed long takes, so as to give them a chance to perform and not to break up speeches and soliloquies. Branagh also insisted on

a proper read through and, as with theatre productions, there were full rehearsals for a week or so in advance of shooting. To enable him to focus on both the role of lead actor and director, Branagh employed the services of another actor, whose job it was to learn his words and perform them while Branagh and the crew were setting the shots. Branagh would direct the actor, take a step back, see how it worked on camera, and then go in and do it himself. To aid his actors further, Branagh ensured that the film was shot entirely in sequence.

Henry V was made in the wintertime and the production was blessed with good weather. Indeed at times the sky was actually too clear and bright for shooting outside. The production also prompted a royal visit to the Studios and a slight headache for the manage-ment, as David Parfitt recalls: "In the late 1980s the studios were just scraping through. There was a great management team, but some of the site had seen better days. I remember Prince Charles coming to Shepperton to visit the set of *Henry V*. I had been chosen to be his guide for the day. We worked out in advance precisely where he would arrive, where he'd be taken, what he'd see on the stages and the backlot. I walked the route in advance with the Studios' management. When I came to take him round on the day itself, everything on that route had been painted. But only that and nothing else. So Prince Charles arrived at one end of the studios, walked through stages "A" and "B" and all the corridors through to the backlot smelled of paint. If we'd turned right or left off that route at any time, we'd have been in trouble."

Left and above
Henry V (1988)

"You walk into the studio sometimes and think, from here you can create any world you want indoor or outdoor. That sense of magic being created is very strongly present at Shepperton."

Running to 137 minutes, exactly the same length as Olivier's 1944 production, Branagh's *Henry V* was generally well received and, aside from the obvious comparisons between the two actors and their productions, was given due credence by many as being at least the equal of its precursor. For his first attempt to put the Bard on the screen, Branagh was nominated for two Oscars® – best actor and best director. He won neither but did pick up the Bafta for best director. The film won an Oscar® for best costume design. Branagh seemed more than satisfied with his film: "The more I thought about it, the more convinced I became that here was a play to be reclaimed from jingoism and its World War II associations."

After *Henry V*, Branagh, Parfitt and Renaissance returned to the theatre, where a world tour took them out on the road for nine months. After marrying actress Emma Thompson Branagh set off to make a film in Hollywood, the thriller, *Dead Again*. On his return he suggested to Parfitt, that the company should be making other films as well as their favoured Shakespearean adaptations "Ken felt that we should be trying to do other films – not just Shakespeare. So we had an amazing year in 1992 when we made three films literally back-to-back: the short film *Swan Song*, the comedy *Peter's Friends*, and then *Much Ado About Nothing*. It was an incredible work rate, and we achieved it by keeping the same team rolling from one production to the next." *Much Ado About Nothing* was not filmed at Shepperton. Made in the summer of 1992, it was shot entirely on location at a fourteenth century villa in the centre of the Chianti wine region of central Italy, though the play itself is set in Messina, Sicily. As Branagh explains: "There's a lot of sex in it. I felt it should be surrounded by nature and grapes and sweat and horses and just that kind of lusty, bawdy thing." Certainly the film looks

good and once again succeeds in proving to audiences that Shakespeare can be fun. Among those stars who seemed to be enjoying themselves in the production were Denzel Washington, Michael Keaton and Keanu Reeves, who joined Branagh as Benedick, and his wife Emma Thompson as Beatrice, in the tale of a man and a woman who have sworn never to marry but who are tricked into falling in love. As *Time* magazine declared: "This isn't the best Shakespeare on film... but it may be the best movie on Shakespeare." *The New York Times* went further: "Triumphantly romantic, comic and emotionally alive."

Mary Shelley's Frankenstein (1993) brought Kenneth Branagh's back to Shepperton studios, though for this production much was to change. It was to be his first movie without Emma Thompson – the couple divorced shortly afterwards – and his relationship with Renaissance was also coming to an end, as producer David Parfitt recalls: "At the end of *Much Ado*, the film company Renaissance disbanded. I stayed with Ken during *Frankenstein*, which was really his bid for Hollywood – a classic story with an interpretation that hadn't been seen before. The film's backers brought in their own people for the film and there was very little for me to do, so I left that production at the end of the shoot. I didn't stay for post-production. Instead I joined forces with Stephen Evans and we went off and made *The Madness of Kind George*, also, I'm glad to say, at Shepperton." Parfitt was correct about the style of the production. *Mary Shelley's Frankenstein*, the tale of a scientist giving life to a creature who, when refused another creature to mate with, wreaks havoc. It was a bold and stunningly stylish attempt to breathe new life into the oft filmed story. Branagh played Frankenstein, with American acting legend Robert De Niro taking on the role of the monster, after it was supposedly turned down by Gerard Depardieu. They were joined in the cast by Tom Hulce, Helena Bonham Carter, Ian Holm, John Cleese, Robert Hardy, and Branagh-film stalwart and admired comedy actor Richard Briers, who played the blind hermit. Branagh was delighted to be back making his film at the Surrey studios. "Shepperton is very welcoming to film-makers, it has

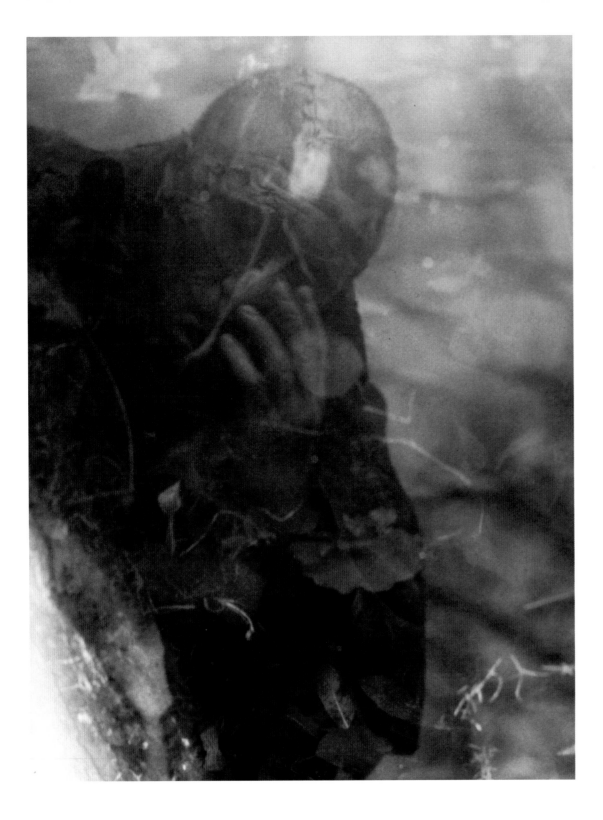

a great sense of community. I like being able to bump into people who are also working on films and for the atmosphere to be friendly. It's an old fashioned thing. Part of what we feel about movies is that though it's exciting to be out on location and it's exciting to travel, it's also very thrilling to be involved in the purest form of old fashioned cinema – studio based filming, where you can 'create' magic. When we made Frankenstein at Shepperton we constructed an enormous village and outdoor mansion set which required us to borrow some land at the back for a short time. You walk into the studio sometimes and think, from here you can create any world you want indoor or outdoor. That sense of magic being created is very strongly present at Shepperton."

The creation of magic and special effects is not always comfortable for the actor. The amniotic fluid in which Frankenstein's Creature is brought to life was a messy gelatinous concoction which had both Branagh and De Niro slipping all over the set, so much so, that at one stage a split appeared in De Niro's costume, which had to be skillfully avoided by the cameras. Branagh's worst moment was having a mould taken of his head, the memory of which still gives him shivers. "I had a prosthetic head made for *Frankenstein* and also recently for *Five Children and It* (2004). Scary process to have that go on. Your face gets covered in gel but it's not until the last minute when everything goes over and you've just got a straw in your nose that there's suddenly this rather coffin-like feeling as the 'lights go out.' I must say the first time they did it, I shouted 'get it off, get it off'. It was only actually on for a few seconds. It's then pretty weird to walk through a props department at Shepperton a few days later and think 'I know that face... oh my goodness, it's me!'"

As with many of Branagh's productions, the reviews for *Mary Shelley's Frankenstein* were mixed. Former Hammer Horror star Ingrid Pitt described the film as, "A gargoyle short of the Gothic horror that made the original unforgettable." *Screen International* was kinder: "A highly paced costume drama that propels us along the trajectory of Frankenstein's ambition with a speed reminiscent of Indiana Jones."

In 1995, Kenneth Branagh was involved in two major productions at Shepperton studios. The first was as an actor in Oliver Parker's directorial debut *Othello*, and the second, as writer/director of *In the Bleak Midwinter*. *Othello* had been filmed for mainstream cinemas twice before. The first production was made by and starred Orson Welles in 1951. Welles had wanted to make *Othello* for several years and had taken many roles – including that of Harry Lime in *The Third Man* – to help finance the project, which was cash-strapped from its inception and remained so throughout its difficult production and beyond. The final black and white version ran for just 91 minutes. The later 1965 colour version of the film was almost twice as long as the Orson Welles version. The film became a record of the National Theatre production, it starred Laurence Olivier, Frank Finlay, Maggie Smith and Derek Jacobi. It's not great cinema, but a very useful record of Olivier's much respected performance (for which he received an Oscar® nomination).

The 1995 version of *Othello* was to be an altogether whole new experience for audiences. For the first time on film an African-American (Laurence Fishburne) was cast in the title role. Previously, both Welles and Olivier had 'blacked up' for the part. The film was to be good-looking and accessible, its trailer colourfully selling the story using modern PR parlance: "In the time of heroes there was but one great general. His bravery in battle was legendary, his devotion to his love unchallenged. His name was Othello. Under the cover of darkness and against her father's will, he took Desdemona into his heart. The great general and his true love were secretly wed. Some men die for glory, some men fight for love. One man lives for revenge. His was the soul of a traitor, and the opportunity he seized will change their lives forever..."

A strong trailer was matched by strong performances, particularly from Branagh as Iago. Ironically, in an effort to make the film more accessible to a mass

"Pitched at audiences as a sort of psychological thriller about sexual jealousy: *Basic Instinct* with better dialogue and a handkerchief instead of an ice pick."

Above
Laurence Fishburne as Othello
and Irene Jacob as Desdemona,
in *Othello* (1995)

Opposite
Robert De Niro as the Creature, in
Mary Shelley's Frankenstein (1993)

audience, much of Shakespeare's dialogue was excised, only one third remaining in place. Director Oliver Parker explained: "I thought it would be interesting to make it more of a punchy, pacey number." The critics didn't seem to mind, *Variety* declaring: "Colourful and intimate production is relatively conventional and unremarkable as an interpretation, but it is well performed by its two males leads and clearly staged and enunciated for ready comprehension by a mass audience." *The Sunday Times* went further: "Pitched at audiences as a sort of psychological thriller about sexual jealousy: *Basic Instinct* with better dialogue and a handkerchief instead of an ice pick."

In complete contrast was Branagh's own Shepperton production that year. *In the Bleak Midwinter* is a small sentimental comedy about an out of work actor who attempts to save his sister's local church by gathering together a motley bunch of unemployed actors to put on a production of *Hamlet* in the village – aptly-named Hope. Written and directed by Branagh, the cast included Michael Maloney, Richard Briers and Joan Collins. Branagh had wanted to make the film for four years but had no time and even less opportunity to work on the script and production before the autumn of 1994. He chose not to act in the film, writing the lead role instead for Michael Maloney who had played the Dauphin in Branagh's *Henry V*. Shooting took place at Shepperton in the early summer of 1995, which made things a little difficult on the days when the weather was bright and warm – in direct contradiction to the name and theme of the film. Behind the camera, Branagh would look for a setting in and around the studios that would not seem out of place whatever the time of year. As he commented during production: "Occasionally there are crisp, bright days. We're trying to shoot wherever there's an evergreen so the logic Nazis don't write in."

In the Bleak Midwinter was made, in black and white, for just $1.6 million, somewhat less than the $44 million that had been spent on *Frankenstein* the year before. Yet Branagh felt equally at home at Shepperton on both productions. "I think we had eleven stages when

we were filming *Frankenstein* – either building on them, shooting, de-rigging, sometimes at the same time. Yet I've also enjoyed the filming when doing perhaps a smaller picture such as *In the Bleak Midwinter*, which we shot in just five weeks in offices at Shepperton. But that's what the Studios is like. They've always been very good about saying, 'use the Studio, not just the stages, just come and be shooting at Shepperton'."

The resurgence of big-screen adaptations of plays by William Shakespeare continued unabated throughout the 1990s. Cynics proclaimed that it was due to copyright of the playwright's work being well out of date, while many big-star names were keen to appear in such prestigious and "award-friendly" productions at a fraction of their usual fees – thus keeping costs

Above

Famed American comedy actor, Billy Crystal, plays the Gravedigger, in *Hamlet* (1995)

Opposite

Oliver Parker's 1995 screen version of Shakespeare's tragedy, *Othello*

down. With the cast that Kenneth Branagh had planned for his film version of *Hamlet*, the latter would be more than helpful. Also made at Shepperton in 1995, Branagh's epic four-hour production boasted some of the biggest acting names in the business on either side of the water, including: Derek Jacobi, Julie Christie, Jack Lemmon, Billy Crystal, Robin Williams, Gerard Depardieu, Charlton Heston, Judi Dench and John Gielgud. Branagh played the nineteenth century Danish prince, who is slow to take revenge when he discovers that his stepfather and uncle has usurped his father's throne. Kate Winslet played Ophelia, a role for which she did not even have to audition. She had previously auditioned for the role of Elizabeth in Branagh's *Frankenstein*, the part going to Helena Bonham Carter.

Hamlet was not only sumptuous to look at but was the first time that it had been filmed unabridged. Part of the film was shot at Blenheim Palace, which is owned by the Duke of Marlborough, who received a small role as Fortinbras' General by way of thanks. Most of the production was filmed at Shepperton. It was a huge project and not without the odd hitch, as Kenneth Branagh recalls: "Thankfully the infrastructure at Shepperton means that if a piece of equipment breaks – a camera goes down or some lights explode – everything's there on site. When we made *Hamlet*, we had to shoot across two sound stages, "A" and "B", which have a double door between them (which we used as part of the set) and a corridor which went from one set of suites and rooms into an enormous courtroom. I remember we were shooting on 65mm with a huge number of lights. There needed to be a four minute tracking shot that went from the

Left
Derek Jacobi prepares for his next scene as Claudius, on the Shepperton set for *Hamlet* (1995)

Opposite
One of the most spectacular sets built for a filmed staging of Shakespeare, was at Shepperton for *Hamlet*, in 1995

Above
Kenneth Branagh behind the
camera, during production of
Love's Labours Lost (1999)

Opposite
Kenneth Branagh places
Shakespeare in the 1930s and 40s,
and adds song and dance
routines, turning *Love's Labours
Lost* (1999) into a romantic musical comedy

far end of one stage through the suite of rooms, through the corridor into the other stage and all the way up to the other end. Alex Thompson, who lit it said 'I'm a bit worried about this governor, there's a lot of lights on here'. Halfway through the day we blew the sub-station at Shepperton." *Hamlet* was nominated for four Oscars®, for best screenplay, music, cinematography and costumes, but left empty-handed from the 1996 awards.

The advertising for Branagh's 1999 production of *Love's Labours Lost* declared it: 'A New Spin on the Old Song and Dance.' The old story was that of the King of Navarre and his three companions who swear an oath to study together and renounce women and whose honour is put to the test by the arrival of the Princess of France and her three female companions.

The new spin was to set the tale in 1939 and to turn the production into a musical with famous song-and-dance numbers of the era, including. *I Get A Kick Out of You*, *Cheek to Cheek*, *The Way You Look Tonight*, *There's No Business Like Showbusiness* and *They Can't Take That Away From Me*. It was an interesting take on trying to do something fresh with Shakespeare. As Derek Malcolm wrote in *Screen International*: "The result is not a classic, but it is fun: short, sharp and fast-paced." However the film was not successful. Stung by the failure of *Love's Labours Lost*, Branagh immediately shelved plans for two other films based on Shakespeare plays. It had been reported that he was planning a version of *Macbeth*, in which the title character would have been represented as a Wall Street Broker, and a version of *As You Like It* set in a Japanese tea garden.

Kenneth Branagh has continued to be a regular visitor to Shepperton over the past few years. He has won deserved critical acclaim for his acting in television productions; as explorer and expedition leader Sir Henry Shackleton, and as the Nazi general Rienhard Heydrich, in the award-winning *Conspiracy*. Ever one to poke fun at himself, Branagh has found a whole new legion of fans in his portrayal of Gilderoy Lockhart in *Harry Potter and the Chamber of Secrets* – in a role originally planned for Hugh Grant.

By his own admission, Branagh is a great fan of Shepperton, and he is the first to admit that, at times, he has been in awe of the studios and its output. "We were shooting *Hamlet* at Shepperton and I remember walking in one day and there was Cruella De Vil standing in the middle of Elsinor. It was Glenn Close who was shooting next door. Then I walked outside and Sylvester Stallone was walking along in a funny helmet because they were in the middle of *Judge Dredd* (1995) and there were strange monorails going over my head. Even hardened film types were pretty excited by that. What was it that Orson Welles called it?... "The biggest toy box in the world."

Above
Veteran Hollywood actor Jack
Lemmon, plays Marcellus, in
Hamlet (1995)

Opposite
Kenneth Branagh adapted
William Shakespeare's play
for the big screen, as well as
directing and appearing as
Berowne, in his 1999 rendering
of *Love's Labours Lost*

David Parfitt

Producer

I started in the business as a child actor over 30 years ago. My first major role was playing Wendy Craig's son in the television sitcom *...and Mother Makes Three*. It would have been around that time that I first went to Shepperton for a television production, *Anita in Jumbleland* starring Anita Harris. It was an independent production, which was rare in those days, and was directed by Peter Frazer-Jones who also directed *...and Mother Makes Three*. Unfortunately, the show wasn't fully financed and was never broadcast. It was shot over many months on a permanent set on one of the larger stages. I went in originally to do a guest spot in one episode as a French boy but, during the inevitable waiting around, I used to wander all over the Studios looking into the workshops and exploring the backlot. The remains of the *Oliver!* set were still standing and I remember risking death by climbing over the raised walkways (no Health and Safety Officers then!). My limited experience was of TV studios so the scale of the film studios and sets were something completely different.

Over the years I moved away from acting into producing. The role of the producer can be very broad, starting from an original idea or buying the rights to a book, to commissioning a screenwriter and attaching a director, as well as raising all the necessary money along the way. You may oversee the casting, get the key crew together – it doesn't stop until the finished product, the film, is out on release.

Having co-founded the Renaissance Theatre Company, with Kenneth Branagh, in 1987 my ambitions were mainly in theatre but after a year or so we decided that the natural extension to our theatre work was to broaden our audience through film. You can take a theatre company on the road, as we did, and tour for nine months, and still not reach the number of people who see a film on its opening weekend. It's such a different medium. From that point of view, you can do everything you can do in the theatre and then some. I do like the intimacy of film. It's not dissimilar from the feeling you can derive from a good theatre

production – it's something that takes you over and makes you feel involved in the action. When as film-makers we get it right, it's an unbeatable experience.

My first production job at Shepperton was on *Henry V* in 1989. As Ken and I were coming from the world of theatre, we brought in the hugely experienced Bruce Sharman as our producer. Ken had talked about our first film being *Hamlet* but Mel Gibson's production was just ahead of us so we changed course. There were some in the industry who were, let us say, cautious about these outsiders and their ambitions in film. This was not surprising as we'd never done anything like it before. There was already a "definitive" version by Laurence Olivier and nobody was making Shakespeare films. I'm sure I would give the same advice to new film-makers myself and I would hope very much that they would ignore me!

At the time, the management at Shepperton seemed to have an unofficial policy of encouraging film-makers by giving them offices in the studio at a peppercorn rent, in the hope that if their projects went forward they would bring the film to the Studios. This policy was incredibly useful to those of us who were new to the industry, and I will always be thankful to everyone at Shepperton for that.

I soon realised that film-making, at least in the practical areas, was in many ways slightly easier for a producer than theatre. In theatre, or at least the sort of theatre I had been involved in, you have tiny budgets and very few people doing all the jobs. At least in film you can delegate to your department heads to a much greater extent. The pyramid is a lot broader based.

I'll always remember shooting *Henry V* at Shepperton. We shot in the winter yet the weather was amazing. In fact it was too bright and too blue for us when we were shooting rain sequences outside. All but one scene was filmed in or around Shepperton, as keeping the production contained, was important for us as new filmmakers.

I've been back to Shepperton many times since then with *Mary Shelley's Frankenstein*, *The Madness of King George*, *The Wings of the Dove* and *Shakespeare in Love*. I have always tried to keep my productions in the UK because of the quality of the crews, and I always try to use Shepperton because I appreciate the workmanlike feel of the place and, of course the team who run the studio. It all makes my life as a producer very much easier.

Working Title

The rise and rise of Working Title Films seems quite spectacular. The company has produced some of the most successful films of recent times. Its commercial hits include *Four Weddings and a Funeral*, *Bridget Jones's Diary* and *Billy Elliot*, while critical acclaim has come in the shape of many awards, including Oscars® for films such as *Fargo* and *Elizabeth*. Over the past ten years, almost all Working Title's UK films have been based at Shepperton Studios, and from those sound stages have emanated some tremendous British cinema.

Of course it wasn't always that way. Indeed Working Title was to make some 20 films before it had a big hit – *Four Weddings and a Funeral* – which has seen its success escalate ever since.

Working Title co-founder Tim Bevan began his career producing pop music videos in the early 1980s. This new "art form" had rapidly taken off and many aspiring film-makers were using it as a launch pad into television and film production. Bevan started the company back in 1984 with Sarah Radclyffe, whom he met when she was working on an early Channel Four commission, *The Comic Strip Presents...* Both of them wanted to make films. Both vehemently believed that if you could make a video, you could make a film. Using his persuasive personality, Bevan enticed established film-makers – such as Nic Roeg and Derek Jarman – to make videos for him. Former documentary and drama director Stephen Frears had just finished the 1984 British cinema suspenser *The Hit* when Bevan approached him to produce a pop video for Heaven 17. Shortly after, Frears found himself directing Working Title's first production, *My Beautiful Launderette*.

"We couldn't really afford to go into studios before then. We had always made location-based films because that's all we could afford. In a class-room or school hall somewhere. Or we would have to convert a shop into a launderette and make sure that every other location was within walking distance, to keep the costs down."

Tim Bevan, Working Title

Above

Working Title's Tim Bevan

Opposite

The set at Shepperton studios for the filming of Working Title's huge commercial hit, *Notting Hill* (1998)

My Beautiful Launderette was originally intended for television – commissioned under the film arm of the recently launched network station Channel Four. The film received such wide acclaim at the Edinburgh Film Festival that the broadcaster decided to give it a theatrical release. The story of a young Asian man from south London who manages his uncle's launderette and falls for a white racist boy, proved fashionable and popular. The film's screenplay was nominated for a British Academy award. More importantly, Bevan was quickly learning how the film industry worked. He was particularly interested to discover that each country had their own independent film distributors who would pay up-front for the purchase of distribution rights. This meant that there could be money available to make a film before the film went into production, if those rights were pre-sold. Armed with this newly-acquired knowledge, Working Title used the funds from pre-sales distribution, as well as monies from a host of tax schemes, to help meet the costs of its films during the rest of the 1980s. The music video business was left behind, as Tim Bevan and his growing team worked harder and harder to establish themselves as truly independent filmmakers. "I enjoyed the early days a lot. There was an anarchy about it all which was terrific but then I was in my 20s and I enjoyed an anarchic life style." At Cannes, for example, Bevan would cram in as many meetings as he could, not sleeping for much of the festival, if at all, working all day, doing deals, partying all night, and regularly bumping into fellow producer and future Working Title chairman, Eric Fellner who was dashing around equally as fast in the opposite direction.

Working Title's output throughout the 80s and into the 90s was varied. Some of its films were good – *Wish You Were Here* (1987), *Personal Services* (1987) – some productions less so. *The Tall Guy* starring Jeff Goldblum was neither one nor the other. The story of a stooge who escapes the restrictions of working with a sadistic comedian to try and make it on his own, was not a huge success. Yet, unbeknown to anyone in 1989, *The Tall Guy* would inadvertently help secure the future survival of Working Title. The screenplay was the first

feature film-script by the writer of the classic BBC comedy *Blackadder*, Richard Curtis. Two years later, with *The Tall Guy* all but forgotten, a large royalty cheque from the film's financiers arrived at Working Title's door. For a struggling independent production company, the money could not have come at a better time. Bevan admits he was surprised. Surely, not that many people had been to see *The Tall Guy*? He brushed aside his first instinct to bank the cheque immediately and set about working out who was entitled to a share of this unexpected windfall. Richard Curtis was equally surprised when a royalty cheque arrived through his letterbox soon afterwards. Curtis had enjoyed the experience of working on his first film. The extra money was now a bonus. He thanked Bevan by sending Working Title his next screenplay... *Four Weddings and a Funeral.*

In 1992, Working Title was bought out by music company PolyGram which had been looking to diversify into film. The investment allowed Working Title to evolve with greater stability. Co-founder Sarah Radclyffe decided to remain an independent producer and left Working Title to form her own company, and producer Eric Fellner came on board as co-chairman with Tim Bevan. The style of the two men proved an instant success. Their knowledge and experience of the industry complemented each other, while personally they brought different skills to the table – Bevan the more impulsive, Fellner more wary, Bevan a great reader, Fellner a better 'people person.' Working Title reached an agreement with PolyGram which meant that, whilst the two companies would be tied together in matters of finance and distribution, Working Title would maintain its autonomy in deciding on the sorts of films that they were to make. For Bevan and Fellner this was a remarkable opportunity. The team would be able to oversee their films from inception and continue to be part of the process of production all the way through to marketing and distribution.

By the time *Four Weddings and a Funeral* was released, Working Title had made 20 films during their first 10 years. Success can hardly have been claimed to have arrived overnight. But this film was the one. The combination of a strong production team, including director Mike Newell, an excellent script by Richard Curtis and the perfect casting of, among others, Hugh Grant and Kristin Scott Thomas (both of whom won BAFTAs for their roles), ensured that *Four Weddings* would be regarded as one of the best pieces of original cinema in Britain in a generation, although Richard Curtis admits he never envisaged his screenplay would be such a hit. "*Four Weddings and a Funeral* had a much harder birth than *The Tall Guy*, because we were just above that line financially when things started to matter. And it never felt particularly like a hit. When I handed the script in to Tim he probably thought, as did we all, 'Here's another one like the last one, let's hope it does a little better than *The Tall Guy*'."

The story of a confirmed bachelor who chases the woman of his dreams from one wedding to another cost less than $5 million to make and grossed $250 million worldwide. *Four Weddings* was the first feature on which Working Title had spent a consistent amount of time shooting at a film studio – Shepperton – as Tim Bevan remembers: "We couldn't really afford to go into studios before then. We had always made location-based films because that's all we could afford. In a class-room or school hall somewhere. Or we would have to convert a shop into a launderette and make sure that every other location was within walking distance, to keep the costs down. I hadn't really 'got' the purpose of using studios before then. We hadn't had the money to spend on studios, other than the odd day's filming here and there; so we hadn't experienced being able to go onto a stage, build a set, and come back at any time to film on it. There was a great flexibility and freedom working on a stage that we hadn't known before. It was really as we began to think of bigger movies that we thought of studios-based films. I had been happy on location. I thought that's the way you were supposed to do it if you were truly independent. So it was an education for me. All part of the process."

Working Title's new found recognition allowed the company to go film-making with greater ease across the water. In America, they teamed up with the Coen

Brothers on *The Hudsucker Proxy* (1994), *Fargo* (1996) and *The Big Lebowski* (1998); with Tim Robbins on Bob Roberts and *Dead Man Walking* (1995); and back in Europe with Larry Kasdan on *French Kiss* (1995), and with Rowan Atkinson on the big worldwide hit, *Bean* (1997). The next Shepperton-based production was to be *The Borrowers*, in 1996. Based on Mary Norton's children's stories about a family of tiny people who live below the floorboards and survive by "borrowing" items from an unknowing family of normal-size humans who live above ground, this delightful family film, directed by Peter Howitt, starred Jim Broadbent as the minute father and John Goodman as an unscrupulous lawyer attempting to take over their home. Unlike *Four Weddings and a Funeral*, which comprised studio shooting and location work, the nature of *The Borrowers* meant the entire film had to be shot at Shepperton. Its huge, larger-than-life sets, took up several sound stages and, while computer generated images (CGI) were used to help create the convincing backgrounds and skylines, the oversized props and sets needed to be built by hand, by the studios' craftsmen. Tim Bevan insists that that was the only way to make the film at the time: "The film was about small people in a big world. And we had to build huge sets – like a 50ft washing machine. In reality we couldn't actually afford the CGI. Also CGI wasn't as advanced then as it is now and we didn't really trust it. CGI has changed so much over the past ten years. If, for example, we had been making *Thunderbirds* (2003) when we made *The Borrowers*, there's no way we would have created all the ships using CGI. We would have had to use models."

Making *The Borrowers* was another learning curve for Bevan and his team. "We learnt that you need to take on a number of sound stages on which to build a number of large sets. As a producer, there was a whole new set of criteria to learn – how long it would take to build a set, how long to shoot, how long to strike the sets and juggling all the stages and schedules to make it all work. And then we had to work out how to keep costs down by turning one set into another set by taking down a wall here and there and putting something else up in its place, and generally moving things

about. That's one of the things I love about a good production designer. They build the fabric of a set and then, after you've shot on that set, they'll change it around so that when you return five weeks later, you're shooting in a completely different environment. It's like being on a completely new set."

If *The Borrowers* was to prove a learning curve for Working Title, their next film would be even more testing. *Elizabeth* (1997) was intended to be a classic production but Bevan and Fellner were convinced from the start that they did not want the film to follow in the footsteps of a traditional British "frock flick." The feel they wanted for the piece was altogether something different – harder, grittier and more akin to a thriller. For inspiration, Bevan screened his favourite film, *The Godfather* (1972), to the staff: "From the start I wanted to buck the trend. I suggested that it would be good to make a movie genre inside an historic film, rather than an historic film which was part of a genre." Buck the trend Working Title did. They actively sought a director, Shekhar Kapur, who knew little about English history. His voyage to discover and learn what had happened to the Queen during her reign, became the film's journey of discovery. As Bevan puts it: "I wanted everyone on the film to be learning about Elizabeth rather than passing on their received knowledge about her." An American production designer, John Myhre, was chosen and proved inventive. He suggested the film should have the texture of stone rather than wood, which was, of course, entirely inaccurate historically, but which worked incredibly well on screen. Says Bevan: "We went to Durham Cathedral and the look and feel of its stone texture was used for the feel of the studio sets at Shepperton. And the sets were amazing; each of them was used two or three times – Queen Mary's death chamber was revamped as Queen Elizabeth's bedroom, which was then revamped as

Opposite

Actor Jim Broadbent as the diminutive head of a family of minute people, is literally swamped by over-sized props in the film, *The Borrowers* (1996)

one of her court rooms." *Elizabeth* was shot both at Shepperton Studios and on location; partly because the company couldn't afford to be on location all of the time and needed to get back into town, and partly because it made sense to do so, as much of the film was interior-based, ideal then for filming on a sound stage.

One big problem that the production faced early on, was finding a lead actress to play the title role. Several star names turned the film down. A relatively unknown actress at that time, Cate Blanchett, found herself undertaking a screen test. The actress was delighted to win the role. "My outstanding memory of filming is storming up and down long, dark corridors at Shepperton. Making the film was an exciting and fluid process. When people ask me about *Elizabeth* and what a success it was, they forget it was a risk and no one really knew whether it was going to work or not." The financial success of its most recent films, *Bean* and *The Borrowers*, meant that Working Title was able to stretch the budget for *Elizabeth* and ensure that the sets and costumes looked as regal and grand as they possibly could. The film opened to great acclaim and duly received seven Oscar® nominations and won one, for make-up. It also received five British Academy Awards including Best British Film and Best Actress for Cate Blanchett, who lost out on Oscar® night – as did the film in several other categories – to *Shakespeare In Love*. Tim Bevan remains philosophical: "The one fault with *Elizabeth* was that we didn't go quite far enough with the script. If we'd gone a couple more rounds with it, we would have had a film that would have been as definitive and as good as we could have made it, and probably would have won the Oscar® that year instead of just being nominated. But we loved the ambition of it and so did the audiences."

Right

Tricks of the trade – the Duke of Norfolk (Christopher Eccleston) faces beheading, courtesy of the executioner's axe, and a funnel and hosepipe of red coloured fluid running up his back to his neck, during filming of *Elizabeth* (1997)

The Queen holds court, in *Elizabeth* (1997)

Notting Hill came next out of Working Title's Shepperton stable. Described by *Empire* magazine as "Solid, crowd-pleasing entertainment," Julia Roberts starred opposite Hugh Grant in this slight but clever and witty romantic comedy penned by Richard Curtis. The film tells the story of a diffident English bookseller who becomes romantically involved with a famous American film star. The crowds that gathered to catch a glimpse of the two attractive leads when filming went out on location, made the production team ever more thankful when they could decamp back to Shepperton for a calmer shooting environment. The film did big box office, some 350 million worldwide. Ironically, Working Title's backers, PolyGram, were not to share in the film's success. At the end of the 1990s, PolyGram was sold to Seagrams, which had been keen to take over PolyGram's music assets. The film interests were taken over by Universal (also part of Seagrams). Tim Bevan and Eric Fellner sought to ensure that the future of their company, and its independence, was secure. They both wanted to be able to choose the sorts of films they wished to make and continue to support and promote new talent across the industry. At the same time, the pair realised, that a worldwide distribution structure was essential to their future success. A deal was struck which allowed European media company, Canal Plus, to part-finance Working Title films, with Universal running and overseeing the arrangement. Bevan and Fellner accepted that, in order to be able to make some of the smaller or more risky films that they wanted to shoot, they must produce big earners too, as Bevan admits: "If you're going to be making an *Elizabeth* you need to be making a *Bean*. Because *Elizabeth* was a very risky film, whereas with *Bean* and Rowan you know early on that it's going to be alright. That may not always be the case. Next year we could be making lower budget films. It's like a slate with a bullseye drawn on it. Sometimes the bullseye is bigger and so easier to hit. That's how I see the films. *Bridget Jones II* has a bigger bullseye, easier to hit for it to be successful. But we also like to make small films, risky sort of films, and their success is never assured." Inheriting a $350 million hit like *Notting Hill* assured that Working Title's new relationship with Universal bedded down smoothly and quickly.

The end of the 1990s also saw Working Title create a new company for the production of smaller films. Called WT2, the express aim was to produce first films by first-time directors, writers and other creative talent. Their first production was to be *Billy Elliot*. Eric Fellner had long been an admirer of stage director Stephen Daldry, and offered him a deal to develop ideas for film. Daldry's debut feature told the story of an 11-year-old boy from the north-east of England who wants to become a ballet dancer. The film is set against the harsh backdrop of the 1984 British coal miners' strike. *Billy Elliot* was shot mostly on location. Thanks to astute marketing, the film found a huge audience across the world. It was also nominated for three Oscars®, and won three BAFTAs; for best British film, best supporting actress for Julie Walters, and most amazingly of all, best actor for the young Jamie Bell, who beat off big names such as Russell Crowe in *Gladiator* (1998) and Tom Hanks in *Castaway* (1999).

If for every *Elizabeth* there needed to be a *Bean* then it's probably true to say that for every *Captain Corelli's Mandolin* there needs to be a *Bridget Jones's Diary*. Working Title had the manuscripts to both these films some years before they were made. The adaptations on both took some years to get right. *Bridget Jones* was Eric Fellner's project and *Captain Corelli's Mandolin* (2000) was Tim Bevan's. There were production hitches on both projects but one was always more likely to be a hit than the other. *Bridget Jones's Diary* was made on location and at Shepperton studios in 2000. This enjoyable romantic comedy starred Rene Zellweger as a single woman in her 30s, looking for love in all the wrong places. Somewhat rarely, the film is often funnier than the book on which it was based, though not all critics gave it the thumbs up. *Variety* declared: "Despite being edited down to a bare-bones 90-odd minutes, forcing the elimination of key characters and scenes and the underdevelopment of others, the pic manages to feel, paradoxically, as dramatically flabby as the 10 pounds Bridget cannot seem to shed!" The *Evening Standard* was a little kinder: "Not big, clever or remotely grown up – but it is tremendous fun." Audiences seemed to think so. They lapped up the exploits of the Oscar®-nominated

Zellweger and her hilarious cohorts, Colin Firth and Hugh Grant, ensuring that *Bridget Jones's Diary* made it into the top ten highest grossing films of all time in the UK.

Working Title's next Shepperton-based film was another Hugh Grant vehicle, *About A Boy* (2001). Based on the novel by Nick Hornby, Grant stars as an idle playboy who is forced to learn about commitment when he befriends an unhappy 12-year-old. Following along shortly afterwards was another link-up with the rubbery-faced *Bean* star, Rowan Atkinson. *Johnny English* (2002) was a spy comedy adventure film which overplays on its typically British style of schoolboy humour as it sends up another institution, the Bond-esque super-spy. By this time, Tim Bevan was finding

the use of studios more and more appealing. "What I've learnt is that a location picture doesn't necessarily make a better picture. I was recently out in New York making a picture with Sydney Pollack. We were out on location a lot of the time. So you've got Sydney Pollack, Sean Penn and Nicole Kidman, all in Manhattan, with helicopters whizzing over head all the time and ruining the scene. You don't get that at Shepperton – unless the Atlantic jumbos are going in a certain direction. I prefer using the studios now to be honest. When we were making *Johnny English* it was so much easier knowing where you're going in the morning – hopping in a car and getting to the Studios. It's so easy."

Love Actually was filmed during 2002. Starring Liam

Neeson, Martine McCutcheon, Rowan Atkinson and Emma Thompson, this was another romantic comedy from the pen of Richard Curtis. This time round, Curtis was also given his first chance to direct a feature, a situation he found quite daunting. "It must have been unbelievably difficult to have me around – directing a film is complicated and the director is always making little compromises in his mind, thinking, 'Well I can't do this because of time, or because of how the actor is, or because of the location.'" Location wasn't a problem when filming got underway at Shepperton for key scenes. From an interior set of No.10 Downing Street to the apartment where Mark (Andrew Lincoln) lives and stores pictures from his art gallery, Shepperton's workmanship once again came up trumps. Bevan and his crew were glad to be back

filming at the Studio on sound stage "B": "One of the things I now love about sound stages is that you step onto them and remember what's been filmed there in the past. That's what I remember about "B" stage: it had *Elizabeth*'s bedroom built in it. We also filmed the light bulb scene from *The Borrowers* on it. That's also where the expensive apartment set was built for *Love Actually*. All those moments come back the moment you step onto it."

Ten years after first hiring a sound stage at Shepperton, Working Title still returns there to make its British films. Perhaps a dash of production super-stition – returning to the Studios where its biggest successes have been created – sprinkled over the knowledge and experience that the Studios offer by

Above

Renee Zellweger plays the heroine in the hit romantic drama, *Bridget Jones's Diary* (2000)

Opposite

Super duo Colin Firth (left) and Hugh Grant (right) as the competing would-be suitors, Mark Darcy and Daniel Cleaver, in *Bridget Jones's Diary* (2000)

Opposite

5,4,3,2,1... almost 40 years after International Rescue first arrived on British television, Lady Penelope and friends were given the big screen treatment by Working Title, in *Thunderbirds* (2003)

Below

Paul Bettany on set in Working Titles *Wimbledon* (2003)

Right

Rowan Atkinson creates his own version of Bond in *Johnny English* (2002)

Below right

Paul Bettany in *Wimbledon* (2003)

way of quality service and facilities. Most recently, those facilities included taking over the backlot at Shepperton and converting it into Centre Court for the romantic comedy, *Wimbledon*, starring Paul Bettany and Kirsten Dunst. According to Tim Bevan, the original plan was to build the world-renowned tennis arena indoors. "We shot *Wimbledon* out on the back lot, reproducing Centre Court. We couldn't shoot the film at the real Wimbledon in south-west London. We had to be in a completely controlled environment and also to be able to stick a green screen all around it for the special effects. We were going to build Centre Court on "H" stage at one time, but we needed the sky to make it feel real."

Working Title has been running now for 20 years and between them Tim Bevan and Eric Fellner have been responsible for some 70 films. Each production brings greater respect from the industry and more success for the company and those who work with and for it. But there's no time to stand still and Tim Bevan takes nothing for granted: "You have to re-invent all the time. You've got to take risks. Yes, you'll fail occasionally. But if you fail, do it brilliantly. Because that's what this industry is about. Do your best, try and keep the quality control. Sometimes the audience will engage with it, sometimes they won't. But take risks. Most importantly you have to try and find fresh ideas. Back the good writers, back the good directors, find the new talent, because they'll come up with good ideas. And when you find something good, stick with it."

After twelve films made at Shepperton and with plans advanced for a sequel to *Elizabeth*, as well as the possibility of more comedy and perhaps a British Hitchcock-style thriller in the offing, will Working Title be sticking with the studios? "Of course," insists Bevan, "I feel comfortable at Shepperton. We've had a good run at the studios. I like its earthiness, which says to me that we're not just here to be in the 'movie' business. We're here to do a job of work."

Working Title's Shepperton Filmography

Four Weddings and a Funeral 1993

The Borrowers 1996

Elizabeth 1997

Notting Hill 1998

Billy Elliot 1999

Bridget Jones's Diary 2000

About A Boy 2001

Johnny English 2002

Love Actually 2002

Wimbledon 2003

Thunderbirds 2003

Bridget Jones: The Edge of Reason 2003

Gemma Jackson

Production Designer

Opposite
The set of the 1996 children's fantasy adventure, *The Borrowers*

Left
Gemma Jackson

Page 312
A set from *Finding Neverland*

Page 313
The Office from *Bridget Jones's Diary*

My initial training was as a painter at Saint Martin's School of Art. However, early on it became clear to me that I responded as much to the word as to the image. So I did a postgraduate in theatre design and was employed for some years before moving over to design films. Once I'd tasted cinema there was no going back! For someone who relishes good story-telling cinema has the potential to be the perfect medium. During the 70s there was The Academy cinema on Oxford Street and there I absorbed magnificent films such as Bertolucci's *1900* (1976), Fellini's *La Dolce Vita* (1960) or the magnificent *Fanny and Alexander* (1982). Seeing Neil Jordan's *Company of Wolves* (1984) later, I realized that the forest was created on a stage, and I knew I wanted to be involved with telling such stories.

So it was with enormous pleasure that I accepted a movie that was to be designed and shot at Shepperton Studios. For me the satisfaction of being in the Studios is the possibility of what I can create on one or more of those stages. Found locations around London are all very well once the nervous home owners have been convinced that if we paint their dining room walls shocking pink we can definitely return them to oyster white with a couple of coats of best Dulux. On stage at Shepperton studios I can create anything and paint it any colour knowing that the ultimate destination for these walls is a big skip. There is also an extensive backlot which means that exterior sets can be built exactly as wanted but outside with the sky as a natural backdrop.

As the production designer I head up a team which, given the appropriate budget, can number quite a few people. There is the immediate art department, particularly the supervising art director who runs the art department and liaises between me and everyone else. I will have art directors with responsibility for particular sets. I will have draughtsmen and women drawing in meticulous detail all aspects of my designs and

there will be someone responsible for all the graphics. There will be workshops headed up by a construction manager and as many carpenters, painters and plasterers as are necessary to create the magic. Once the sets are up and looking amazing they need to be dressed. Enter the set decorator and her or his team. I also work very closely with this department as life is breathed into the architecture, the space takes on its own character and we can hand over to the director and the shooting crew.

I have recently designed *Bridget Jones: The Edge of Reason* and before that *Bridget Jones' Diary* at Shepperton Studios. What most audiences were unaware of was that we built Bridget's flat (apparently above the pub) on stage at Shepperton and her office too. (Her parents' house in the Cotswolds was also a set as soon as Bridget set foot in the hallway!) A lot of time was spent in her flat in both films so a very particular character was given to the architecture, colour and texture. I found some wonderful old end-of-line wallpapers. The views out of the windows had to be immaculately reproduced to describe her neighborhood and also to lull the audience into not even questioning any aspect of the reality of Bridget's home. In the first film the huge backings were painted and we had one for day and one for night. This slowed the filming down a little so for the second film we had a giant translit which, with specific lighting, could switch from day to night at random. To accommodate the camera, the crew, the soundman's boom, walls have to move, night becomes day, day becomes night, rain falls, it snows, trains rumble by. All these elements are tightly controlled and this is only possible on stage.

A few years ago I designed another Working Title film, *The Borrowers*. This was probably a designer's dream (and potentially worst nightmare)! The story was of a family barely six inches tall who lived beneath the floorboards of the Lender's family home. We had many of Shepperton's finest stages bursting with some extraordinary sets. And we also used the backlot for some huge exterior sets as well. My team grew. We needed specialist graphic painters, an army of skilled model makers and sculptors and a team of scenic artists, all of whom were kept busy for months.

We created two worlds, a normal sized one and an oversized one where the Borrowers lived. We created oversized cotton reels to sit on. Scaled up they were fifteen inches high. A snakes and ladders board made a very fine carpet. One Borrower gets trapped in the fridge alongside a bag of peas and a large pot of chocolate ice cream. Another falls into a milk bottle and nearly comes to a very tragic end. The milk bottle had to be over twelve-feet high, the oversized ice cream carton needed to have allocations of edible ice-cream. We had a ten-foot Action Man and a six-foot lightbulb. I particularly loved the set of a toyshelf in the human boy's bedroom, which had elephant mouldings round the ceiling, which Arrietty, the little Borrower girl, could open to access the so-called real world.

The following list shows the films I have designed at Shepperton Studios, and I would be delighted if the phone rang this minute inviting me back there to create a new world!

My films at Shepperton Studios:

Blame it on the Bellboy
The Borrowers
Bridget Jones's Diary
Killing Me Softly
Bridget Jones: The Edge of Reason
Finding Neverland

Small Budget
Big Box Office

"Small Budget films are fantastic. They give film-makers freedom to express themselves without having people breathing down their necks worrying about how they're going to get their money back."

Gurinder Chadha, Director – *Bend It Like Beckham*

When the British film industry first began production before the outbreak of World War I, the cost of the average picture was £4,000. In the early 1920s, that figure rose to £6,000. By the time Shepperton's doors opened a disparity was appearing between the types of features being made and the cost of making them. Supporting features at the beginning of the 1930s would cost anything up to £10,000. Yet future Ealing Studios head Michael Balcon was quoted as saying that anything up to £35,000 was reasonable for a quality picture. The maths weren't helped by the vast number of quota quickies whose budgets were determined, not by quality, but by length of screened film, estimated at £1 per foot – more akin perhaps to buying carpet than making memorable movies. The average length of a 1930s quota quickie was 6,000ft, and so the average budget was £6,000 for a film that had just a 12 day shooting schedule. Scientific if not artistic.

In America, budgets for films actually decreased when productions moved over to sound. The average silent film in the 1920s cost $300,000 dollars to make. That figure almost halved at the beginning of the 1930s to $153,000. Some claim that this fall was due to the number of cheap 'B' pictures that suddenly flooded the picture houses. Others blame the drop on the economies, forced on studios by the great Depression. It's also fair to surmise that the early talkie films tended to have smaller casts and far less elaborate sets than their silent predecessors – audiences bowled over by being able to hear their heroes speak, thought more about what was being said than how the movie looked.

Left

Gurinder Chadha on the set of
Bend It Like Beckham (2001)

By the end of the 1950s, the average budget for a British film had risen to around £125,000 (or £2 million in today's money) – not a great deal by American standards, where average movie costs could be up to five times higher. Of course, averages were just that and in both countries some films would inevitably cost more than others. Peter Rogers would produce a black and white Carry On film for around £80,000 in 1959, while his wife Betty Box would produce a Doctor film in colour for £125,000 in the same year. Meanwhile, Richard Attenborough would have trouble raising the £124,000 needed to make *The Angry Silence* at Shepperton Studios, having to trim his budget back so far that the only lead actor he could afford was himself. *The Angry Silence* – a classic of its generation – was made for just £100,000. At the same time, average American film budgets had risen to around £1 million each. Yet the period had also seen a vogue for expensive historical epics, the demise of the "B" movie, and a substantial increase in the use of colour. This meant that a film such as *Ben Hur* was produced at above the average cost, its budget coming in at $15 million (around $100 million today). *Ben Hur* – the Titanic of its time – went on to win eleven Oscars® and, more importantly for its producers, took more than $70 million dollars at the US box office.

Much has changed in the world of film since then. The rare has become the commonplace and the average cost of production of a Hollywood feature film is now around $60 million, with many of the big block-busters costing well in excess of $100 million. Britain sees its fair share of blockbuster films made in its studios. The 2002 Bond outing, *Die Another Day*, was made at Pinewood, and at a cost of $142 million was the sixth most expensive film ever made. It is interesting to note that of the top ten highest-grossing film franchises of all time, five are series made in Britain: James Bond, Star Wars, Harry Potter, Batman and Indiana Jones. There have also been – and continue to be – many occasions over the past 30 years when a British film made on little more than a shoestring has, pro rata, outperformed its blockbuster counterparts both here and across the water. Rarely have these films been made with even the intention of

attempting to become a blockbuster. The majority of them tell a story and do so in a way that captures the audience's attention through good writing, great acting and simple but usually eye-catching cinematography. The motive behind the production of these films is very often about vision rather than cash, which tends to stifle ideas with the need to make huge profits. Director and co-writer of the smash hit British film, *Bend It Like Beckham* (2001), Gurinder Chadha explains: "Small budget films are fantastic. They give film-makers freedom to express themselves without having people breathing down their necks worrying about how they're going to get their money back. It also gives you the freedom not to have to commit yourself to stars who may not be right for the roles but are there for the sales figures. The films are also a great way of learning. You need the space as a film-maker to explore and express yourself. You don't always get it right. Low budget films allow you that space."

Bend It Like Beckham was filmed at Shepperton and on location around west London in the summer of 2001. The film tells the story of an 18-year-old football-crazy Indian girl who can play the game better than any boy she knows. Yet while Jess is determined to play for a top women's football team, her traditional parents have very different ideas for her future. The film was Gurinder Chadha's third production, yet getting it off the ground did not prove easy. "I was determined to write the most commercial movie I possibly could with an Indian girl in the lead. Everyone said that was impossible and that I had to have a name in my movie, a star, and preferably an American star to make a successful commercial film. But the experiences of films like *Billy Elliot*, *The Full Monty* (1997) and *East is East* (1999) proved that you could have great British successes without American stars. We came up with the script for *Bend It Like Beckham*. It was still

Left

Jess Bhamra (Parminder Nagra) dreams of football stardom in the 2001 hit comedy film, *Bend It Like Beckham*

tough to get the finance for the film – it took us two years – even though I was telling everyone it was going to be really successful. I knew that the British public would warm to it. But everyone was saying, 'No no, we've had *East is East*, we don't want to do another one.' Luckily, I was able to make it as a low budget film."

The *Bend It Like Beckham* production was helped, in no small part, by the encouragement of the Shepperton Studios management. Gurinder Chadha is very appreciative of how the studios try to help film-makers: "Shepperton were great to us. We got the best possible rate we could from them. We wanted to set up our offices there and the management were very co-operative. We were lucky in that it was fairly quiet at the time. *Gosford Park* (2001) was at the Studios but not any big American pictures, which is why we were able to be there and build what we needed for as long as we did. There was a great amount of goodwill towards me as a British film-maker. At the time we didn't know Bend It was going to be the big success that it became, so I guess to everyone around us we were probably just a small little film with Indians in it." It certainly may have looked that way during production at Shepperton. Chadha had already taken the film's production designers and art department to visit the homes of her relatives to give them ideas of how to recreate Jess's house as an interior at the studios. But as well as using their homes, Chadha also employed the services of her relatives as extras on the film. As she recalls: "There were quite a few scenes that needed Indian relatives to be present in the house. The set was on Stage "I" at Shepperton. It was very funny seeing all these doddery old Indian ladies walking round the studios over to the cafeteria, or just sitting outside on chairs, when you'd normally see English blokes with their bellies out having a mug of tea or taking a rest in between building. The whole experi-ence was great for me. I was on a proper studio lot. Shepperton has such great history in movies and at lunch I would enjoy walking around looking at stages, seeing what else was going on. Robert Altman was shooting *Gosford Park* at the same time, so we had a look round his set. It was spectacular. They had a lot more money than we did."

Bend It Like Beckham, which starred Parminder Nagra, Keira Knightley, Jonathan Rhys Meyers, and acting stalwarts Anupam Kher and Juliet Stevenson, took just five weeks to shoot. The schedule was tight and not without its problems. "The film cost £3 million. I would have been happier with a budget of £5 million. We shot it in 30 days. I was given a few extra days because the lead, Parminder Nagra, who was playing Jess, got a cold sore on her lip and couldn't work. The only scene I could do with her was the one where she was in the car changing out of a sari into football shorts and I shot it with her face the other way round, so you could just see her bum. I remember there was one shot we had filmed outside what was Jess's house, on location in Heston, near Heathrow. It was a close up of the Dad when he warns her not to go and talk to Joe. There were trees and the sky and so on, behind him. When the lab report came back, we saw that the shot was soft. I was very worried. I knew we couldn't go back out on location for that one shot. We ended up shooting it on the sound stage at Shepperton in one little corner. I was shocked how well it worked. You just can't tell. That's the wonder of stages for me. They look like big empty rooms but they become transformed into anything and everything – day becomes night, night becomes day. It really is magic."

Bend It Like Beckham certainly weaved its magic on audiences worldwide, taking over £13 million at the British box office and a further $33 million in America. The film also played on hundreds of screens across Italy, Spain, France and Germany. Bend It also received a warm reception in India, helped no doubt by the casting of Anupam Kher, one of the superstars of Hindi cinema, as Jess's father, Mr Bhamra.

One of the biggest costs in making a film has traditionally been the amounts spent on cast – big names taking up a sizable swathe of the production budget. On many occasions over the years, stars have taken a smaller salary in exchange for a percentage of the film's box office gross. Gregory Peck did that in order to help keep the costs down on the production of *The Omen*, which was made at Shepperton Studios in 1975. Fast approaching 60 years of age and with cinema roles drying up – only two films in the previous five years – Peck gambled on a pay cut to play the part of American ambassador to London, Richard Thorn, whose son turns out to be the devil-child. *The Omen* took less than 12 weeks to film and was made for around $2.8 million, at a time when the average American film cost at least $4 million, with big productions and big name stars costing many times more that. Yet the gamble paid off, as the variation on *The Exorcist* (1973) became the fourth most commercially successful film of 1973, taking $60 million at the US box office alone. Ironically, several star names turned the lead role down, including Charlton Heston, Roy Scheider and William Holden (who then proceeded to take the lead role in *Damien: Omen II* (1978)). Peck's fee of $250,000 was boosted by a guaranteed ten per cent of the box office gross, making *The Omen*, the highest-paid performance of his career.

Doing a deal with lead actors was not the only way to keep film production costs down. Famed satirist, comedy writer and performer, Mel Brooks, was very keen for his production company to make the biographical drama, *The Elephant Man* (1980) – the true story of the horrifically disfigured John Merrick, who battles against the prejudices of Victorian society. The average cost of American productions had begun to spiral, almost doubling to around $8 million within a few years. Brooks decided to bring *The Elephant Man* to Shepperton and to further reduce the cost of production by shooting the film in black and white. Brooks hired David Lynch to direct and renowned cinematographer Freddie Francis to shoot the film. John Hurt played the role of John Merrick – the British actor unrecognisable after 12 hours of make up. The real John Merrick (born Joseph Carey Merrick) died in 1890, aged just 27. Following Merrick's death, parts of his body were preserved for medical science. Internal organs were kept in jars and plaster casts were made of his head, an arm and a foot. The organs were destroyed during German air raids in World War II,

Above

Gregory Peck and Patrick Troughton in Richard Donner's *The Omen* (1975)

The sets by Ken Adams were beautiful. He deserved the Oscar® that he won. Madness wasn't a big budget film. It was very tight for what we were trying to achieve.

but the casts survived and the make up for John Hurt was designed by careful study of the original casts. Hurt, who won a Bafta for the film, was joined in the cast by Anthony Hopkins and John Gielgud, as well as Mel Brooks', wife, actress Anne Bancroft. In order that audiences didn't get the wrong idea about the film – perhaps mistaking it for a comedy or spoof – Brooks had his own name left off the credits. *The Elephant Man* surprised many when it took some $26 million at the US box office.

In 1994, two very different types of small-budget films were made at Shepperton; one which was to win huge critical acclaim, the other, huge financial reward. *The Madness of King George* (1994) was the film version of the stage play by acclaimed writer Alan Bennett. It tells the story of the increasingly parlous mental state of George III, who is eventually diagnosed as mad and almost loses his royal power as a result. The cast, which included Helen Mirren, Ian Holm and Rupert Everett, was headed by Nigel Hawthorne. He had played the part on stage for some time and so had honed the role down to such a level that his performance as George III was a delight from start to finish. Hawthorne was nominated for the Oscar® as best actor, and won a British Academy award for the role. As Derek Malcolm wrote in *The Guardian*: "Essentially it is Hawthorne's triumph and no one else's, since he provides the holding centre without which the rest might have seemed an ephemeral romp, uncertain as to whether to comment on its own times or ours and drifting towards parody in both instances." The title of Bennett's play was actually *The Madness of George III*, but was changed for the cinema version after it was felt that some audiences may have thought it was the third film in a series, of which they had not seen the first two instalments.

The film's producer David Parfitt recalls working on *The Madness of King George* at Shepperton. "We filmed

the House of Lords' interior and the king's apartments at Shepperton on the two stages next to "H". At the time they weren't sound-proofed which caused us a few problems. There were no other stages available. We knew they weren't sound stages and we had to accept that. But inevitably when you're shooting an intimate scene in the king's bedroom and a truck goes trundling past outside, there's a few wobblies thrown. But we knew what we were letting ourselves into. The sets by Ken Adams were beautiful. He deserved the Oscar® that he won. Madness wasn't a big budget film. It was very tight for what we were trying to achieve. But it had the most amazing script and stunning performances and I think I knew when we were shooting that it was good. Though that's not the same as being successful." The film, though, was successful, taking a combined box office in America and Britain of more than $22 million.

Shepperton's second small budget offering of 1994 was *Four Weddings and A Funeral*. The film was intended to be a modest, very British, almost Ealing-esque type of episodic comedy, as a confirmed bachelor chases the woman of his dreams from one wedding to another. The film was made by Working Title and, though the company had been producing pictures for ten years, it was the first proper chance that they had had to use a studio to shoot many of the interior scenes. As Working Title co-founder and producer Tim Bevan recalls: "We couldn't really afford to go into studios before then. We had always made location-based films because that's all we could afford." Not that Working Title could afford a great deal more on Four Weddings. The budget for the film came in at around £5 million. Costs were pared to the minimum. The Scottish wedding scenes weren't filmed in Scotland at all, the location being too far away and consequently, too expensive for the cast and crew to decamp there. Extras were asked to bring their own suits for the shooting of wedding scenes. Actors Hugh Grant, Andie McDowell, Kristin Scott Thomas joined the rest of the cast and crew in giving their all for not a great deal of financial reward. And then *Four Weddings and A Funeral* became something that no one had expected. A huge hit.

"I do like the feeling when you come to Shepperton that it's a working place. And of course the quality of crews in this country is still the best anywhere." That certainly proved to be the case as 115 construction crew took just eight weeks to put up the 17 different buildings, including The Rose and Curtain theatres, used as the sets for the film

Indeed, it became the highest-grossing British film in cinema history, taking more than £130 million at the box-office worldwide. The film served to make even bigger stars of its cast and turned Working Title into a highly respected name in film production across the world. Even the recitation of a love poem

by W H Auden during the film ensured that a slim volume of his work, published shortly after the film was released, also became a best-seller. Ten years on and Tim Bevan still ponders long and hard when it comes to budgeting a production: "It used to be that we wouldn't spend a penny more than say $10 million. Now we look at how a film has connected with an audience. So we have to pay more for actors and put more into the production to make it feel bigger for the audience who have come to expect it. Instead of 20 extras you now have 50 extras on the street, so the frame feels bigger. We've done that well recently – making a British film feel bigger. It's a balancing act. Even on a bigger budget film I like there to be hunger everywhere because I think it gives the film an edge. Everyone works to get the most out of what we've got."

Founded in 1979 by brothers Harvey and Bob Weinstein and named after their parents Miriam and Max, Miramax is a production and distribution company that has been part of the Walt Disney company since 1993. Its films are both critically and commercially successful, attracting independent film-makers in their droves to its doors. In just over a decade, Miramax has garnered almost 200 Oscar® nominations for its films. To date, Miramax's highest grossing film is *Shakespeare In Love*, which was made at Shepperton in the spring and summer of 1998. An intelligent, passionate and very funny romantic comedy about the life and loves of a young Will Shakespeare, this huge box-office hit was almost never made at all, as producer David Parfitt explains: "Each time we went out to try and sell a film we were told there was no market for it. I would say, well what about *Henry V* or Much Ado, or *The Madness of King George*? Each time we're told, well that's the exception. The script for *Shakespeare in Love* had been floating around for some time. It had first arrived at my desk during the shooting of *The Madness of King George*. It was due to be made at Pinewood but the project collapsed. We were approached and said we couldn't do it for the price that was on offer. We could never understand why there wasn't enough money to make it – of course, the costs of its first incarnation had

Left

Queen Elizabeth (Judi Dench) on the throne, in a scene from the multi-award winning *Shakespeare in Love* (1998)

Opposite

A scene shot on the Shepperton sets for *Shakespeare in Love*, in 1998

been so hefty that people were trying to make it more cheaply to make sense of the overall numbers. It came across my desk three times. The third time was by Miramax who were the first to ask us – rather than tell us – how much we could make it for."

Parfitt and his team put their heads together and concluded that the film could be reasonably made on a budget of around £13 million. After having worked many times on several productions at Shepperton over the previous ten years, Parfitt decided to bring *Shakespeare In Love* to Shepperton. "We made it at Shepperton because we had good relationships at the Studios. Shepperton is a very workmanlike studio. No pretension. It's a very different feeling to the Hollywood stages which are painted brilliant white,

with not a piece of litter around, not a fag end, and are absolutely perfect. I do like the feeling when you come to Shepperton that it's a working place. And of course the quality of crews in this country is still the best anywhere." That certainly proved to be the case, as 115 construction crew took just eight weeks to put up the 17 different buildings, including The Rose and Curtain theatres, used as the sets for the film.

Shakespeare In Love was written by Tom Stoppard and Marc Norman, directed by John Madden and starred Gwyneth Paltrow, Joseph Fiennes and Geoffrey Rush, with a regal performance by Judi Dench, whose eight minutes on-screen was memorable enough for the much-loved actress to win the Oscar® for best supporting actress. The film won a total of seven Oscars®,

including best picture and best actress for Gwyneth Paltrow, who had not been the original choice for the lead role of Viola (Julia Roberts was cast when the film was originally mooted for production). The film also won four British Academy awards. *Shakespeare In Love* was the ninth most popular film of 1998 and has taken almost $300 million at the box office worldwide to date. David Parfitt was always confident the film would be well received. "We thought *Shakespeare In Love* was good. We all felt there was a danger that people would look on it as an in joke – with all those nods to the theatre. We were worried audiences might react against that. But they didn't. As soon as we got it into preview, we knew the film was going to be okay. And nobody promotes a film like Harvey Weinstein at Miramax. He makes sure people see the film. He'll carry a tape up Everest if there's a member of the American Academy up there who hasn't seen it."

Three of Miramax's top ten films have been based at Shepperton. As well as *Shakespeare In Love*, they also acted as distributor for Working Title's hugely successful *Bridget Jones's Diary*, made at the studios in 2000, and the smaller-budget romantic comedy *Chocolat* – which was filmed in France and at Shepperton during the same year. Starring Juliette Binoche, Lena Olin, Johnny Depp, Judi Dench and Alfred Molina, *Chocolat* is a whimsical tale of the impact that a striking young mother has on a tranquil and staid French town when

she opens up an unusual chocolate shop during Lent. Directed by Lasse Hallstrom, most of the film was shot at Flavigny-sur-Ozerain (ironically, a French town without a chocolate shop) with cast and crew returning to Shepperton, where the film's production designer worked with the art department to construct scale models of the village and reproductions of the buildings, as well as all the interior sets. *Chocolat* was nominated for five Oscars® and took around $100 million at the worldwide box office.

Tag-lined "They dropped everything for a good cause", the surprise hit of 2003, was director Nigel Cole's comedy drama, *Calendar Girls* (2003). A marvellous cast of British acting stalwarts, including Helen Mirren, Julie Walters, Annette Crosbie, Celia Imrie and Penelope Wilton, star as members of a Women's Institute whose foray into the world of glamour photography to produce a 'girly' calendar for charity, becomes an unexpected worldwide sensation, with the Yorkshire ladies' poses outselling those of Britney Spears and Cindy Crawford. Exteriors for the film were shot predominantly in Yorkshire, and interiors shot at Shepperton. This charming film had all the same ingredients which saw *The Full Monty* score so highly with audiences in 1997. *Calendar Girls* took $31 million at the American box office and more than £20 million in Britain.

Of course not all small-budget films do big numbers, even when perhaps some would insist that they deserve to. Stephen Frear's *Dirty Pretty Things*, telling the story of illegal immigrants living on the edge in London, was made at Shepperton in 2002. The film is engrossing, combining all the elements of a dark thriller with an insight into the harsh realty that is life for some unfortunates in the capital in the twenty-first century. *Variety* described the film as. "An intelligent and extremely well-made romantic drama," while *The Independent* declared: "A gently entertaining crowd-pleaser." Yet the film was not a huge success in monetary terms, although making its money back and a little more on top. Certainly nothing like the scale of financial success that other British small-budget films have had in recent years.

But more often than not small-budget film-makers do not intend to make huge sums, they are there for the story not for the money.

Director Gurinder Chadha has recently made a £12 million feature – a musical version of Jane Austen's *Pride and Prejudice*, cleverly entitled *Bride and Prejudice*. But she does not lose sight of the importance of small-budget films for both the British film industry and audiences alike. "My first film had a budget of £1.1 million, my second was about £2 million and Bend It was around £3 million. With *Bride and Prejudice* it shot up to £12 million. It's more difficult with a higher budget because there are a lot more people to please and a lot more people being nervous about everything around you. You have to be very clear at all times about what you're doing and making sure you convey with clarity to everybody so that everyone knows what's going on. I have a hand in the schedules and the budgets but I also have to work to what I'm given. For *Bend It Like Beckham* I could certainly have done with a bit extra for the football scenes and perhaps I could have taken longer in the sound mix, but I didn't have the time. You have to cut your cloth don't you? I still want to make low budget films. Yes, I'd like to make a couple of big ones. But I've still got three or four fantastic ideas on the same level as *Bend It Like Beckham*, maybe a little more money, say between £5 and £8 million. I think it's important as a film-maker that you make films that are close to your heart and that allow you to expand your horizons and explore your instincts and vision, in a way without all the glare and publicity of the higher profile big budget films."

Opposite

Star-struck lovers Viola De Lesseps (Gwyneth Paltrow) and Will Shakespeare (Joseph Fiennes), in John Madden's period romantic drama, *Shakespeare in Love* (1998)

Below

Dirty Pretty Things (2001) director, Stephen Frears

Bottom

Audery Tautou as Turkish Asylum seeker Senay, in *Dirty Pretty Things* (2001)

Oscar® and Bafta winning *Gosford Park* (2001) used studio sets at Shepperton to create this multi layered drama set in 1932, showing the lives of the upstairs guests and downstairs servants. Julian Fellowes won the Oscar® for Best Screenplay.

Above right
Below stairs with the servants, in *Gosford Park* (2001)

Opposite
Upstairs with the guests, in *Gosford Park* (2001)

Right
Clive Owen is Robert Parks in *Gosford Park* (2001) and Robert Altman

Far right
Gosford Park director Robert Altman

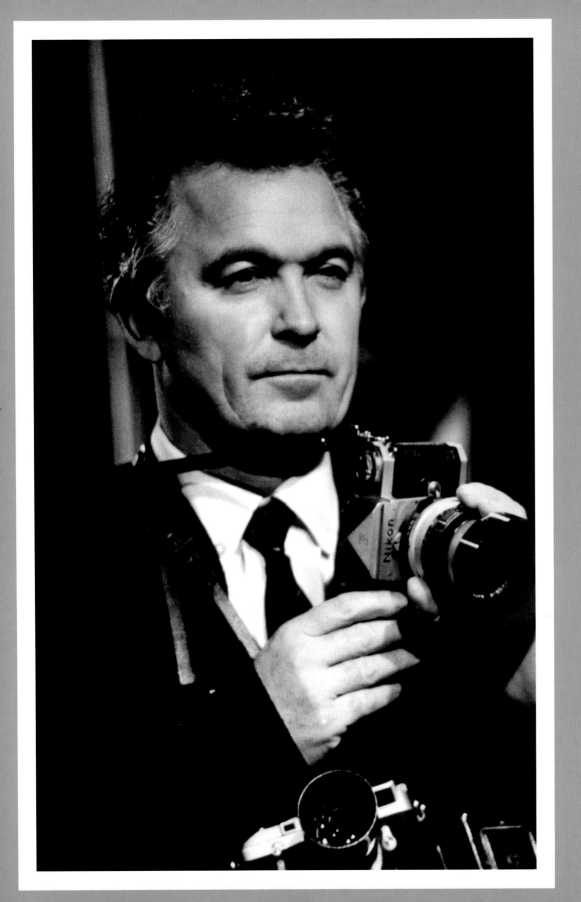

Left
Bob Penn

Bob Penn
Stills Photographer
1926 – 2002

By common consent Bob Penn, was for many years the British Film industry's top stills photographer. He was also recognised on the international stage and his talents were in demand from directors such as Kubrick, Houston, Wilder, Milius, Scott, Cameron and Cukor.

Visconti, who refused to allow any photographer on his sets made an exception for Penn and on the last night of his work on *The Leopard*, described him as a fine photographer and a true professional. In 1963, whilst working on the set of *Dr Strangelove*, Penn was presented with a picture of him at work with Stanley Kubrick.

The caption read,

To Bob...

The Worlds Greatest Photographer

England 1963.

It was signed by Weegee who like Stanley Kubrick was a highly respected photographer from New York and whose work enjoys cult status to this day.

Bob Penn's impressive list of films included many classics that were filmed at Shepperton studios and these included:

Dr Strangelove (1963)
Becket (1963)
The Spy Who Came in from the Cold (1965)
Oliver! (1967)
The Omen (1975)
Alien (1978)
Flash Gordon (1979)
Ragtime (1980)

Many of his haunting images are included in this book. Bob Penn always thought of himself as an ordinary bloke – but then extraordinary people often do.

Above
The set of *Dr Strangelove* photographed
by Bob Penn

Above
Bob Penn with James Cagney on
the set of *Ragtime* (1980) at
Shepperton Studios

Awards

1948

British Film Academy Awards

Best British Film: *The Fallen Idol*

1949

British Film Academy Awards

Best British Film: *The Third Man*

1950

Academy Awards

Cinematography (Black & White): *The Third Man*

1951

Academy Awards

Best Actor: Humphrey Bogart (*The African Queen*)

1952

British Film Academy Awards

Best Film: *The Sound Barrier*
Best British Film: *The Sound Barrier*
Best British Actor: Ralph Richardson (*The Sound Barrier*)
United Nations Award: *Cry the Beloved Country*

Academy Awards

Sound: *The Sound Barrier*

1954

British Film Academy Awards

Best British Film: *Hobson's Choice*

1955

British Film Academy Awards

Best Film: *Richard III*
Best British Film: *Richard III*
Best British Actor: Laurence Olivier (*Richard III*)

1958

British Film Academy Awards

Best Film: *Room at the Top*
Best British Film: *Room at the Top*
Best Foreign Actress: Simone Signoret (*Room at the Top*)
Best Screenplay: Paul Dehn (*Orders to Kill*)
Most Promising Newcomer: Paul Massie (*Orders to Kill*)

1959

British Film Academy Awards

Best British Actor: Peter Sellers (*I'm All Right Jack*)
Best British Screenplay: Frank Harvey, Alan Hackney, John
Boulting (*I'm All Right Jack*)

Academy Awards

Best Actress: Simone Signoret (*Room at the Top*)
Writing (Screenplay Based on Material from Another Medium):
Neil Paterson (*Room at the Top*)

1960

British Film Academy Awards

Best British Screenplay: Bryan Forbes (*The Angry Silence*)

1961

British Film Academy Awards

Best British Screenplay: Wolf Mankowitz, Val Guest (*The Day
the Earth Caught Fire*)

Academy Awards

Effects – Visual and Sound: Bill Warrington and Vivian
Greenham (*The Guns of Navarone*)

1962

British Film Academy Awards

Best British Actress: Leslie Caron (*The L-Shaped Room*)

1963

British Film Academy Awards

Best British Film: *The Servant*
Best British Actor: Dirk Bogarde (*The Servant*)
Most Promising Newcomer to Leading Film Roles: James Fox
(*The Servant*)
Best British Cinematography (Black and White): Douglas
Slocombe (*The Servant*)

1964

British Film Academy Awards

Best Film: *Dr Strangelove, or How I Learned to Stop Worrying
and Love the Bomb*
Best British Film: *Dr Strangelove, or How I Learned to Stop
Worrying and Love the Bomb*
United Nations Award: *Dr Strangelove, or How I Learned to
Stop Worrying and Love the Bomb*
British Screenplay: Harold Pinter (*The Pumpkin Eater*)
Best Foreign Actress: Anne Bancroft (*The Pumpkin Eater*)
Best British Cinematography (Colour): Geoffrey Unsworth
(*Becket*)
Best British Cinematography (Black and White): Oswald Morris
(*The Pumpkin Eater*)
Best British Art Direction (Colour): John Bryan (*Becket*)
Best British Art Direction (Black and White): Ken Adam (*Dr
Strangelove*)
Best British Costume Design (Colour): Margaret Furse (*Becket*)
Best British Costume Design (Black and White): Motley (*The
Pumpkin Eater*)

Academy Awards

Writing (Screenplay Based on Material from Another Medium):
Edward Anhalt (*Becket*)

1965

British Film Academy Awards

Best British Actor: Dirk Bogarde (*Darling*)
Best British Actress: Julie Christie (*Darling*)
Best British Screenplay: Frederic Raphael (*Darling*)
Best British Art Direction (Black and White): Ray Simm
(*Darling*)

Academy Awards

Best Actress: Julie Christie (*Darling*)
Writing (Screenplay Written Directly for the Screen): Frederic Raphael (*Darling*)
Costume Design (Black and White): Julie Harris (*Darling*)

1966
British Film Academy Awards

Best British Film: *The Spy Who Came In from the Cold*
Best British Actor: Richard Burton (*The Spy Who Came In from the Cold*)
Best British Cinematography (Black and White): Oswald Morris (*The Spy Who Came In from the Cold*)
Best British Art Direction: Tambi Larsen (*The Spy Who Came In from the Cold*)

Academy Awards

Best Picture: *A Man for All Seasons*
Directing: Fred Zinnemann (*A Man for All Seasons*)
Actor: Paul Scofield (*A Man for All Seasons*)
Writing (Screenplay Based on Material from Another Medium): Robert Bolt (*A Man for All Seasons*)
Cinematography (Colour): Ted Moore (*A Man for All Seasons*)
Costume Design (Colour): Joan Bridge/Elizabeth Haffenden (*A Man for All Seasons*)

1967
British Films Academy Awards

Best Film: *A Man for All Seasons*
Best British Film: *A Man for All Seasons*
Best British Actor: Paul Scofield (*A Man for All Seasons*)
Best British Screenplay: Robert Bolt (*A Man for All Seasons*)
Best British Cinematography (Colour): Ted Moore (*A Man for All Seasons*)
Best British Art Direction (Colour): John Box (*A Man for All Seasons*)
Best British Costume Design (Colour): Elizabeth Haffenden, Joan Bridge (*A Man for All Seasons*)

1968
British Academy of Film and Television Arts Awards

Best Supporting Actress: Billie Whitelaw (*Twisted Nerve* and also for her performance in *Charlie Bubbles*)

Academy Awards

Best Picture: *Oliver!*
Directing: Carol Reed (*Oliver!*)
Art Direction: John Box, Terry Marsh, Vernon Dixon, Ken Muggleston (*Oliver!*)
Sound: Shepperton Studios Sound Department (*Oliver!*)
Score: Johnny Green (*Oliver!*)

1969
Academy Awards

Costume Design: Margaret Furse (*Anne of the Thousand Days*)

1970
Academy Awards

Costume Design: Vittorio Novaresse (*Cromwell*)

1972
British Academy of Film and Television Arts Awards

Cinematography: Geoffrey Unsworth (*Alice's Adventures in Wonderland* and also for his work on *Cabaret*)
Costume Design: Anthony Mendelson (*Young Winston/Alice's Adventures in Wonderland* and also for his work on *Macbeth*)

1973
British Academy of Film and Television Arts Awards

Best Film Editing: Ralph Kemplen (*The Day of the Jackal*)

1976
Academy Awards

Score: Jerry Goldsmith (*The Omen*)

1979
British Academy of Film and Television Arts Awards

Production Design: Michael Seymour (*Alien*)
Soundtrack: Derrick Leather/Jim Shield/Bill Rowe (*Alien*)

Academy Awards

Visual Effects: Nick Allder, Denys Ayling, H. R. Giger, Brian Johnson, Carlo Rambaldi (*Alien*)

1980
British Academy of Film and Television Arts Awards

Best Film: *The Elephant Man*
Best Actor: John Hurt (*The Elephant Man*)
Production Design: Stuart Craig (*The Elephant Man*)

1982
British Academy of Film and Television Arts Awards

Best Film: *Gandhi*
Best Director: Richard Attenborough (*Gandhi*)
Best Actor: Ben Kingsley (*Gandhi*)
Best Supporting Actress: Rohini Hattangady (*Gandhi*)
Outstanding Newcomer to Leading Film Roles: Ben Kingsley (*Gandhi*)

Academy Awards

Best Picture: *Gandhi*
Directing: *Gandhi*
Actor in a Leading Role: Ben Kingsley – *Gandhi*
Writing (Screenplay Written Directly for the Screen): John Briley (*Gandhi*)
Cinematography: Ronny Taylor, Billy Williams (*Gandhi*)
Film Editing: John Bloom (*Gandhi*)
Art Direction: Stuart Craig, Bob Laing, Michael Seirton (*Gandhi*)
Costume Design: Bhanu Athaiya, John Mollo (*Gandhi*)

1984

Academy Awards

Actress in a Supporting Role: Peggy Ashcroft (*A Passage to India*)
Score: Maurice Jarre (*A Passage to India*)

1985

British Academy of Film and Television Arts Awards

Best Actress: Peggy Ashcroft (*A Passage to India*)

Academy Awards

Best Picture: *Out of Africa*
Directing: Sydney Pollack (*Out of Africa*)
Writing (Screenplay Based on Material from Another Medium): Kurt Luedtke (*Out of Africa*)
Cinematography: David Watkin (*Out of Africa*)
Art Direction: Stephen Grimes, Josie MacAvin (*Out of Africa*)
Sound: Gary Alexander, Peter Handford, Chris Jenkins, Larry Stensvold (*Out of Africa*)
Score: John Barry (*Out of Africa*)

1986

British Academy of Film and Television Arts Awards

Adapted Screenplay: Kurt Luedtke (*Out of Africa*)
Cinematography: David Watkin (*Out of Africa*)
Sound: Tom McCarthy Jnr/Peter Handford/Chris Jenkins (*Out of Africa*)

1987

British Academy of Film and Television Arts Awards

Best Actress in a Leading Role: Anne Bancroft (*84 Charing Cross Road*)
Sound: Jonathan Bates/Simon Kaye/Gerry Humphreys (*Cry Freedom*)

1988

British Academy of Film and Television Arts Awards

Best Actress in a Leading Role: Maggie Smith (*The Lonely Passion of Judith Hearne*)

1989

British Academy of Film and Television Arts Awards

Best Achievement in Direction: Kenneth Branagh (*Henry V*)

Academy Awards

Costume Design: Phyllis Dalton (*Henry V*)

1991

British Academy of Film and Television Arts Awards

Best Actor in a Supporting Role: Alan Rickman (*Robin Hood: Prince of Thieves*)

1992

British Academy of Film and Television Arts Awards

The Michael Balcon Award for Outstanding British Contribution to Cinema: Kenneth Branagh
The Alexander Korda Award for the Outstanding British Film of the Year: *The Crying Game*
Best Actress in a Supporting Role: Miranda Richardson (*Damage*)

Academy Awards

Writing (Screenplay Written Directly for the Screen): Neil Jordan (*The Crying Game*)

1993

British Academy of Film and Television Arts Awards

The Alexander Korda Award for the Outstanding British Film of the Year: *Shadowlands*

1994

British Academy of Film and Television Arts Awards

Best Film: *Four Weddings and a Funeral*
The David Lean Award for the Best Achievement in Direction: Mike Newell *(Four Weddings and a Funeral)*
Best Performance by an Actor in a Leading Role: Hugh Grant (*Four Weddings and a Funeral*)
Best Performance by an Actress in a Supporting Role: Kristin Scott Thomas (*Four Weddings and a Funeral*)

Academy Awards

Art Direction: Ken Adam, Carolyn Scott (*The Madness of King George*)

1995

British Academy of Film and Television Arts Awards

Best Film: *Sense and Sensibility*
The Alexander Korda Award for the Outstanding British Film of the Year: *The Madness of King George*
Best Performance by an Actor in a Leading Role: Nigel Hawthorne (*The Madness of King George*)
Best Performance by an Actress in a Leading Role: Emma Thompson (*Sense and Sensibility*)
Best Performance by an Actress in a Supporting Role: Kate Winslet (*Sense and Sensibility*)
Make Up/Hair: Lisa Westcott (*The Madness of King George*)

Academy Awards

Writing (Screenplay Based on Material Previously Produced or Published): Emma Thompson (*Sense and Sensibility*)

1997

British Academy of Film and Television Arts Awards

Cinematography: Eduardo Serra (*The Wings of the Dove*)
Make Up/Hair: Sallie Jaye/Jan Archibald (*The Wings of the Dove*)

1998

British Academy of Film and Television Arts Awards

Best Film: *Shakespeare in Love*
The Alexander Korda Award for the Outstanding British Film of the Year: *Elizabeth*
Best Performance by an Actress in a Leading Role: Cate Blanchett (*Elizabeth*)
Best Performance by an Actor in a Supporting Role: Geoffrey Rush (*Shakespeare in Love*)
Best Performance by an Actress in a Supporting Role: Judi Dench (*Shakespeare in Love*)
The Anthony Asquith Award for Achievement in Film Music: David Hirschfielder (*Elizabeth*)
Cinematography: Remi Adefarasin (*Elizabeth*)
Editing: David Gamble (*Shakespeare in Love*)
Make Up/Hair: Jenny Shircore (*Elizabeth*)

Academy Awards

Best Picture: *Shakespeare in Love*
Actress in a Leading Role: Gwyneth Paltrow (*Shakespeare in Love*)
Actress in a Supporting Role: Judi Dench (*Shakespeare in Love*)
Writing (Screenplay Written Directly for the Screen): Marc Norman, Tom Stoppard (*Shakespeare in Love*)
Art Direction: Martin Childs, Jill Quertier (*Shakespeare in Love*)
Costume Design: Sandy Powell (*Shakespeare in Love*)
Make Up: Jenny Shircore (*Elizabeth*)
Score: Stephen Warbeck (*Shakespeare in Love*)

1999

British Academy Film Awards

Best Screenplay (Adapted): Neil Jordan (*The End of the Affair*)
Production Design: Rick Heinrichs (*Sleepy Hollow*)
Costume Design: Colleen Atwood (*Sleepy Hollow*)

Academy Awards

Art Direction: Rick Heinrichs, Peter Young (*Sleepy Hollow*)

2000

British Academy Film Awards

Best Film: *Gladiator*
The Alexander Korda Award for the Outstanding British Film of the Year: *Billy Elliot*
Best Performance by an Actor in a Leading Role: Jamie Bell (*Billy Elliot*)
Best Performance by an Actress in a Supporting Role: Julie Walters (*Billy Elliot*)
Cinematography: John Mathieson (*Gladiator*)
Production Design: Arthur Max (*Gladiator*)
Editing: Pietro Scalia (*Gladiator*)

Academy Awards

Best Picture: *Gladiator*
Actor in a Leading Role: Russell Crowe (*Gladiator*)
Costume Design: Janty Yates (*Gladiator*)
Sound: Bob Beemer, Scott Millan, Ken Weston (*Gladiator*)
Visual Effects: Tim Burke, Neil Corbould, Rob Harvey, John Nelson (*Gladiator*)

2001

British Academy Film Awards

The Alexander Korda Award for the Outstanding British Film of the Year: *Gosford Park*
Costume Design: Jenny Beavan (*Gosford Park*)

Academy Awards

Writing (Screenplay Written Directly for the Screen): Julian Fellowes (*Gosford Park*)

2002

British Academy Film Awards

Best Performance by an Actress in a Leading Role: Nicole Kidman (*The Hours*)
The Anthony Asquith Award for Achievement in Film Music: Philip Glass (*The Hours*)

Academy Awards

Actress in a Leading Role: Nicole Kidman (*The Hours*)

2003

British Academy Film Awards

Best Performance by an Actor in a Supporting Role: Bill Nighy (*Love Actually*)

2004

British Academy Film Awards

The Orange Film of the Year: *Harry Potter and The Prisoner of Azkaban*

Academy Awards

Best Score: Jan Kaczmarek (*Finding Neverland*)

Stanley Kubrick on the Shepperton
set of *Dr Strangelove* (1963)

Filmography

Using the best available sources for reference, the following film-ography attempts to list details of every film made at Shepperton from the start of production at the Studios, back in 1932. A film's title, along with director and actor's credits are included for each production. The date given for a film is the year of production at the Studios – which is not necessarily the year of release. Where a film may have had one or more alternative titles, i.e. for American or international release, the most widely recognised film name is listed.

Drawing up such a list is not without its potential pitfalls. For example, deciding just how much of a film needs to have been produced at Shepperton for it to be included within the filmography, has led to an interesting debate. The author and publishers have concluded that if Shepperton played any part in the production of a film, it should rightfully be included in the filmography.

In recent years, several major productions have come to Shepperton after a film has been made to use the Studios' excellent sound facilities for dubbing, soundtrack work and so on. Titles of such major productions are also included within the body of the filmography.

Finally, with the increasing popularity of studios use for television production, it seems only right and fitting to at least include a list of titles made for that medium. Therefore, television shows and programme titles from the year 2000, have been appended at the end of this list.

Should readers feel that there are any omissions or inaccuracies, the author and publishers would be happy to receive such details, for consideration and possible use in any future updated editions of this book.

1932

Reunion
Director: Ivar Campbell
Starring: George Bishop, Harry Blue, Noel Dainton, Bernard Dudley

Watch Beverley
Director: Arthur Maude
Starring: Dorothy Bartlam, Francis X. Bushman, Frederic de Lara, Anthony Holles

Plus five shorts:
Aerobatics, Capture, Pursuit of Priscilla, Reward, The Safe

1933

Colonel Blood
Director W. P. Lipscomb
Starring Frank Cellier, Anne Grey, Mary Lawson, Allan Jeayes

Doss House
Director John Baxter
Starring Frank Cellier, Arnold Bell, Herbert Franklyn, Mark Daly

Drake of England
Director Arthur Woods
Starring Matheson Lang, Athene Seyler, Jane Baxter, Donald Wolfit

Eyes of Fate
Director Ivar Campbell
Starring Allan Jeayes, Valerie Hobson, Terence de Marney, Faith Bennett

Golden Cage
Director Ivar Campbell
Starring Anne Grey, Anthony Kimmins, Frank Cellier, Jillian Sande

Moorland Tragedy
Director M. A. Wetherell
Starring Haddon Mason, Barbara Coombes, Moore Marriott, Griffith Humphreys

Paris Plane
Director John Paddy Carstairs
Starring Edwin Ellis, James Harcourt, Allan Jeayes, Molly Lamont

She Was Only A Village Maiden
Director Arthur Maude
Starring Anne Grey, Lester Matthews, Carl Harbord, Barbara Everest

Side Streets
Director Ivar Campbell
Starring Aline MacMahon, Paul Kelly, Ann Dvorak, Helen Lowell

Song of the Plough
Director John Baxter
Starring Stewart Rome, Rosalinde Fuller, Allan Jeayes, Hay Petrie

Taking Ways
Director John Baxter
Starring Leonard Morris, Daisy Crossley, Harry Terry, Freddie Watts

The Wishbone
Director Arthur Maude
Starring Nellie Wallace, Davy Burnaby, A. Bromley Davenport, Jane Wood

1934

By-Pass to Happiness
Director Anthony Kimmins
Starring Tamara Desni, Maurice Evans, Kay Hammond, Mark Daly

Designing Women
Director Ivar Campbell
Starring Stewart Rome, Valerie Taylor, Tyrell Davis, D.A. Clarke-Smith

How's Chances
Director Anthony Kimmins
Starring Harold French, Tamara Desni, Davy Burnaby, Morton Selten

Lest We Forget
Director John Baxter
Starring George Carney, Wilson Coleman, Roddy Hughes, Esmond Knight

Once in a New Moon
Director Anthony Kimmins
Starring Eliot Makeham, Rene Ray, Morton Selten, Wally Patch

Rolling Home
Director Ralph Ince
Starring Will Fyffe, Ralph Ince, Molly Lamont, James Raglan

Sanders of the River
Director Zoltan Korda
Starring Leslie Banks, Paul Robeson, Nina Mae, Robert Cochran

White Ensign
Director John L. F. Hunt
Starring Anthony Kimmins, Molly Lamont, Kenneth Villiers, Ivan Samson

Youthful Folly
Director Miles Mander
Starring Irene Vanbrugh, Jane Carr, Mary Lawson, Arthur Chesney

1935

Birds of a Feather
Director John Baxter
Starring George Robey, Horace Hodges, Eve Lister, Jack Melford

Emil and the Detectives
Director Milton Rosmer
Starring Rolf Wenkhaus, Fritz Rasp, Kaethe Haack, Olga Engl

Father O'Flynn
Director Wilfred Noy/ Walter Tennyson
Starring Tom Burke, Jean Adrienne, Robert Chisholm, Henry Oscar

Maria Marten, aka The Murder in the Red Barn
Director George King
Starring Tod Slaughter, Sophie Stewart, DJ Williams, Eric Portman

Radio Pirates
Director Ivar Campbell
Starring Leslie French, Mary Lawson, Warren Jenkins, Enid Stamp-Taylor

Two Hearts in Harmony
Director William Beaudine
Starring Bernice Claire, George Curzon, Enid Stamp-Taylor, Nora Williams

1936

The Captain's Table
Director Percy Marmont
Starring Percy Marmont, Marian Spencer, Louis Goodrich, Mark Daly

The Crimes of Stephen Hawke
Director   George King
Starring   Tod Slaughter, Marjorie Taylor,
           Eric Portman, Gerald Barry

The Crimson Circle
Director   George King
Starring   Hugh Wakefield, Alfred Drayton,
           Niall MacGinnis, June Duprez

David Livingstone
Director   James A. Fitzpatrick
Starring   Percy Marmont, Marian Spencer,
           James Carew, Pamela Stanley

Grande Finale
Director   Ivar Campbell
Starring   Mary Glynne, Guy Newall, Eric
           Cowley, Glen Alyn

Happy Days are Here Again
Director   Norman Lee
Starring   Renee Houston, Billie Houston,
           Shirley Houston, Harry Milton

Hearts of Humanity
Director   John Baxter
Starring   Bransby Williams, Wilfrid Walter,
           Cathleen Nesbitt, Eric Portman

King of the Castle
Director   Redd Davis
Starring   June Clyde, Claude Dampier, Billy
           Milton, Cynthia Stock

Men of Yesterday
Director   John Baxter
Starring   Stewart Rome, Sam Livesey, Hay
           Petrie, Cecil Parker

Mill on the Floss
Director   Tim Whelan
Starring   Frank Lawton, Victoria Hopper,
           Fay Compton, Geraldine
           Fitzgerald

Murder by Rope
Director   George Pearson
Starring   Constance Godridge, D.A. Clarke-
           Smith, Sunday Wilshin, Wilfrid
           Hyde-White

On the Top of the World (aka Everything Okay)
Director   Redd Davis
Starring   Leslie Bradley, Ben Field, Betty
           Fields, Wally Patch

Reasonable Doubt
Director   George King
Starring   John Stuart, Nancy Burne, Ivan
           Brandt, Marjorie Taylor

The Robber Symphony
Director   Freidrich Feher
Starring   George Graves, Magda Sonja,
           Hans Feher, Michael Martin-
           Harvey

Sabotage (aka While London Sleeps, and Menace)
Director   Adrian Brunel
Starring   Victor Varconi, Joan Maude, D. A.
           Clarke-Smith, Hubert Leslie

Second Bureau
Director   W. Victor Hanbury
Starring   Marta Labarr, Charles Oliver,
           Arthur Wontner, Meinhart Maur

Secret of Stamboul
Director   Andrew Marton
Starring   Valerie Hobson, Frank Vosper,
           James Mason, Kay Walsh

Show Flat
Director   Bernard Mainwaring
Starring   Eileen Munro, Anthony Hankey,
           Clifford Heatherley, Max Faber

Sporting Love
Director   J. Elder Wills
Starring   Stanley Lupino, Laddie Cliff,
           Henry Carlisle, Eda Peel

Such is Life
Director   Randall Faye
Starring   Gene Gerrard, Claude Dampier,
           Jean Colin, Eve Gray

Sweeney Todd
Director   George King
Starring   Tod Slaughter, Eva Lister, Bruce
           Seton, Davina Craig

Wings Over Africa
Director   Ladislau Vajda
Starring   Joan Gardner, Ian Colin, James
           Harcourt, James Carew

Wolf's Clothing
Director   Andrew Marton
Starring   Claude Hulbert, Gordon Harker,
           Lilli Palmer, George Graves

1937

The Academy Decides
Director   John Baxter
Starring   Harry Oscar, April Vivian, John
           Oxford, Wensley Russell

Auld Land Syne
Director   James A. Fitzpatrick
Starring   Andrew Cruickshank, Christine
           Adrian, Richard Ross, Marian
           Spencer

Bells of St. Mary's
Director   Redd Davis
Starring   Kathleen Gibson, Sylvia Marriott,
           J. Fisher White, Stella Bonheur

Double Exposures
Director   John Paddy Carstairs
Starring   Julien Mitchell, Ruby Miller, Basil
           Langton, Mavis Clair

The Elder Brother
Director   Frederick Hayward
Starring   John Stuart, Marjorie Taylor,
           Basil Langton, Stella Bonheur

For Valour
Director   Tom Walls
Starring   Tom Walls, Ralph Lynn, Veronica
           Rose, Joan Marion

House of Silence
Director   R. K. Neilson Baxter
Starring   Tom Helmore, Jenny Laird,
           Terence de Marney, Roddy
           Hughes

It's Never Too Late to Mend
Director   David MacDonald
Starring   Tod Slaughter, Marjorie Taylor,
           Jack Livesey, Ian Colin

Last Adventurers
Director   Roy Kellino
Starring   Niall MacGinnis, Roy Emerton,
           Linden Travers, Peter Gawthorne

Last Rose of Summer
Director   James A. Fitzpatrick
Starring   John Garrick, Kathleen Gibson,
           Malcolm Graham, Marian
           Spencer

Merry Comes to Town
Director   George King
Starring   ZaSu Pitts, Guy Newall, Betty Ann
           Davies, Muriel George

Mr. Stringfellow Says No
Director   Randall Faye
Starring   Neil Hamilton, Claude Dampier,
            Muriel Aked, Kathleen Gibson

Overcoat Sam
Director   Wallace Orton
Starring   George Mozart, Vera Sherburne,
            Frederick Peisley, Stanley Kirkby

Return of a Stranger
Director   W. Victor Hanbury
Starring   Griffith Jones, Rosalyn Boulter,
            Ellis Jeffreys, Athole Stewart

School for Husbands
Director   Andrew Marton
Starring   Rex Harrison, Diana Churchill,
            June Clyde, Henry Kendall

Screen-Struck
Director   Lawrence Huntington
Starring   Julien Vedey, Diana Beaumont,
            Richard Norris, John Oxford

Song of the Road
Director   John Baxter
Starring   Bransby Williams, Ernest
            Butcher, Muriel George, Davy
            Burnaby

Talking Feet
Director   John Baxter
Starring   Hazel Ascot, Jack Barty, Davy
            Burnaby, Enid Stamp-Taylor

Thunder in the City
Director   Marion Gering
Starring   Edward G. Robinson, Luli Deste,
            Nigel Bruce, Ralph Richardson

Ticket of Leave Man
Director   George King
Starring   Tod Slaughter, Marjorie Taylor,
            John Warwick, Robert Adair

Under a Cloud
Director   George King
Starring   Edward Rigby, Betty Ann Davies,
            Bernard Clifton, Renee Gadd

Wake up Famous
Director   Gene Gerrard
Starring   Nelson Keys, Gene Gerrard, Bela
            Mila, Josephine Huntley Wright

Wanted
Director   George King
Starring   Stella Bonheur, Billy Bray, Finlay
            Currie, Mark Daly

When the Poppies Bloom Again
Director   David MacDonald
Starring   Derek Gorst, Nancy Burne, Jack
            Livesey, John Warwick

Wife of General Ling
Director   Ladislau Vajda
Starring   Griffith Jones, Valery Inkijinoff,
            Adrianne Renn, Alan Napier

1938

George Bizet Composer of Carmen
Director   James A. Fitzpatrick
Starring   Dino Galvani, Peter Gawthorne

John Halifax, Gentleman
Director   George King
Starring   John Warwick, Nancy Burne,
            Ralph Michael, D.J. Williams,

Kate Plus Ten
Director   Reginald Denham
Starring   Jack Hulbert, Genevieve Tobin,
            Noel Madison, Francis L. Sullivan

Old Bones of the River
Director   Marcel Varnel
Starring   Will Hay, Moore Marriott,
            Graham Moffatt, Robert Adams

Old Iron
Director   Tom Walls
Starring   Tom Walls, Eva Moore, Cecil
            Parker, Richard Ainley

Second Best Bed
Director   Tom Walls
Starring   Tom Walls, Jane Baxter, Veronica
            Rose, Greta Gynt

Sexton Blake and the Hooded Terror
Director   George King
Starring   George Curzon, Tod Slaughter,
            Greta Gynt, Charles Oliver

Silver Top
Director   George King
Starring   Marie Wright, Betty Ann Davies,
            Marjorie Taylor, David Farrar

Stepping Toes
Director   John Baxter
Starring   Hazel Ascot, Enid Stamp-Taylor,
            Jack Barty, Edgar Driver

Plus musical shorts:
Dream of Love, and The Life of Chopin
(both directed by James A. Fitzpatrick)

1939

French Without Tears
Director   Anthony Asquith
Starring   Ray Milland, Ellen Drew, Janine
            Darcey, Roland Culver

Riding High
Director   David MacDonald
Starring   Claude Dampier, John Garrick,
            Kathleen Gibson, Helen Haye

Spy for a Day
Director   Mario Zampi
Starring   Duggie Wakefield, Paddy Browne,
            Jack Allen, Albert Lieven

1946

London Town
Director   Wesley Ruggles
Starring   Sid Field, Greta Gynt, Petula
            Clark, Jerry Desmonde

The Shop at Sly Corner
Director   George King
Starring   Oscar Homolka, Derek Farr,
            Muriel Pavlow, Kenneth Griffith

White Cradle Inn
Director   Harold French
Starring   Madeleine Carroll, Michael
            Rennie, Ian Hunter, Anne Marie
            Blanc

1947

An Ideal Husband
Director   Alexander Korda
Starring   Paulette Goddard, Michael
            Wilding, Hugh Williams, Diana
            Wynyard

Bonnie Prince Charlie
Director   Anthony Kimmins
Starring   David Niven, Margaret Leighton,
            Judy Campbell, Jack Hawkins

The Courtneys of Curzon Street
Director   Herbert Wilcox
Starring   Anna Neagle, Michael Wilding,
            Gladys Young, Coral Browne

A Man About the House
Director   Leslie Arliss
Starring   Margaret Johnston, Dulcie Gray,
            Kieron Moore, Felix Aylmer

Mine Own Executioner
Director   Anthony Kimmins
Starring   Burgess Meredith, Dulcie Gray,
            Kieron Moore, Barbara White

1948

Anna Karenina
Director   Julian Duvivier
Starring   Vivien Leigh, Ralph Richardson,
            Kieron Moore, Sally Ann Howes

Call of the Blood
Director   John Clements, Ladislas Vajda
Starring   Kay Hammond, John Clements,
            John Justin, Hilton Edwards

The Fallen Idol
Director   Carol Reed
Starring   Ralph Richardson, Michele
            Morgan, Bobby Henrey, Sonia
            Dresdel

Night Beat
Director   Harold Huth
Starring   Anne Crawford, Maxwell Reed,
            Ronald Howard, Christine
            Norden

Spring in Park Lane
Director   Herbert Wilcox
Starring   Anna Neagle, Michael Wilding,
            Tom Walls, Peter Graves

The Winslow Boy
Director   Anthony Asquith
Starring   Robert Donat, Margaret Leighton,
            Cedric Hardwicke, Basil Radford

1949

Britannia Mews
Director   Jean Negulesco
Starring   Dana Andrews, Maureen O'Hara,
            Sybil Thorndike, Wilfrid Hyde-
            White

Elizabeth of Ladymead
Director   Herbert Wilcox
Starring   Anna Neagle, Hugh Williams,
            Bernard Lee, Michael Laurence

I Was a Male War Bride
Director   Howard Hawks
Starring   Cary Grant, Ann Sheridan,
            William Neff, Marion Marshall

The Last Days of Dolwyn
Director   Emlyn Williams
Starring   Edith Evans, Emlyn Williams,
            Richard Burton, Anthony James

Saints and Sinners
Director   Leslie Arliss
Starring   Kieron Moore, Christine Norden,
            Sheila Manahan, Michael Dolan

The Small Back Room
Director   Michael Powell, Emeric
            Pressburger
Starring   David Farrar, Kathleen Byron,
            Jack Hawkins, Leslie Banks

That Dangerous Age
Director   Gregory Ratoff
Starring   Roger Livesey, Myrna Loy, Peggy
            Cummins, Richard Greene

The Third Man
Director   Carol Reed
Starring   Joseph Cotten, Orson Welles,
            Alida Valli, Trevor Howard

1950

The Angel with the Trumpet
Director   Anthony Bushell
Starring   Eileen Herlie, Basil Sydney,
            Norman Wooland, Anthony
            Bushell

The Black Rose
Director   Henry Hathaway
Starring   Tyrone Power, Orson Welles,
            Cecile Aubry, Jack Hawkins

Circle of Danger
Director   Jacques Tourneur
Starring   Ray Milland, Patricia Roc, Marius
            Goring, Hugh Sinclair

Cure for Love
Director   Robert Donat
Starring   Robert Donat, Renee Asherson,
            Marjorie Rhodes, Thora Hird

Curtain Up
Director   Ralph Smart
Starring   Robert Morley, Margaret
            Rutherford, Olive Sloane, Joan
            Rice

Flesh and Blood
Director   Anthony Kimmins
Starring   Richard Todd, Glynis Johns, Joan
            Greenwood, Andre Morell

Gone to Earth
Director   Michael Powell
Starring   Jennifer Jones, David Farrar, Cyril
            Cusack, Esmond Knight

The Happiest Days of Your Life
Director   Frank Launder
Starring   Alastair Sim, Margaret
            Rutherford, Joyce Grenfell,
            Richard Wattis

Into the Blue
Director   Herbert Wilcox
Starring   Michael Wilding, Odile Versois,
            Jack Hulbert, Constance
            Cummings

The Late Edwina Black
Director   Maurice Elvey
Starring   Geraldine Fitzgerald, David
            Farrar, Roland Culver, Jean Cadell

The Lost Hours
Director   Malcolm MacDonald
Starring   Mark Stevens, Jean Kent, John
            Bentley, Dianne Foster

The Mudlark
Director   Jean Negulesco
Starring   Irene Dunne, Alec Guinness,
            Andrew Ray, Beatrice Campbell

My Daughter Joy
Director   Gregory Ratoff
Starring   Edward G. Robinson, Peggy
            Cummings, Nora Swinburne,
            Richard Greene

Night and the City
Director   Jules Dassin
Starring   Richard Widmark, Gene Tierney,
            Googie Withers, Herbert Lom

Seven Days to Noon
Director   John Boulting
Starring   Barry Jones, Olive Sloane, Andre
            Morell, Sheila Manahan

State Secret
Director   Sidney Gilliat
Starring   Douglas Fairbanks Jnr, Glynis
            Johns, Herbert Lom, Jack
            Hawkins

The Wonder Kid
Director   Karl Hartl
Starring   Bobby Henrey, Elwyn Brook-
            Jones, Muriel Aked, Oskar Werner

The Wooden Horse
Director   Jack Lee
Starring   Leo Genn, David Tomlinson,
            Anthony Steel, David Greene

1951

The Elusive Pimpernel
Director   Michael Powell
Starring   David Niven, Margaret Leighton,
            Cyril Cusack, Jack Hawkins

Lady Godiva Rides Again
Director   Frank Launder
Starring   Dennis Price, John McCallum,
            Stanley Holloway, Pauline Stroud,

The Lady with a Lamp
Director   Herbert Wilcox
Starring   Anna Neagle, Michael Wilding,
            Gladys Young, Felix Aylmer

Pandora and the Flying Dutchman
Director   Albert Lewin
Starring   James Mason, Ava Gardner, Nigel
            Patrick, Sheila Sim

The Tales of Hoffman
Director   Michael Powell
Starring   Moira Shearer, Robert
            Rounseville, Robert Helpmann,
            Pamela Brown

1952

The African Queen
Director   John Huston
Starring   Humphrey Bogart, Katharine
            Hepburn, Robert Morley, Peter
            Bull

Outcast of the Islands
Director   Carol Reed
Starring   Trevor Howard, Ralph
            Richardson, Kerima, Robert
            Morley

The Beggar's Opera
Director   Peter Brook
Starring   Laurence Olivier, Stanley
            Holloway, Dorothy Tutin,
            Daphne Anderson

Circumstantial Evidence
Director   Don Birt
Starring   Rona Anderson, Patrick Holt,
            John Arnatt, John Warwick

Cry the Beloved Country
Director   Zoltan Korda
Starring   Canada Lee, Charles Carson,
            Sidney Poitier, Joyce Carey

Derby Day
Director   Herbert Wilcox
Starring   Anna Neagle, Michael Wilding,
            Googie Withers, Gordon Harker

The Gift Horse
Director   Compton Bennett
Starring   Trevor Howard, Richard
            Attenborough, Sonny Tufts,
            James Donald

The Holly and the Ivy
Director   George More O'Ferrall
Starring   Ralph Richardson, Celia Johnson,
            Margaret Leighton, Denholm
            Elliott

Home at Seven
Director   Ralph Richardson
Starring   Ralph Richardson, Margaret
            Leighton, Jack Hawkins,
            Campbell Singer

Mr Denning Drives North
Director   Anthony Kimmins
Starring   John Mills, Phyllis Calvert, Sam
            Wanamaker, Herbert Lom

The Sound Barrier
Director   David Lean
Starring   Ralph Richardson, Nigel Patrick,
            Ann Todd, John Justin

Trent's Last Case
Director   Herbert Wilcox
Starring   Margaret Lockwood, Michael
            Wilding, Orson Welles, John
            McCallum

Who Goes There?
Director   Anthony Kimmins
Starring   Peggy Cummins, Valerie Hobson,
            George Cole, Nigel Patrick

1953

Appointment in London
Director   Philip Leacock
Starring   Dirk Bogarde, Ian Hunter, Dinah
            Sheridan, Bryan Forbes

Beautiful Stranger
Director   David Miller
Starring   Ginger Rogers, Stanley Baker,
            Herbert Lom, Jacques Bergerac

The Captain's Paradise
Director   Anthony Kimmins
Starring   Alec Guinness, Yvonne De Carlo,
            Celia Johnson, Charles Goldner,

Folly to be Wise
Director   Frank Launder
Starring   Alastair Sim, Roland Culver,
            Elizabeth Allan, Martita Hunt

The Intruder
Director   Guy Hamilton
Starring   Jack Hawkins, Michael Medwin,
            Hugh Williams, George Cole

Laughing Anne
Director   Herbert Wilcox
Starring   Wendell Corey, Margaret
            Lockwood, Forrest Tucker,
            Ronald Shiner

The Man Between
Director   Carol Reed
Starring   James Mason, Claire Bloom,
            Hildegarde Neff, Geoffrey Toone

Moulin Rouge
Director   John Huston
Starring   Jose Ferrer, Colette Marchand,
            Suzanne Flon, Zsa Zsa Gabor

Profile
Director   Francis Searle
Starring   John Bentley, Kathleen Byron,
            Thea Gregory, Stuart Lindsell

The Red Beret
Director   Terence Young
Starring   Alan Ladd, Susan Stephen, Leo
            Genn, Harry Andrews

The Ringer
Director   Guy Hamilton
Starring   Herbert Lom, Donald Wolfit, Mai
            Zetterling, Greta Gynt

Single-Handed
Director   Roy Boulting
Starring   Jeffrey Hunter, Michael Rennie, Wendy Hillier, Bernard Lee

The Story of Gilbert and Sullivan
Director   Sidney Gilliat
Starring   Robert Morley, Maurice Evans, Peter Finch, Dinah Sheridan

They Who Dare
Director   Lewis Milestone
Starring   Dirk Bogarde, Denholm Elliott, Akim Tamiroff, Gerard Oury

Twice Upon a Time
Director   Emeric Pressburger
Starring   Hugh Williams, Elizabeth Allan, Jack Hawkins, Yolande Larthe

1954

An Inspector Calls
Director   Guy Hamilton
Starring   Alastair Sim, Arthur Young, Olga Lindo, Eileen Moore

Aunt Clara
Director   Anthony Kimmins
Starring   Ronald Shiner, Margaret Rutherford, A.E. Matthews, Fay Compton

Bang, You're Dead
Director   Lance Comfort
Starring   Jack Warner, Derek Farr, Veronica Hurst, Michael Medwin

Beat the Devil
Director   John Huston
Starring   Humphrey Bogart, Gina Lollobrigida, Jennifer Jones, Robert Morley

The Belles of St. Trinian's
Director   Frank Launder
Starring   Alastair Sim, George Cole, Joyce Grenfell, Hermione Baddeley

The Colditz Story
Director   Guy Hamilton
Starring   John Mills, Eric Portman, Christopher Rhodes, Lionel Jeffries

Devil Girl from Mars
Director   David MacDonald
Starring   Patricia Laffan, Hugh McDermott, Joseph Tomelty, Adrienne Corri

Eight O'Clock Walk
Director   Lance Comfort
Starring   Richard Attenborough, Cathy O'Donnell, Derek Farr, Ian Hunter

The Green Scarf
Director   George More O'Ferrall
Starring   Michael Redgrave, Ann Todd, Leo Genn, Kieron Moore

The Heart of the Matter
Director   George More O'Ferrall
Starring   Trevor Howard, Elizabeth Allan, Maria Schell, Denholm Elliott

Hobson's Choice
Director   David Lean
Starring   Charles Laughton, John Mills, Brenda de Banzie, Prunella Scales

It's a Great Day
Director   John Warrington
Starring   Ruth Dunning, Edward Evans, Sidney James, Vera Day

Josephine and Men
Director   Roy Boulting
Starring   Glynis Johns, Jack Buchanan, Donald Sinden, Peter Finch

Malaga
Director   Richard Sale
Starring   Trevor Howard, Dorothy Dandridge, Edmund Purdom, Michael Hordern

Prince Valiant
Director   Henry Hathaway
Starring   James Mason, Janet Leigh, Robert Wagner, Debra Paget

Raising a Riot
Director   Wendy Toye
Starring   Kenneth More, Shelagh Fraser, Mandy Miller, Fusty Bentine

The Teckman Mystery
Director   Wendy Toye
Starring   Margaret Leighton, John Justin, Roland Culver, Michael Medwin

1955

Carrington VC
Director   Anthony Asquith
Starring   David Niven, Margaret Leighton, Noelle Middleton, Laurence Naismith

Cockleshell Heroes
Director   Jose Ferrer
Starring   Jose Ferrer, Trevor Howard, Anthony Newley, Victor Maddern

The Constant Husband
Director   Sidney Gilliat
Starring   Rex Harrison, Margaret Leighton, Kay Kendall, Cecil Parker

The Deep Blue Sea
Director   Anatole Litvak
Starring   Vivien Leigh, Kenneth More, Eric Portman, Emlyn Williams

The End of the Affair
Director   Edward Dmytryk
Starring   Deborah Kerr, Van Johnson, John Mills, Peter Cushing

Gentlemen Marry Brunettes
Director   Richard Sale
Starring   Jane Russell, Jeanne Crain, Alan Young, Scott Brady

Geordie
Director   Frank Launder
Starring   Bill Travers, Alastair Sim, Norah Gorsen, Raymond Huntley

The Good Die Young
Director   Lewis Gilbert
Starring   Laurence Harvey, Gloria Grahame, Richard Basehart, Joan Collins

I am a Camera
Director   Henry Cornelius
Starring   Julie Harris, Laurence Harvey, Shelley Winters, Ron Randell

It's a Wonderful World
Director   Val Guest
Starring   Terence Morgan, George Cole, Kathleen Harrison, Mylene Demongeot

The Man Who Loved Redheads
Director   Harold French
Starring   Moira Shearer, John Justin, Roland Culver, Gladys Cooper

Privates Progress
Director   John Boulting
Starring   Ian Carmichael, Terry-Thomas, Richard Attenborough, Dennis Price

Summer Madness aka Summertime
Director   David Lean
Starring   Katherine Hepburn, Rossano Brazzi, Isa Miranda, Darren McGavin

They Can't Hang Me
Director   Val Guest
Starring   Terence Morgan, Yolande Donlan, Andre Morrell, Ursula Howells

Three Cases of Murder
Director   Wendy Toye, David Eady & George More O'Ferrall
Starring   Alan Badel, Hugh Pryse, John Salew, Leueen MacGrath

1956

The Admirable Crichton
Director   Lewis Gilbert
Starring   Kenneth More, Diane Cilento, Cecil Parker, Sally Ann Howes

The Baby and the Battleship
Director   Jay Lewis
Starring   John Mills, Richard Attenborough, Bryan Forbes, Harold Siddons

Charley Moon
Director   Guy Hamilton
Starring   Max Bygraves, Dennis Price, Michael Medwin, Shirley Eaton

Dry Rot
Director   Maurice Elvey
Starring   Ronald Shiner, Brian Rix, Peggy Mount, Lee Patterson

The Extra Day
Director   William Fairchild
Starring   Richard Basehart, Simone Simon, George Baker, Josephine Griffin

The Green Man
Director   Robert Day
Starring   Alastair Sim, George Cole, Jill Adams, Terry-Thomas

A Hill in Korea
Director   Julian Amyes
Starring   George Baker, Harry Andrews, Stanley Baker, Michael Medwin

Loser Takes All
Director   Ken Annakin
Starring   Rossano Brazzi, Glynis Johns, Robert Morley, Tony Britton

Manuela
Director   Guy Hamilton
Starring   Trevor Howard, Elsa Martinelli, Pedro Armendariz, Donald Pleasance

The March Hare
Director   George More O'Ferrall
Starring   Peggy Cummins, Terence Morgan, Martita Hunt, Cyril Cusack

My Teenage Daughter
Director   Herbert Wilcox
Starring   Anna Neagle, Sylvia Sims, Kenneth Haigh, Wilfrid Hyde-White

The Passionate Stranger
Director   Muriel Box
Starring   Ralph Richardson, Margaret Leighton, Carlo Justini, Patricia Dainton

Richard III
Director   Laurence Olivier
Starring   Laurence Olivier, Ralph Richardson, Claire Bloom, John Gielgud

Sailor Beware
Director   Gordon Parry
Starring   Peggy Mount, Esma Cannon, Cyril Smith, Shirley Eaton

The Secret Tent
Director   Don Chaffey
Starring   Donald Gray, Andree Melly, Jean Anderson, Sonia Dresdel

Three Men in a Boat
Director   Ken Annakin
Starring   Laurence Harvey, Jimmy Edwards, David Tomlinson, Shirley Eaton

1957

Behind the Mask
Director   Brian Desmond Hurst
Starring   Michael Redgrave, Tony Britton, Carl Mohner, Niall MacGinnis

The Birthday Present
Director   Pat Jackson
Starring   Tony Britton, Sylvia Syms, Jack Watling, Walter Fitzgerald

Blue Murder at St. Trinians
Director   Frank Launder
Starring   Terry-Thomas, George Cole, Joyce Grenfell, Alastair Sim

Bonjour Tristesse
Director   Otto Preminger
Starring   Deborah Kerr, David Niven, Jean Seberg, Mylene Demongeot

Fortune is a Woman
Director   Sidney Gilliat
Starring   Jack Hawkins, Arlene Dahl, Dennis Price, Geoffrey Keen

Happy is the Bride
Director   Roy Boulting
Starring   Ian Carmichael, Janette Scott, Cecil Parker, Joyce Grenfell

A King in New York
Director   Charles Chaplin
Starring   Charles Chaplin, Dawn Addams, Oliver Johnston, Maxine Audley

The Long Haul
Director   Ken Hughes
Starring   Victor Mature, Gene Anderson, Patrick Allen, Diana Dors

A Novel Affair
Director   Muriel Box
Starring   Ralph Richardson, Margaret Leighton, Patricia Dainton, Carlo Giustini

Saint Joan
Director   Otto Preminger
Starring   Jean Seberg, Richard Widmark, Richard Todd, John Gielgud

Second Fiddle
Director   Maurice Elvey
Starring   Adrienne Corri, Thorley Walters, Lisa Gastoni, Richard Wattis

Seven Waves Away
Director   Richard Sale
Starring   Tyrone Power, Mai Zetterling, Lloyd Nolan, Stephen Boyd

The Smallest Show on Earth
Director   Basil Dearden
Starring   Bill Travers, Virginia McKenna, Leslie Phillips, Peter Sellers,

The Story of Esther Costello
Director   David Miller
Starring   Joan Crawford, Rossano Brazzi, Heather Sears, Lee Patterson,

Town on Trial
Director   John Guillerman
Starring   Charles Coburn, John Mills, Barbara Bates, Derek Farr

1958

Carlton-Browne of the FO
Director   Roy Boulting
Starring   Terry-Thomas, Peter Sellers, Ian Bannen, Thorley Walters

Danger Within
Director   Don Chaffey
Starring   Richard Todd, Bernard Lee, Michael Wilding, Richard Attenborough

The Horse's Mouth
Director   Ronald Neame
Starring   Robert Beatty, Joseph Tomelty, Mervyn Johns, Michael Medwin

The Iron Petticoat
Director   Ralph Thomas
Starring   Bob Hope, Katharine Hepburn, James Robertson Justice, Robert Helpmann

Jack the Ripper
Director   Robert S. Baker
Starring   Lee Patterson, Eddie Byrne, Betty McDowall, Ewen Solon

The Killers of Kilimanjaro
Director   Richard Thorpe
Starring   Robert Taylor, Anthony Newley, Anne Aubrey, Gregoire Aslan

Law and Disorder
Director   Charles Crichton
Starring   Michael Redgrave, Robert Morley, Elizabeth Sellars, Ronald Squire

Life is a Circus
Director   Val Guest
Starring   Bud Flanagan, Nervo & Knox, Naughton & Gold, Shirley Eaton

The Man Upstairs
Director   Don Chaffey
Starring   Richard Attenborough, Bernard Lee, Donald Houston, Dorothy Alison

Orders to Kill
Director   Anthony Asquith
Starring   Eddie Albert, Paul Massie, Lillian Gish, James Robertson Justice

The Silent Enemy
Director   William Fairchild
Starring   Laurence Harvey, Dawn Addams, Michael Craig, John Clements

Tread Softly Stranger
Director   Gordon Parry
Starring   Diana Dors, George Baker, Terence Morgan, Patrick Allen

The Truth about Women
Director   Muriel Box
Starring   Laurence Harvey, Julie Harris, Diane Cilento, Mai Zetterling

The Whole Truth
Director   John Guillerman
Starring   Stewart Granger, Donna Reed, George Sanders, Gianna Maria Canale

1959

The Angry Silence
Director   Guy Green
Starring   Richard Attenborough, Pier Angeli, Michael Craig, Bernard Lee

Friends and Neighbours
Director   Gordon Parry
Starring   Arthur Askey, Megs Jenkins, Peter Illing, Tilda Thamar

Idle on Parade
Director   John Gilling
Starring   William Bendix, Anthony Newley, Lionel Jeffries, Sidney James

I'm All Right Jack
Director   John Boulting
Starring   Ian Carmichael, Peter Sellers, Terry-Thomas, Richard Attenborough

Jetstorm
Director   C. Raker Endfield
Starring   Richard Attenborough, Stanley Baker, Hermione Baddeley, Bernard Braden

Left, Right and Centre
Director   Sidney Gilliat
Starring   Patricia Bredin, Eric Barker, Jack Hedley, Leslie Dwyer

A Model for Murder
Director   Terry Bishop
Starring   Keith Andes, Hazel Court, Jean Aubrey, Michael Gough

The Mouse that Roared
Director   Jack Arnold
Starring   Peter Sellers, Jean Seberg, David Kossoff, William Hartnell

The Mummy
Director   Terence Fisher
Starring   Peter Cushing, Christopher Lee, Yvonne Furneaux, Eddie Byrne

Next to No Time
Director   Henry Cornelius
Starring   Kenneth More, Betsy Drake, Harry Green, Patrick Barr

Our Man in Havana
Director   Coral Reed
Starring   Burl Ives, Alec Guinness, Maureen O'Hara, Noel Coward

Room at the Top
Director   Jack Clayton
Starring   Laurence Harvey, Simone Signoret, Heather Sears, Donald Wolfit

Subway in the Sky
Director   Muriel Box
Starring   Van Johnson, Hildegarde Neff, Albert Lieven, Cec Linder

Suddenly Last Summer
Director   Joseph L. Mankiewicz
Starring   Elizabeth Taylor, Montgomery Clift, Katharine Hepburn, Albert Dekker

Tarzan's Greatest Adventure
Director   John Guillerman
Starring   Gordon Scott, Anthony Quayle,
            Sara Shane, Niall MacGinnis

1960

City Of The Dead
Director   John Moxey
Starring   Patricia Jessel, Betta St John,
            Christopher Lee, Dennis Lotis

Cone Of Silence
Director   Charles Frend
Starring   Michael Craig, Bernard Lee, Peter
            Cushing, George Sanders

Dead Lucky
Director   Montgomery Tully
Starring   Vincent Ball, Betty McDowall,
            John Le Mesurier, Alfred Burke

Offbeat
Director   Cliff Owen
Starring   William Sylvester, Mai Zetterling,
            John Meillon, Anthony Dawson

The Entertainer
Director   Tony Richardson
Starring   Laurence Olivier, Joan Plowright,
            Brenda de Banzie, Alan Bates

Expresso Bongo
Director   Val Guest
Starring   Laurence Harvey, Sylvia Syms,
            Yolande Donlan, Cliff Richard

Faces in the Dark
Director   David Eady
Starring   John Gregson, Mai Zetterling,
            Michael Denison, John Ireland

The Flesh and The Fiends
Director   John Gilling
Starring   Peter Cushing, June Laverick,
            George Rose, Donald Pleasance

A French Mistress
Director   Roy Boulting
Starring   James Robertson Justice, Cecil
            Parker, Raymond Huntley, Agnes
            Laurent

The Grass is Greener
Director   Stanley Donen
Starring   Cary Grant, Deborah Kerr, Robert
            Mitchum, Jean Simmons

The Greengage Summer
Director   Lewis Gilbert
Starring   Kenneth More, Susannah York,
            Danielle Darrieux, Claude Nollier

Greyfriars Bobby
Director   Don Chaffey
Starring   Donald Crisp, Laurence
            Naismith, Alex Mackenzie, Kay
            Walsh

The Guns of Navarone
Director   J. Lee-Thompson
Starring   Gregory Peck, David Niven,
            Anthony Quinn, Stanley Baker

The Hands of Orlac
Director   Edmond T. Greville
Starring   Mel Ferrer, Christopher Lee, Dany
            Carrel, Felix Aylmer

Mysterious Island
Director   Cy Endfield
Starring   Michael Craig, Joan Greenwood,
            Michael Callan, Gary Merrill

Nearly a Nasty Accident
Director   Don Chaffey
Starring   Jimmy Edwards, Kenneth
            Connor, Shirley Eaton, Richard
            Wattis

The Night we Got the Bird
Director   Darcy Conyers
Starring   Brian Rix, Dora Bryan, Ronald
            Shiner, Irene Handl

The Pure Hell at St. Trinians
Director   Frank Launder
Starring   Cecil Parker, Joyce Grenfell,
            George Cole, Thorley Walters

The Queen's Guards
Director   Michael Powell
Starring   Daniel Massey, Raymond Massey,
            Robert Stephens, Jack Watson

The Risk
Director   Roy Boulting, John Boulting
Starring   Tony Britton, Virginia Maskell,
            Peter Cushing, Ian Bannen

Spare the Rod
Director   Leslie Norman
Starring   Max Bygraves, Geoffrey Keen,
            Donald Pleasance, Richard
            O'Sullivan

Surprise Package
Director   Stanley Donen
Starring   Yul Brynner, Bill Nagy, Mitzi
            Gaynor, Lionel Murton

Tarzan the Magnificent
Director   Robert Day
Starring   Gordon Scott, Jock Mahoney,
            Betta St. John, John Carradine

The Trunk
Director   Donovan Winter
Starring   Philip Carey, Julia Arnall, Dermot
            Walsh, Vera Day

Tunes of Glory
Director   Ronald Neame
Starring   Alec Guinness, John Mills, Dennis
            Price, Susannah York

The Unstoppable Man
Director   Terry Bishop
Starring   Cameron Mitchell, Marius
            Goring, Harry H. Corbett, Lois
            Maxwell

Weekend with Lulu
Director   John Paddy Carstairs
Starring   Bob Monkhouse, Leslie Phillips,
            Alfred Marks, Shirley Eaton

Yesterday's Enemy
Director   Val Guest
Starring   Stanley Baker, Guy Rolfe, Leo
            McKern, Gordon Jackson

1961

The Barber Of Stamford Hill
Director   Casper Wrede
Starring   Megs Jenkins, John Bennett,
            Maxwell Shaw, John Graham

The Day of the Triffids
Director   Steve Sekely, Freddie Francis
            (uncredited)
Starring   Howard Keel, Nicole Maurey,
            Janette Scott, Kieron Moore

The Day the Earth Caught Fire
Director   Val Guest
Starring   Janet Munro, Leo McKern,
            Edward Judd, Michael Goodliffe

Dentist on the Job
Director   C.M. Pennington-Richards
Starring   Bob Monkhouse, Kenneth Connor, Shirley Eaton, Eric Barker

The Devil's Daffodil
Director   Akos Rathony
Starring   Christopher Lee, Marius Goring, Penelope Horner, Ingrid Van Bergen

Foxhole in Cairo
Director   John Moxey
Starring   James Robertson Justice, Adrian Hoven, Niall MacGinnis, Peter Van Eyck

The Frightened City
Director   John Lemont
Starring   Herbert Lom, John Gregson, Sean Connery, Alfred Marks

The Girl on the Boat
Director   Henry Kaplan
Starring   Norman Wisdom, Millicent Martin, Richard Briers, Sheila Hancock

The Golden Rabbit
Director   David MacDonald
Starring   Timothy Bateson, Maureen Beck, Willoughby Goddard, Dick Bentley

Hair of the Dog
Director   Terry Bishop
Starring   Reginald Beckwith, Dorinda Stevens, John Le Mesurier, Brian Oulton

HMS Defiant
Director   Lewis Gilbert
Starring   Alec Guinness, Dirk Bogarde, Anthony Quayle, Tom Bell

Information Received
Director   Robert Lynn
Starring   Sabina Sesselmann, William Sylvester, Hermione Baddeley, Edward Underdown

The Innocents
Director   Jack Clayton
Starring   Deborah Kerr, Megs Jenkins, Pamela Franklin, Martin Stephens

It's Trad, Dad
Director   Dick Lester
Starring   Helen Shapiro, Craig Douglas, Felix Felton, Arthur Mullard

A Kind of Loving
Director   John Schlesinger
Starring   Alan Bates, June Ritchie, Thora Hird, Bert Palmer

The Kitchen
Director   James Hill
Starring   Carl Mohner, Mary Yeomans, Brian Phelan, Tom Bell

Nothing Barred
Director   Darcy Conyers
Starring   Brian Rix, Leo Franklyn, Naunton Wayne, Charles Heslop

On the Fiddle
Director   Cyril Frankel
Starring   Alfred Lynch, Sean Connery, Cecil Parker, Stanley Holloway

Only Two Can Play
Director   Sidney Gilliat
Starring   Peter Sellers, Virginia Maskell, Mai Zetterling, Richard Attenborough

Over the Odds
Director   Michael Forlong
Starring   Marjorie Rhodes, Glenn Melvyn, Cyril Smith, Esma Cannon

The Painted Smile
Director   Lance Comfort
Starring   Liz Fraser, Kenneth Griffith, Peter Reynolds, Anthony Wickert

The Prince and the Pauper
Director   Don Chaffey
Starring   Kenny Morse, Barry Pearl, Gene Bua, Barbara Huston

The Road to Hong Kong
Director   Melvin Frank
Starring   Bing Crosby, Bob Hope, Joan Collins, Dorothy Lamour

Take Me Over
Director   Robert Lynn
Starring   Temperance Seven, John Paul, John Rutland, Diane Aubrey

Two and Two Make Six
Director   Freddie Francis
Starring   George Chakiris, Janette Scott, Alfred Lynch, Jackie Lane

The Valiant
Director   Roy Baker
Starring   John Mills, Ettore Manni, Roberto Risso, Robert Shaw

The War Lover
Director   Philip Leacock.
Starring   Steve McQueen, Robert Wagner, Shirley Ann Field, Gary Cockrell

1962

The Amorous Prawn
Director   Anthony Kimmins
Starring   Joan Greenwood, Cecil Parker, Ian Carmichael, Robert Beatty

Billy Liar
Director   John Schlesinger
Starring   Tom Courtenay, Julie Christie, Wilfred Pickles, Mona Washbourne

The Break
Director   Lance Comfort
Starring   Tony Britton, William Lucas, Eddie Byrne, Robert Urquhart

Danger By My Side
Director   Charles Saunders
Starring   Anthony Oliver, Maureen Connell, Alan Tilvern, Bill Nagy

The Dock Brief
Director   James Hill
Starring   Peter Sellers, Richard Attenborough, Beryl Reid, David Lodge

Doomsday at Eleven
Director   Theodore Zichy
Starring   Carl Jaffe, Stanley Morgan, Alan Heywood, Derrick de Marney

Heavens Above!
Director   John Boulting
Starring   Peter Sellers, Isabel Jeans, Cecil Parker, Brock Peters

Hide and Seek
Director   Cy Endfield
Starring   Ian Carmichael, Janet Munro, Curt Jurgens, George Pravda

I Could Go on Singing
Director   Ronald Neame
Starring   Judy Garland, Dirk Bogarde, Aline MacMahon, Jack Klugman

The L-Shaped Room
Director   Bryan Forbes
Starring   Leslie Caron, Anthony Booth, Avis Bunnage, Tom Bell

The Main Attraction
Director   Daniel Petrie.
Starring   Pat Boone, Nancy Kwan, Mai Zetterling, Yvonne Mitchell

Mix Me a Person
Director   Leslie Norman
Starring   Anne Baxter, Donald Sinden, Adam Faith, Walter Brown

Mystery Submarine
Director   C.M. Pennington-Richards
Starring   Edward Judd, James Robertson Justice, Laurence Payne, Joachim Fuchsberger

Night of the Prowler
Director   Francis Searle
Starring   Patrick Holt, Colette Wilde, Bill Nagy, Mitzi Rogers

Night Without Pity
Director   Theodore Zichy
Starring   Sarah Lawson, Neil McCallum, Alan Edwards, Dorinda Stevens

Sammy Going South
Director   Alexander Mackendrick
Starring   Edward G. Robinson, Fergus McClelland, Constance Cummings, Harry H. Corbett

Serena
Director   Peter Maxwell
Starring   Patrick Holt, Emrys Jones, Honor Blackman, Bruce Beeby

The Small World of Sammy Lee
Director   Ken Hughes
Starring   Anthony Newley, Julia Foster, Robert Stephens, Wilfrid Brambell

Station Six-Sahara
Director   Seth Holt
Starring   Carroll Baker, Peter Van Eyck, Ian Bannen, Denholm Elliott

Stolen Hours
Director   Daniel Petrie
Starring   Susan Hayward, Michael Craig, Diane Baker, Edward Judd

Two Left Feet
Director   Roy Baker
Starring   Michael Crawford, Nyree Dawn Porter, Julia Foster, Michael Craze

The Victors
Director   Carl Foreman
Starring   Vince Edwards, Albert Finney, George Hamilton, Melina Mercouri

1963

Becket
Director   Peter Glenville
Starring   Richard Burton, Peter O'Toole, Donald Wolfit, John Gielgud

Catacombs
Director   Gordon Hessler
Starring   Gary Merrill, Neil McCallum, Georgina Cookson, Jane Merrow

The Comedy Man
Director   Alvin Rakoff
Starring   Kenneth More, Cecil Parker, Dennis Price, Angela Douglas

Dr Strangelove, or How I Learned to Stop Worrying and Love the Bomb
Director   Stanley Kubrick
Starring   Peter Sellers, George C. Scott, Sterling Hayden, Keenan Wynn

The Eyes of Annie Jones
Director   Reginald Le Borg
Starring   Richard Conte, Francesca Annis, Joyce Carey, Myrtle Reed

First Men in the Moon
Director   Nathan Juran
Starring   Edward Judd, Lionel Jeffries, Martha Hyer, Eric Chitty

A Jolly Bad Fellow
Director   Don Chaffey
Starring   Leo McKern, Janet Munro, Maxine Audley, Duncan Macrae

The Horror of it All
Director   Terence Fisher
Starring   Pat Boone, Erica Rogers, Dennis Price, Valentine Dyall

It's all Happening
Director   Don Sharp
Starring   Tommy Steele, Angela Douglas, Michael Medwin, Bernard Bresslaw

Lord Jim
Director   Richard Brooks
Starring   Peter O'Toole, James Mason, Curt Jurgens, Eli Wallach

A Matter of Choice
Director   Vernon Sewell
Starring   Anthony Steel, Jeanne Moody, Ballard Berkeley, Malcolm Gerard

Psyche 59
Director   Alexander Singer
Starring   Patricia Neal, Curt Jurgens, Samantha Eggar, Ian Bannen

The Pumpkin Eater
Director   Jack Clayton
Starring   Anne Bancroft, Peter Finch, James Mason, Janine Gray

Ring of Spies
Director   Robert Tronson
Starring   Bernard Lee, William Sylvester, Margaret Tyzack, David Kossoff

Saturday Night Out
Director   Robert Hartford-Davis
Starring   Heather Sears, Bernard Lee, Erika Remberg, John Bonney

The Servant
Director   Joseph Losey
Starring   Dirk Bogarde, Sarah Miles, Wendy Craig, James Fox

Walk a Tightrope
Director   Frank Nesbitt
Starring   Dan Duryea, Patricia Owens, Terence Cooper, Richard Leech

The Yellow Teddybears
Director   Robert Hartford-Davis
Starring   Jill Adams, John Bonney, Victor Brooks, Jacqueline Ellis

1964

Allez France!
Director   Robert Dhery
Starring   Pierre Tornade, Pierre Doris, Raymond Bussieres, Jean Richard

The Amorous Adventures of Moll Flanders
Director   Terence Young
Starring   Kim Novak, Claire Ufland, Richard Johnson, Angela Lansbury

The Bedford Incident
Director   James B. Harris
Starring   Richard Widmark, Sidney Poitier, James MacArthur, Martin Balsam

The Black Torment
Director   Robert Hartford-Davis
Starring   John Turner, Heather Sears, Ann Lynn, Peter Arne

Curse of the Fly
Director   Don Sharp
Starring   Brian Donlevy, George Baker, Carole Gray, Yvette Rees

Darling
Director   John Schlesinger
Starring   Julie Christie, Dirk Bogarde, Laurence Harvey, Roland Curram

Do You Know This Voice?
Director   Frank Nesbitt
Starring   Dan Duryea, Isa Miranda, Gwen Watford, Peter Madden

Dr Terror's House of Horrors
Director   Freddie Francis
Starring   Peter Cushing, Christopher Lee, Roy Castle, Donald Sutherland

The Earth Dies Screaming
Director   Terence Fisher
Starring   Willard Parker, Virginia Field, Dennis Price, Vanda Godsell

East Of Sudan
Director   Nathan Juran
Starring   Anthony Quayle, Sylvia Syms, Derek Fowlds, Jenny Agutter

Every Day's a Holiday
Director   James Hill
Starring   Freddie and the Dreamers, John Leyton, Mike Sarne, Ron Moody

King and Country
Director   Joseph Losey
Starring   Tom Courtenay, Dirk Bogarde, Leo McKern, Barry Foster

I've Gotta Horse
Director   Kenneth Hume
Starring   Billy Fury, Amanda Barrie, Michael Medwin, Marjorie Rhodes

Joey Boy
Director   Frank Launder
Starring   Harry H. Corbett, Stanley Baxter, Bill Fraser, Reg Varney

Just For You
Director   Douglas Hickox
Starring   Peter Asher, Gordon Waller

Khartoum
Director   Basil Dearden
Starring   Charlton Heston, Laurence Olivier, Richard Johnson, Ralph Richardson

Night Train to Paris
Director   Robert Douglas
Starring   Leslie Nielsen, Alizia Gur, Dorinda Stevens, Eric Pohlmann

The Projected Man
Director   Ian Curteis
Starring   Bryant Halliday, Mary Peach, Norman Wooland, Ronald Allen

Rotten to the Core
Director   John Boulting
Starring   Anton Rodgers, Thorley Walters, Eric Sykes, Ian Bannen

The Sicilians
Director   Ernest Morris
Starring   Robert Hutton, Reginald Marsh, Ursula Howells, Alex Scott

Spaceflight IC-1
Director   Bernard Knowles
Starring   Bill Williams, Norma West, John Cairney, Jeremy Longhurst

The Tomb of Ligeia
Director   Roger Corman
Starring   Vincent Price, Elizabeth Shepherd, John Westbrook, Oliver Johnston

Troubled Waters
Director   Stanley Goulder
Starring   Tab Hunter, Zena Walker, Andy Myers, Michael Goodliffe

Witchcraft
Director   Don Sharp
Starring   Jack Hedley, Lon Chaney Jnr, Marie Ney, Jill Dixon

1965

Casino Royale
Directors   John Huston, Ken Hughes, Robert Parrish, Val Guest, Joseph McGrath
Starring   Peter Sellers, Ursula Andress, David Niven, Orson Welles

Cul de Sac
Director   Roman Polanski
Starring   Donald Pleasence, Francoise Dorleac, Lionel Stander, Jack MacGowran

Daleks – Invasion Earth 2150 A.D.
Director   Gordon Flemyng
Starring   Peter Cushing, Bernard Cribbins, Ray Brooks, Jill Curzon

Doctor Who and the Daleks
Director   Gordon Flemyng
Starring   Peter Cushing, Roy Castle, Jennie Linden, Roberta Tovey

Georgy Girl
Director   Silvio Narizzano.
Starring   James Mason, Alan Bates, Lynn Redgrave, Charlotte Rampling

The Great St. Trinian's Train Robbery
Director   Frank Launder
Starring   George Cole, Frankie Howerd, Dora Bryan, Reg Varney

Monster of Terror (aka Die, Monster, Die!)
Director   Daniel Haller
Starring   Boris Karloff, Nick Adams, Freda Jackson, Patrick Magee

Life at the Top
Director   Ted Kotcheff
Starring   Laurence Harvey, Jean Simmons, Honor Blackman, Michael Craig

Mr Moto and the Persian Oil Case
Director   Ernest Morris
Starring   Henry Silva, Martin Wyldeck, Terence Longden, Sue Lloyd

Modesty Blaise
Director   Joseph Losey
Starring   Monica Vitti, Terence Stamp, Dirk Bogarde, Harry Andrews

The Murder Game
Director   Sidney Salkow
Starring   Ken Scott, Marla Landi, Trader Faulkner, Conrad Phillips

The Night Caller
Director   John Gilling
Starring   John Saxon, Maurice Denham, Patricia Haines, Alfred Burke

Othello
Director   Stuart Burge
Starring   Laurence Olivier, Frank Finlay, Maggie Smith, Robert Lang

The Psychopath
Director   Freddie Francis
Starring   Patrick Wymark, Margaret Johnston, John Standing, Alexander Knox

Sands of the Kalahari
Director   Cy Endfield
Starring   Stuart Whitman, Stanley Baker, Susannah York, Harry Andrews

The Skull
Director   Freddie Francis
Starring   Peter Cushing, Patrick Wymark, Christopher Lee, Jill Bennett

The Spy Who Came In from the Cold
Director   Martin Ritt
Starring   Richard Burton, Claire Bloom, Oskar Werner, Peter Van Eyke

A Study in Terror
Director   James Hill
Starring   John Neville, Donald Houston, John Fraser, Anthony Quayle

1966

Berserk!
Director   Jim O'Connolly
Starring   Joan Crawford, Ty Hardin, Diana Dors, Michael Gough

Calamity the Cow
Director   David Eastman
Starring   John Moulder-Brown, Elizabeth Dear, Stephen Brown, Philip Collins

The Family Way
Director   Roy Boulting
Starring   Hayley Mills, Hywel Bennett, John Mills, Marjorie Rhodes

Fathom
Director   Leslie Martinson
Starring   Anthony Franciosa, Raquel Welch, Ronald Fraser, Greta Chi

Half a Sixpence
Director   George Sidney
Starring   Tommy Steele, Julia Foster, Penelope Horner, Cyril Ritchard

A Man for All Seasons
Director   Fred Zinnemann
Starring   Paul Scofield, Wendy Hiller, Leo McKern, Orson Welles

The Spy With a Cold Nose
Director   Daniel Petrie
Starring   Laurence Harvey, Lionel Jeffries, Daliah Lavi, Eric Sykes

Torture Garden
Director   Freddie Francis.
Starring   Jack Palance, Burgess Meredith, Beverly Adams, Peter Cushing

The Trygon Factor
Director   Cyril Frankel
Starring   Stewart Granger, Susan Hampshire, Robert Morley, Cathleen Nesbitt

1967

Danger Route
Director   Seth Holt
Starring   Richard Johnson, Carol Lynley, Barbara Bouchet, Sylvia Syms

Don't Raise the Bridge, Lower the River
Director   Jerry Paris
Starring   Jerry Lewis, Terry-Thomas, Jacqueline Pearce, Bernard Cribbins

Duffy
Director   Robert Parish
Starring   James Coburn, James Mason, James Fox, Susannah York

Girl on a Motorcycle
Director   Jack Cardiff
Starring   Alain Delon, Marianne Faithfull, Roger Mutton, Marius Goring

Great Catherine
Director   Gordon Flemyng
Starring   Peter O'Toole, Zero Mostel, Jeanne Moreau, Jack Hawkins

Hostile Witness
Director   Ray Milland
Starring   Ray Milland, Sylvia Syms, Felix Aylmer, Raymond Huntley

Mrs Brown, You've Got a Lovely Daughter
Director   Saul Swimmer
Starring   Peter Noone and Herman's Hermits, Stanley Holloway, Mona Washbourne, Lance Percival

Oliver!
Director   Carol Reed
Starring   Ron Moody, Oliver Reed, Harry Secombe, Mark Lester

Salt & Pepper
Director   Richard Donner
Starring   Sammy Davis Jnr, Peter Lawford, Michael Bates, Ilona Rodgers

1968

The Adding Machine
Director   Jerome Epstein
Starring   Phyllis Diller, Milo O'Shea, Billie Whitelaw, Sydney Chaplin

Anne of a Thousand Days
Director   Charles Jarrott
Starring   Richard Burton, Genevieve Bujold, Irene Papas, Anthony Quayle

The Birthday Party
Director   William Friedkin
Starring   Robert Shaw, Patrick McGee, Dandy Nichols, Sydney Tafler

The Body Stealers
Director   Gerry Levy
Starring   George Sanders, Maurice Evans, Patrick Allen, Neil Connery

The File of the Golden Goose
Director   Sam Wanamaker
Starring   Yul Brynner, Charles Gray, Edward Woodward, John Barrie

The Looking Glass War
Director   Frank R. Pierson
Starring   Christopher Jones, Pia Degermark, Ralph Richardson, Anthony Hopkins

Negatives

Director — Peter Medak

Starring — Peter McEnery, Diane Cilento, Glenda Jackson, Maurice Denham

Otley

Director — Dick Clement

Starring — Tom Courtenay, Romy Schneider, Alan Badel, James Villiers

Romeo and Juliet

Director — Franco Zeffirelli

Starring — Leonard Whiting, Olivia Hussey, Laurence Olivier, Milo O'Shea

The Smashing Bird I Used to Know

Director — Robert Hartford-Davis

Starring — Madeline Hinde, Renee Asherson, Dennis Waterman, Patrick Mower

Till Death Us Do Part

Director — Norman Cohen

Starring — Warren Mitchell, Dandy Nichols, Anthony Booth, Una Stubbs

A Touch of Love

Director — Warris Hussein

Starring — Sandy Dennis, Ian McKellen, Michael Coles, John Standing

Twisted Nerve

Director — Roy Boulting

Starring — Hayley Mills, Hywel Bennett, Billie Whitelaw, Phyllis Calvert

2001: A Space Odyssey

Director — Stanley Kubrick

Starring — Keir, Dullea, Gary Lockwood, William Sylvester, Daniel Richter

1969

Cromwell

Director — Ken Hughes

Starring — Richard Harris, Alec Guinness, Robert Morley, Dorothy Tutin

Every Home Should Have One

Director — James Clark

Starring — Marty Feldman, Shelley Bergman, Judy Cornwell, Julie Ege

The Last Grenade

Director — Gordon Flemyng

Starring — Stanley Baker, Alex Cord, Honor Blackman, Richard Attenborough

Loot

Director — Silvio Narizzano

Starring — Richard Attenborough, Lee Remick, Hywel Bennett, Roy Holder

The Mind of Mr. Soames

Director — Alan Cooke

Starring — Terence Stamp, Robert Vaughn, Nigel Davenport, Donal Donnelly

The Oblong Box

Director — Gordon Hessler

Starring — Vincent Price, Christopher Lee, Alastair Williamson, Hilary Dwyer

The Promise

Director — Michael Hayes

Starring — Ian McKellen, John Castle, Susan Macready, Mary Jones

Scream and Scream Again

Director — Gordon Hessler

Starring — Vincent Price, Christopher Lee, Peter Cushing, Judy Huxtable

A Severed Head

Director — Dick Clement.

Starring — Lee Remick, Richard Attenborough, Ian Holm, Claire Bloom

Take a Girl Like You

Director — Jonathan Miller

Starring — Hayley Mills, Oliver Reed, Noel Harrison, Sheila Hancock

Three Sisters

Director — Laurence Olivier

Starring — Jeanne Watts, Joan Plowright, Louise Purnell, Derek Jacobi

1970

Dad's Army

Director — Norman Cohen

Starring — Arthur Lowe, John Le Mesurier, Clive Dunn, John Laurie

Cry of the Banshee

Director — Gordon Hessler

Starring — Vincent Price, Elisabeth Bergner, Essy Persson, Hugh Griffith

A Day in the Death of Joe Egg

Director — Peter Medak

Starring — Alan Bates, Janet Suzman, Peter Bowles, Sheila Gish

Fright

Director — Peter Collinson

Starring — Susan George, Honor Blackman, Ian Bannen, John Gregson

The House that Dripped Blood

Director — Peter John Duffell

Starring — Denholm Elliott, Joanna Dunham, Peter Cushing, Joss Ackland

I, Monster

Director — Stephen Weeks

Starring — Christopher Lee, Peter Cushing, Mike Raven, Richard Hurndall

Macbeth

Director — Roman Polanski

Starring — Jon Finch, Francesca Annis, Martin Shaw, Nicholas Selby

Puppet on a Chain

Director — Geoffrey Reeve

Starring — Sven-Bertil Taube, Barbara Parkins, Alexander Knox, Patrick Allen

Scrooge

Director — Ronald Neame

Starring — Albert Finney, Alec Guinness, Edith Evans, Kenneth More

There's a Girl in my Soup

Director — Roy Boulting

Starring — Peter Sellers, Goldie Hawn, Tony Britton, Nicky Henson

Wuthering Heights

Director — Robert Fuest

Starring — Anna Calder-Marshall, Timothy Dalton, Harry Andrews, Pamela Brown

Zee and Co.

Director — Brian G. Hutton

Starring — Elizabeth Taylor, Michael Caine, Susannah York, Margaret Leighton

1971

Crucible of Horror

Director — Victor Ritelis

Starring — Michael Gough, Yvonne Mitchell, Sharon Gurney, Simon Gough

Mary, Queen of Scots
Director   Charles Jarrot
Starring   Vanessa Redgrave, Glenda
              Jackson, Patrick McGoohan,
              Timothy Dalton

Something to Hide
Director   Alistair Reid
Starring   Peter Finch, Shelley Winters,
              Colin Blakely, John Stride

Who Slew Auntie Roo
Director   Curtis Harrington
Starring   Shelley Winters, Mark Lester,
              Ralph Richardson, Lionel Jeffries

Young Winston
Director   Richard Attenborough
Starring   Simon Ward, Peter Cellier,
              Ronald Hines, John Mills

1972

And Now The Screaming Starts!
Director   Roy Ward Baker
Starring   Peter Cushing, Herbert Lom,
              Patrick Magee, Ian Ogilvy

Alice's Adventures in Wonderland
Director   William Sterling
Starring   Fiona Fullerton, Peter Sellers,
              Michael Crawford, Robert
              Helpmann

The Asphyx
Director   Peter Newbrook
Starring   Robert Stephens, Robert Powell,
              Jane Lapotaire, Alex Scott

Asylum
Director   Roy Ward Baker
Starring   Peter Cushing, Britt Ekland,
              Herbert Lom, Patrick Magee

Bequest to the Nation
Director   James Cellen Jones
Starring   Glenda Jackson, Peter Finch,
              Michael Jayston, Anthony Quayle

The Boy Who Turned Yellow
Director   Michael Powell
Starring   Mark Dightam, Robert Eddison,
              Helen Weir, Brian Worth

The Creeping Flesh
Director   Freddie Francis
Starring   Christopher Lee, Peter Cushing,
              Lorna Heilbron, George Benson

The Day of the Jackal
Director   Fred Zinnemann
Starring   Edward Fox, Terence Alexander,
              Michel Auclair, Alan Badel

Hitler the Last Ten Days
Director   Ennio de Concini
Starring   Alec Guinness, Simon Ward,
              Adolfo Celi, Diane Cilento

The Homecoming
Director   Peter Hall
Starring   Cyril Cusack, Ian Holm, Michael
              Jayston, Vivien Merchant

**It's a 2' 6" Above the Ground World (aka The
Love Ban)**
Director   Ralph Thomas
Starring   Nanette Newman, Hywel Bennett,
              Russell Lewis, Simon Henderson

The Last Chapter
Director   David Tringham
Starring   Denholm Elliott, Susan
              Penhaligon

The Lovers
Director   Herbert Wise.
Starring   Richard Beckinsale, Paula Wilcox,
              Joan Scott, Susan Littler

Luther
Director   Guy Green
Starring   Stacy Keach, Patrick Magee, Hugh
              Griffith, Robert Stephens

Tales that Witness Madness
Director   Freddie Francis
Starring   Jack Hawkins, Donald Pleasance,
              Russell Lewis, Peter McEnery

The Wicker Man
Director   Robin Hardy
Starring   Edward Woodward, Christopher
              Lee, Diane Cilento, Britt Ekland

1973

The Beast Must Die
Director   Paul Annett
Starring   Calvin Lockhart, Peter Cushing,
              Charles Gray, Anton Diffring

Butley
Director   Harold Pinter
Starring   Alan Bates, Jessica Tandy, Richard
              O'Callaghan, Susan Engel

Craze
Director   Freddie Francis.
Starring   Jack Palance, Diana Dors, Julie
              Ege, Edith Evans

The Internecine Project
Director   Ken Hughes
Starring   James Coburn, Lee Grant, Harry
              Andrews, Ian Hendry

Soft Beds and Hard Battles
Director   Roy Boulting
Starring   Peter Sellers, Lila Kedrova, Curt
              Jurgens, Gabriella Licudi

Tales from the Crypt
Director   Freddie Francis
Starring   Ralph Richardson, Geoffrey
              Bayldon, Peter Cushing, Joan
              Collins

1974

Brannigan
Director   Douglas Hickox
Starring   John Wayne, Richard
              Attenborough, Judy Geeson, Mel
              Ferrer

Conduct Unbecoming
Director   Michael Anderson
Starring   Michael York, Richard
              Attenborough, Trevor Howard,
              Stacy Keach

Great Expectations
Director   Joseph Hardy
Starring   Michael York, Sarah Miles,
              Margaret Leighton, James Mason

The Land That Time Forgot
Director   Kevin Conor
Starring   Doug McClure, John McEnery,
              Susan Penhaligon, Keith Barron

Lisztomania
Director   Ken Russell
Starring   Roger Daltrey, Sara Kestleman,
              Paul Nicholas, Fiona Lewis

The Man Who Fell to Earth
Director   Nicolas Roeg
Starring   David Bowie, Rip Torn, Candy
              Clark, Buck Henry

Mr. Quilp
Director   Michael Tuchner
Starring   Anthony Newley, David
Hemmings, David Warner,
Michael Hordern

The Return of the Pink Panther
Director   Blake Edwards
Starring   Peter Sellers, Christopher
Plummer, Catherine Schell,
Herbert Lom

1975

The Adventure of Sherlock Holmes' Smarter Brother
Director   Gene Wilder
Starring   Gene Wilder, Madeline Kahn,
Marty Feldman, Dom DeLuise

The Omen
Director   Richard Donner
Starring   Gregory Peck, Lee Remick, Patrick
Troughton, David Warner

The Pink Panther Strikes Again
Director   Blake Edwards
Starring   Peter Sellers, Herbert Lom, Colin
Blakely, Leonard Rossiter

Sinbad and the Eye of the Tiger
Director   Sam Wanamaker
Starring   Patrick Wayne, Taryn Power,
Margaret Whiting, Jane Seymour

1976

Jabberwocky
Director   Terry Gilliam
Starring   Michael Palin, Max Wall,
Deborah Fallender, Warren
Mitchell

The Marriage of Figaro
Director   Peter Hall
Starring   Frederica Von Stade, Ileana
Cotrubas, Kiri Te Kanawa

Queen Kong
Director   Frank Agrama
Starring   Robin Askwith, Rula Lenska,
Valerie Leon, Roger Hammond

1977

The Boys From Brazil
Director   Franklin Schaffner
Starring   Gregory Peck, Laurence Olivier,
James Mason, Lilli Palmer

Dominique
Director   Michael Anderson
Starring   Jean Simmons, Jenny Agutter,
Cliff Robertson, Simon Ward

Force Ten from Navarone
Director   Guy Hamilton
Starring   Robert Shaw, Harrison Ford,
Edward Fox, Franco Nero

Prey
Director   Norman J Warren
Starring   Barry Stokes, Sally Faulkner,
Glory Annen, Sandy Chinney

The Revenge of the Pink Panther
Director   Blake Edwards
Starring   Peter Sellers, Herbert Lom,
Robert Webber, Dyan Cannon

1978

Alien
Director   Ridley Scott
Starring   Sigourney Weaver, John Hurt, Ian
Holm, Tom Skerritt

Dracula
Director   John Badham
Starring   Laurence Olivier, Donald
Pleasence, Frank Langella, Kate
Nelligan

Murder by Decree
Director   Bob Clark
Starring   James Mason, John Gielgud,
Donald Sutherland, Christopher
Plummer

The Odd Job
Director   Peter Medak
Starring   Graham Chapman, David Jason,
Diana Quick, Simon Williams

Saturn 3
Director   Stanley Donen
Starring   Farrah Fawcett, Kirk Douglas,
Harvey Keitel, Ed Bishop

The Thief of Baghdad
Director   Clive Donner
Starring   Roddy McDowall, Frank Finlay,
Peter Ustinov, Kabir Bedi

1979

Flash Gordon
Director   Michael Hodges
Starring   Sam J. Jones, Max Von Sydow,
Topol, Melody Anderson

SOS Titanic
Director   William Hale
Starring   David Janssen, Cloris Leachman,
Susan St James, David Warner

1980

The Elephant Man
Director   David Lynch
Starring   Anthony Hopkins, John Hurt,
Anne Bancroft, John Gielgud

Eye of the Needle
Director   Richard Marquand
Starring   Donald Sutherland, Kate
Neilligan, Christopher Cazenove,
Ian Bannen

History of the World Part 1
Director   Mel Brooks
Starring   Mel Brooks, Dom DeLuise,
Madeline Kahn, Cloris Leachman

Priest of Love
Director   Christopher Miles
Starring   Ian McKellen, Janet Suzman,
Helen Mirren, Penelope Keith

Ragtime
Director   Milos Forman
Starring   James Cagney, Pat O'Brien, James
Olson, Mary Steenburgen

1981

Brimstone and Treacle
Director   Richard Loncraine
Starring   Sting, Denholm Elliot, Joan
Plowright, Suzanna Hamilton

Five Days One Summer
Director   Fred Zinnemann
Starring   Sean Connery, Betsy Brantley,
Lambert Wilson, Jennifer Hilary

Gandhi
Director   Richard Attenborough
Starring   Ben Kingsley, Candice Bergen, Edward Fox, John Mills

The Hunger
Director   Tony Scott
Starring   Catherine Deneuve, David Bowie, Susan Sarandon, Cliff de Young

The Pirates of Penzance
Director   Wilford Leach
Starring   Kevin Kline, Linda Ronstadt, Patricia Routledge, Angela Lansbury

1982

The Hound of the Baskervilles
Director   Douglas Hickox
Starring   Ian Richardson, Donald Churchill, Denholm Elliott, Nicholas Clay

The Jigsaw Man
Director   Terence Young
Starring   Michael Caine, Laurence Olivier, Susan George, Robert Powell

The Keep
Director   Michael Mann
Starring   Scott Glenn, Alberta Watson, Jurgen Prochnow, Robert Prosky

The Lords of Discipline
Director   Franc Roddam
Starring   David Keith, Robert Prosky, G. D. Spradlin, Barbara Babcock

The Missionary
Director   Richard Loncraine
Starring   Michael Palin, Maggie Smith, Michael Hordern, Trevor Howard

Privates on Parade
Director   Michael Blakemore
Starring   Patrick Pearson, Michael Elphick, John Cleese, Dennis Quilley

The Sender
Director   Roger Christian
Starring   Kathryn Harrold, Zelijko Ivanek, Shirley Knight, Paul Freeman

The Sign of Four
Director   Desmond Davis
Starring   Ian Richardson, David Healy, Thorley Walters, Terence Rigby

1983

Bullshot
Director   Dick Clement
Starring   Alan Shearman, Diz White, Ron House, Frances Tomelty

The Company of Wolves
Director   Neil Jordan
Starring   Angela Lansbury, David Warner, Graham Crowden, Brian Glover

1984

The Bride
Director   Franc Roddam
Starring   Sting, Jennifer Beals, Clancy Brown, David Rappaport

The Doctor and the Devils
Director   Freddie Francis
Starring   Timothy Dalton, Jonathan Pryce, Twiggy, Julian Sands

1984

Director   Michael Radford
Starring   John Hurt, Richard Burton, Suzanna Hamilton, Cyril Cusack

A Passage to India
Director   David Lean
Starring   Judy Davis, Peggy Ashcroft, Alec Guinness, Victor Banerjee

Starship
Director   Roger Christian
Starring   Tyler Coppin, Ralph Cotterill, Adam Cockburn, Tami James

Water
Director   Dick Clement
Starring   Michael Caine, Valerie Perrine, Billy Connolly, Leonard Rossiter

1985

Absolute Beginners
Director   Julien Temple
Starring   Patsy Kensit, David Bowie, Eddie O'Connell, Mandy Rice Davies

Link
Director   Richard Franklin
Starring   Elisabeth Shue, Terrance Stamp, Steven Pinner, Richard Garnett

Out of Africa
Director   Sydney Pollack
Starring   Meryl Streep, Robert Redford, Klaus Maria Brandauer, Michael Kitchen

1986

Cry Freedom
Director   Richard Attenborough
Starring   Kevin Kline, Denzel Washington, Penelope Wilton, Alec McCowen

84 Charing Cross Road
Director   David Jones
Starring   Anne Bancroft, Anthony Hopkins, Judi Dench, Maurice Denham

Hearts of Fire
Director   Richard Marquand
Starring   Bob Dylan, Rupert Everett, Fiona Flanagan, Lesley Donaldson

The Princess Bride
Director   Rob Reiner
Starring   Cary Elwes, Mandy Patinkin, Chris Sarandon, Christopher Guest

Shanghai Surprise
Director   Jim Goddard
Starring   Sean Penn, Madonna, Paul Freeman, Richard Griffiths

1987

Gorillas in the Mist
Director   Michael Apted
Starring   Sigourney Weaver, Bryan Brown, Julie Harris, Iain Cuthbertson

The Lonely Passion of Judith Hearne
Director   Jack Clayton
Starring   Maggie Smith, Bob Hoskins, Wendy Hiller, Prunella Scales

White Mischief
Director   Michael Radford
Starring   Greta Scacchi, Charles Dance, Joss Ackland, Sarah Miles

1988

Bert Rigby, You're a Fool
Director   Carl Reiner
Starring   Robert Lindsay, Robbie Coltrane, Anne Bancroft, Corbin Bernsen

Endless Game
Director   Bryan Forbes
Starring   Albert Finney, George Segal, Ian Holm,

Erik the Viking
Director   Terry Jones
Starring   Tim Robbins, Mickey Rooney, John Cleese, Eartha Kitt

Henry V
Director   Kenneth Branagh
Starring   Derek Jacobi, Kenneth Branagh, Simon Shepherd, James Larkin

How to Get Ahead in Advertising
Director   Bruce Robinson
Starring   Richard E. Grant, Rachel Ward, Richard Wilson, Jacqueline Tong

Mountains of the Moon
Director   Rob Rafelson
Starring   Patrick Bergin, Iain Glen, Richard E. Grant, Fiona Shaw

Strapless
Director   David Hare
Starring   Blair Brown, Bruno Ganz, Bridget Fonda, Alan Howard

1989

About Face
Director   John Henderson
Starring   Amanda Dickinson, Michael Gambon,

The Choice
Director   Idrissa Ouedraogo
Starring   Aoua Guiraud, Moussa Bologo, Ousmana Sawadogo, Fatima Ouedraogo

The Free Frenchmen
Director   Jim Goddard
Starring   Derek de Lint, Corinne Dacla,

Killing Dad
Director   Michael Austin
Starring   Denholm Elliott, Julie Walters, Richard E. Grant, Anna Massey

Nuns on the Run
Director   Jonathan Lynn
Starring   Eric Idle, Robbie Coltrane, Camille Coduri, Janet Suzman

1990

Hamlet
Director   Franco Zeffirelli
Starring   Mel Gibson, Glenn Close, Alan Bates, Paul Scofield

A Kiss Before Dying
Director   James Dearden
Starring   Matt Dillon, Sean Young, Max von Sydow, Jim Fyfe

The Rainbow Thief
Director   Alejandro Jodorowsky
Starring   Peter O'Toole, Omar Sharif, Christopher Lee

Robin Hood Prince of Thieves
Director   Kevin Reynolds
Starring   Kevin Costner, Morgan Freeman, Alan Rickman, Christian Slater

Three Men and a Little Lady
Director   Emile Ardonilo
Starring   Tom Selleck, Steve Guttenberg, Ted Danson, Nancy Travis

1991

Blame it on the Bellboy
Director   Mark Herman
Starring   Dudley Moore, Bryan Brown, Richard Griffiths, Andreas Katsulas

Chaplin
Director   Richard Attenborough
Starring   Robert Downey Jnr, Geraldine Chaplin, Dan Ackroyd, Kevin Dunn

The Crying Game
Director   Neil Jordan
Starring   Forest Whitaker, Miranda Richardson, Stephen Rea, Jim Broadbent

The Other Woman
Director   Simon Moore
Starring   Forest Whitaker, Miranda Richardson,

Wuthering Heights
Director   Peter Kosminski
Starring   Juliette Binoche, Ralph Fiennes, Janet McTeer, Sophie Ward

1992

Damage
Director   Louis Malle
Starring   Jeremy Irons, Juliette Binoche, Miranda Richardson, Rupert Graves

The Muppet Christmas Carol
Director   Brian Henson
Starring   Michael Caine, Steven MacKintosh, Meredith Brown, Robin Weaver

Splitting Heirs
Director   Robert Young
Starring   Eric Idle, Rick Moranis, Barbara Hershey, Catherine Zeta Jones

The Turn of the Screw
Director   Rusty Lemorande
Starring   Patsy Kensit, Stéphane Audran, Julian Sands, Clare Szekeres

1993

Four Weddings and a Funeral
Director   Mike Newell
Starring   Hugh Grant, Simon Callow, Andie MacDowell, Kristin Scott Thomas

Mary Shelley's Frankenstein
Director   Kenneth Branagh
Starring   Robert De Niro, Kenneth Branagh, Tom Hulce, Helena Bonham Carter

The Funny Man
Director   Simon Sprackling
Starring   Christopher Lee, Tim James, Benny Young, Pauline Chan

Intimate with a Stranger
Director   Melanie Woods
Starring   Roderick Mangin-Turner, Daphne Nayer, Amy Tolsky, Lorelei King

The Never Ending Story III
Director   Peter MacDonald
Starring   Jason James Richter, Melody Kay, Freddie Jones, Ryan Bollman

Princess Caraboo
Director Michael Austin
Starring Jim Broadbent, Phoebe Cates, Wendy Hughes, Kevin Kline

Shadowlands
Director Richard Attenborough
Starring Anthony Hopkins, Debra Winger, John Wood, Edward Hardwicke

1994

Carrington
Director Christopher Hampton
Starring Emma Thompson, Jonathan Pryce, Steven Waddington, Samuel West

Haunted
Director Lewis Gilbert
Starring Aidan Quinn, Kate Beckinsale, Anthony Andrews, John Gielgud

Judge Dredd
Director Danny Cannon
Starring Sylvester Stallone, Diane Lane, Armand Assante, Rob Schneider

The Madness of King George
Director Nick Hynter
Starring Nigel Hawthorne, Helen Mirren, Ian Holm, Amanda Donohoe

Restoration
Director Michael Hoffman
Starring Robert Downey Jnr, Sam Neill, Ian McKellen, David Thewlis

1995

Hamlet
Director Kenneth Branagh
Starring Kenneth Branagh, Kate Winslet, Derek Jacobi, Julie Christie

In the Bleak Midwinter
Director Kenneth Branagh
Starring Michael Maloney, Richard Briers, Joan Collins, Nicholas Farrell

Muppet Treasure Island
Director Brian Henson
Starring Tim Curry, Kevin Bishop, Steve Whitmire, Frank Oz

101 Dalmations
Director Steve Herek
Starring Glenn Close, Jeff Daniels, Joan Plowright, Joely Richardson

Othello
Director Oliver Parker
Starring Laurence Fishburne, Kenneth Branagh, Irene Jacob, Nathaniel Parker

Sense and Sensibility
Director Ang Lee
Starring Hugh Grant, Emma Thompson, Alan Rickman, Kate Winslet

The Wind in the Willows
Director Terry Jones
Starring Steve Coogan, Eric Idle, Terry Jones, John Cleese

White Squall
Director Ridley Scott
Starring Jeff Bridges, Caroline Goodall, John Savage, Scott Wolf

1996

Amy Foster
Director Beeban Kidron
Starring Vincent Perez, Rachel Weisz, Ian McKellen, Joss Ackland

The Borrowers
Director Peter Hewitt
Starring John Goodman, Jim Broadbent, Hugh Laurie, Mark Williams

Evita
Director Alan Parker
Starring Madonna, Antonio Banderas, Jonathan Pryce, Jimmy Nail

Fairy Tale – A True Story
Director Charles Sturridge
Starring Peter O'Toole, Harvey Keitel, Florence Hoath. Phoebe Nicholls

G.I. Jane
Director Ridley Scott
Starring Demi Moore, Viggo Mortensen, Anne Bancroft, Jason Beghe

In Love and War
Director Richard Attenborough
Starring Chris O'Donnell, Sandra Bullock, Mackenzie Astin, Ingrid Lacey

London Suite
Director Jay Sandrich
Starring Kelsey Grammer, Michael Richards, Madeline Kahn, Richard Mulligan

Masterminds
Director Roger Christian
Starring Patrick Stewart, Brenda Fricker, Vincent Kartheiser, Bradley Whitford

Mrs Dalloway
Director Marleen Gorris
Starring Vanessa Redgrave, Natascha McElhone, Rupert Graves, Michael Kitchen

Shooting Fish
Director Stefan Schwartz
Starring Dan Futterman, Kate Beckinsale, Stuart Townsend, Nickolas Grace

The Wings of the Dove
Director Iain Softly
Starring Helena Bonham Carter, Charlotte Rampling, Michael Gambon, Linus Roache

1997

An Inch Over the Horizon
Director Robert Young
Starring Bob Hoskins, Gemma Jones, Maureen Lipman, Sadie Frost

The Avengers
Director Jeremiah Chechik
Starring Ralph Fiennes, Uma Thurman, Sean Connery, Jim Broadbent

Elizabeth
Director Shekhar Kapur
Starring Cate Blanchett, Geoffrey Rush, Joseph Fiennes, Richard Attenborough

Lost in Space
Director Stephen Hopkins
Starring William Hurt, Mimi Rogers, Heather Graham, Gary Oldman

The Parent Trap
Director   Nancy Myers
Starring   Lindsay Lohan, Dennis Quaid, Natasha Richardson, Elaine Hendrix

Sliding Doors
Director   Peter Howitt
Starring   Gwyneth Paltrow, John Hannah, John Lynch, Jeanne Tripplehorn Young

1998

Elephant Juice
Director   Sam Miller
Starring   Emanuelle Béart, Sean Gallagher, Daniel Lapaine, Daniela Nardini

Entrapment
Director   Jon Amiel
Starring   Sean Connery, Catherine Zeta-Jones, Will Patton, Ving Rhames

Onegin
Director   Martha Fiennes
Starring   Ralph Fiennes, Toby Stephens, Liv Tyler, Lena Headey

Felicia's Journey
Director   Atom Egoyan
Starring   Bob Hoskins, Arsine Khanjian, Elaine Cassidy, Sheila Reid

Gladiator
Director   Ridley Scott
Starring   Russell Crowe, Joaquin Phoenix, Connie Nielsen, Oliver Reed

Hilary and Jackie
Director   Anand Tucker
Starring   Emily Watson, Rachel Griffiths, David Morrissey, James Frain

The Mummy
Director   Steve Sommers
Starring   Brendan Fraser, Rachel Weisz, John Hannah, Arnold Vosloo

Notting Hill
Director   Roger Michell
Starring   Julia Roberts, Hugh Grant, Hugh Bonneville, James Dreyfus

Shakespeare in Love
Director   John Madden
Starring   Gwyneth Paltrow, Geoffrey Rush, Joseph Fiennes, Martin Clunes

Simon Magus
Director   Ben Hopkins
Starring   Noah Taylor, Stuart Townsend, Sean McGinley, Embeth Davidtz

Sleepy Hollow
Director   Tim Burton
Starrring   Johnny Depp, Christina Ricci, Miranda Richardson, Michael Gambon

1999

Billy Elliot
Director   Stephen Daldry
Starring   Jamie Bell, Jean Haywood, Jamie Draven, Julie Walters

Black Adder (*Millennium Dome Project*)
Director   Paul Weiland
Starring   Rowan Atkinson, Tony Robinson, Miranda Richardson, Tim McInnery

Circus
Director   Robert Walker
Starring   John Hannah, Famke Jenssen, Peter Stormare, Eddie Izzard

The End Of The Affair
Director   Neil Jordan
Starring   Ralph Fiennes, Stephen Rea, Julianne Moore, James Bolam

Eyes Wide Shut
Director   Stanley Kubrick
Starring   Tom Cruise, Nicole Kidman, Madison Eginton, Jackie Sawiris

Kevin & Perry Go Large
Director   Ed Bye
Starring   Harry Enfield, Kathy Burke, Rhys Ifans, Laura Fraser

Leprechauns
Director   John Henderson
Starring   Randy Quaid, Whoopi Goldberg, Roger Daltrey, Zoe Wanamaker

Love's Labours Lost
Director   Kenneth Branagh
Starring   Kenneth Branagh, Alessandro Nivola, Alicia Silverstone, Matthew Lillard

Maybe Baby
Director   Ben Elton
Starring   Joely Richardson, Matthew MacFadyen, Hugh Laurie, Adrian Lester

102 Dalmatians
Director   Kevin Lima
Starring   Glenn Close, Gérard Depardieu, Ioan Gruffud, Alice Evans

Women Talking Dirty
Director   Coky Giedroyc
Starring   Helen Bohnam Carter, Gina McKee, Eileen Atkins, Kenneth Cranham

2000

Bedazzled
Director   Harold Ramis
Starring   Brendan Fraser, Elizabeth Hurley, Frances O'Connor, Miriam Shor

Bridget Jones's Diary
Director   Sharon Maguire
Starring   Renee Zellweger, Hugh Grant, Colin Firth, James Faulkner

The Calling
Director   Richard Caesar
Starring   Laura Harris, Richard Lintern, Francis Magee, Alex Roe-Brown

Chocolat
Director   Lasse Hallstrom
Starring   Alfred Molina, Carrie-Anne Moss, Aurelien Parent-Koenig, Judi Dench

Crush
Director   John McKay
Starring   Andie MacDowell, Imelda Staunton, Anna Chancellor, Kenny Doughty

Dog Eat Dog
Director   Moody Shoaibi
Starring   Mark Tonderai, Nathan Constance, Alan Davies, Gary Kemp

Endgame
Director   Gary Wicks
Starring   Daniel Newman, Corey Johnson, Toni Barry, Mark McGann

Eric & Ramzy – La Tour Montparnasse Infernale
Director   Charles Nemes
Starring   Eric Judor, Ramzy Bedia, Marina Fois, Serge Riaboukine

The Golden Bowl
Director   James Ivory
Starring   Kate Beckinsale, James Fox, Angelica Houston, Nick Nolte

Killing Me Softly
Director   Chen Kaige
Starring   Heather Graham, Joseph Fiennes, Natascha McElhone, Ulrich Thomsen

The Mummy Returns
Director   Stephen Sommers
Starring   Brenden Fraser, Rachel Weisz, John Hannah, Arnold Vosloo

Not I
Director   Neil Jordan
Starring   Julianne Moore

Possession
Director   Neil La Bute
Starring   Gwyneth Paltrow, Aaron Eckhart, Jeremy Northam, Jennifer Ehle

Snatch
Director   Guy Ritchie
Starring   Jason Statham, Alan Ford, Brad Pitt, Vinnie Jones

Spy Game
Director   Tony Scott
Starring   Robert Redford, Brad Pitt, Catherine McCormack, Stephen Dillance

Unconditional Love
Director   P.J. Hogan
Starring   Kathy Bates, Rupert Everett, Meredith Eaton, Peter Sarsgaard

2001

About A Boy
Director   Paul Weitz, Chris Weitz
Starring   Hugh Grant, Toni Collette, Nicholas Hoult, Rachel Weisz

Anita & Me
Director   Metin Hausayn
Starring   Kabir Bedi, Max Beesley, Sanjeev Bhasker, Kathy Burke

Below
Director   David Tuohy
Starring   Chuck Ellswood, Crispin Layfield, Holt McCallany, Bruce Greenwood

Bend It Like Beckham
Director   Gurinder Chadha
Starring   Parminder K. Nagra, Keira Knightley, Jonathan Rhys-Meyers, Anupam Kher

Dirty Pretty Things
Director   Stephen Frears
Starring   Chiwetel Ejiofor, Audrey Tautou, Sergi Lopez, Sophie Okonedo

The Four Feathers
Director   Shekhar Kapur
Starring   Wes Bentley, Heath Ledger, Mohamed Bouich, Campbell Brown

Gosford Park
Director   Robert Altman
Starring   Maggie Smith, Micheal Gambon, Kristin Scott Thomas, Camilla Rutherford

Harry Potter and the Philosopher's Stone
Director   Chris Columbus
Starring   Richard Harris, Maggie Smith, Daniel Radcliffe, Robbie Coltrane

The Hours
Director   Stephen Daldry
Starring   Nicole Kidman, Julianne Moore, Meryl Streep, Stephen Dillane

The Shipping News
Director   Lasse Hallstrom
Starring   Kevin Spacey, Julianne Moore, Judi Dench, Cate Blanchett

Two Men Went To War
Director   John Henderson
Starring   Kenneth Cranham, Leo Bill, Derek Jacobi, Rosanna Lavelle

2002

Blackball
Director   Mel Smith
Starring   Paul Kaye, Bernard Cribbins, James Cromwell, Alice Evans

Calendar Girls
Director   Nigel Cole
Starring   Annette Crosbie, Philip Glenister, Celia Imrie, John-Paul Macleod

Cheeky
Director   David Thewlis
Starring   David Thewlis, Trudie Styler, Johnny Vegas

To Kill a King
Director   Mike Barker
Starring   Tim Roth, Dougray Scott, Rupert Everett, Olivia Williams

Ella Enchanted
Director   Tommy O'Haver
Starring   Anne Hathaway, Hugh Dancy, Cary Elwes

Harry Potter and the Chamber Of Secrets
Director   Chris Columbus
Starring   Daniel Radcliffe, Emma Watson, Rupert Grint, Richard Harris

I Captured the Castle
Director   Tim Flywell
Starring   Romola Garai, Rose Byrne, Henry Thomas, Marc Blucas

If Only
Director   Jil Junger
Starring   Jennifer Love Hewitt, Lucy Davenport, Diana Hardcastle, Paul Nicholls

Johnny English
Director   Peter Howitt
Starring   Rowan Atkinson, John Malkovich, Natalie Imbruglia, Ben Miller

The Life of David Gale
Director   Alan Parker
Starring   Kevin Spacey, Kate Winslet, Laura Linney, Gabriel Mann

Love Actually
Director   Richard Curtis
Starring   Laura Linney, Liam Neeson, Martine McCutcheon, Hugh Grant

My House in Umbria
Director   Richard Loncraine
Starring   Maggie Smith, Chris Cooper,
             Timothy Spall, Ronnie Barker

Neverland
Director   Marc Foster
Starring   Johnny Depp, Kate Winslet, Julie
             Christie, Dustin Hoffman

Second Nature
Director   Ben Bolt
Starring   Alec Baldwin, Powers Boothe,
             Cosima Shaw, Georgina Bouzova

Sylvia
Director   Christine Jeffs
Starring   Gwyneth Paltrow, Daniel Craig,
             Jared Harris, Blythe Danner

Wondrous Oblivion
Director   Paul Morrison
Starring   Sam Smith, Delroy Lindo, Emily
             Woof, Stanley Townsend

2003

Alexander
Director   Oliver Stone
Starring   Anthony Hopkins, Angelina Jolie,
             Val Kilmer, Christopher Plummer

Bridget Jones: The Edge of Reason
Director   Beeban Kidron
Starring   Renee Zellweger, Colin Firth,
             Hugh Grant, Tim Broadbent

Five Children and It
Director   John Stephenson
Starring   Kenneth Branagh, Zoe
             Wanamaker, Freddie Highmore,
             Norman Wisdom

Harry Potter and the Prisoner of Azkaban
Director   Alfonso Cuaron
Starring   Daniel Radcliffe, Robbie
             Coltrane, Michael Gambon, Alan
             Rickman

The Life and Death of Peter Sellers
Director   Stephen Hopkins
Starring   Geoffrey Rush, Charlize Theron,
             Emily Watson, John Lithgow

Shaun of the Dead
Director: Edgar Wright
Starring: Simon Pegg, Kate Ashfield, Nick
             Frost, Lucy Davis

Stage Beauty
Director: Richard Eyre
Starring: Tom Wilkinson, Billy Crudup,
             Ben Chaplin, Claire Danes

Thunderbirds
Director: Jonathan Frakes
Starring: Brady Corbet, Deborah Weston,
             Sophia Myles, Bill Paxton

Troy
Director: Wolfgang Peterson
Starring: Brad Pitt, Julian Glover, Brian
             Cox, Nathan Jones

Wimbledon
Director: Richard Loncraine
Starring: Kirsten Dunst, Paul Bettany, Kyle
             Hyde, Robert Lindsay

2004

Alfie
Director: Charles Shyer
Starring: Jude Law, Jane Krakowski, Marisa
             Tomei, Susan Sarandon

Around the World in 80 Days
Director: Frank Coraci
Starring: Jackie Chan, Steve Coogan,
             Robert Fyfe, Jim Broadbent

Batman Begins
Director: Christopher Nolan
Starring: Christian Bale, Michael Caine,
             Liam Neeson, Morgan Freeman

Bride and Prejudice
Director: Gurinder Chadha
Starring: Aishwarya Rai, Martin
             Henderson, Daniel Gillies,
             Naveen Andrews

Closer
Director: Mike Nichols
Starring: Natalie Portman, Jude Law, Julia
             Roberts, Clive Owen

Colour Me Kubrick
Director: Brian W. Cook
Starring: John Malkovich, Richard E.
             Grant, Leslie Phillips, Ken Russell

The Hitchhiker's Guide to the Galaxy
Director: Garth Jennings
Starring: Martin Freeman, Mos Def, Sam
             Rockwell, Bill Nighy

The Russian Dolls
Director: Cedric Klapisch
Starring: Lucy Gordon, Frederique Bel,
             Kevin Bishop, Cecile de France

Mrs Henderson Presents
Director: Stephen Frears
Starring: Judi Dench, Bob Hoskins, Thelma
             Barlow, Will Young

Sahara
Director: Breck Eisner
Starring: Matthew McConaughey, Penelope
             Cruz, William H. Macy, Delroy
             Lindo

Star Wars: Episode III – Revenge of the Sith
Director: George Lucas
Starring: Ewan McGregor, Hayden
             Christensen, Samuel L. Jackson,
             Christopher Lee

Where the Truth Lies
Director: Atom Egoyan
Starring: Kevin Bacon, Colin Firth, Alison
             Lohman, Sonja Bennett

From the year 2000, the following television productions have also been made at Shepperton Studios:

Being April
Born and Bred
Born to Die
Combat Sheep
Conspiracy
The Cruise
The Crust
Doctor Terrible's House of Horribles
Emma Brodie
Falklands Play
Fame Academy
The Gathering Storm
The Glass
The Heart of Me
Jack
Last of the Summer Wine
Poirot
Pollyanna
Robot Wars
Shackleton
Silent Witness VIII
Sons and Lovers
Sport Relief
State of Play
Strange
Techno Games
Thomas the Tank Engine
U Get Me
Walking with Cavemen
The Young Visitors

Bob Penn

Acknowledgements

The author and publisher would like to thank the following people for their help and support with this book:

Lord Attenborough
Sir John Mills
Sir Ridley Scott
Tony Scott
Tim Bevan
David Parfitt
Gurinder Chadha
The Kubrick Estate
Tony Frewin
Bryan Forbes
Freddie Francis
Pam Francis
Sheila Penn
Angela Douglas
Mike Hodges
Iris Rose
Dick Knapman
John Lee
Bfi Stills Department
Michael Putland at Retna
George Lewis – Designer
Amelia Granger
Richard Blanshard
Charlie Cobb
Adam Blackie
Gareth Snowden-Davies
Alison Parker
Roy Pembroke
Claire Watts
Mark Tan
Victor Morrison
Nick Pollard
Paul Medcalf – Avocet Typeset
Richard Howard
Patricia Horrocks

At Pinewood Shepperton

Michael Grade
Ivan Dunleavy
Steve Jaggs
David Wight
Gary Stone
Dave Godfrey
Nick Smith
Julia Kenny
Emma Budgen
Peter Wicks
Emma Molony
Rob Langridge

At CANAL + IMAGE UK Ltd
Special thanks to John Herron, Dennis Hall and Michael Dunsford

The publisher would particularly like to thank those who contributed personal accounts of their work in the film business and their association with Shepperton studios.

David Parfitt
Gemma Jackson
Robin O' Donoghue
Mark Sanger
Neil Corbould
George Frost
Pat Eustace
Sybil Robinson
Keith Robinson
Roy Pembroke
Terry Sharratt
Pam Francis
Dave Godfrey
Gary Stone

Very special thanks to Tim Forrester at Pinewood Shepperton, without whom this project would not have been possible.

Bibliography

The following publications and associated media have proved most useful in researching this book and ensuring accuracy of both facts and quotes.

I am grateful to each title and each author. However, I single out Derek Threadgall and his book *Shepperton Studios – An Independent View* for special mention. Few books can ever have been quite as encyclopaedic in detail on a subject as this one and it did indeed prove a mighty useful source of reference, which I would recommend to anyone who wants a blow-by-blow account of Shepperton's first 60 years as an independent film studio.

Morris Bright

Books:

Ash, Russell *The Top 10 of Film* (Dorling Kindersley, 2003)

Brewer's Cinema (Cassell, 1995)

Cinema Year by Year 1894–2003 (DK Publishing, 2003)

Cotrell, John & Fergus Cashin *Richard Burton* (Coronet Books, 1974)

Guest, Val *So You Want to be in Pictures* (Reynolds & Hearn, 2001)

Hepburn, Katharine *The Making of The African Queen or How I went to Africa with Bogart, Bacall and Huston and almost lost my mind* (Century, 1987)

Higham, Charles *The Rise and Fall of an American Genius – Orson Welles* (New English Library, 1986)

Lewis, Roger *The Real Life of Laurence Olivier* (Arrow, 1996)

McFarlane, Brian *An Autobiography of British Cinema* (Methuen, 1997)

Niven, David *The Moon's a Balloon* (Hamish Hamilton, 1971)

Olivier, Laurence *Confessions of an Actor* (Orion, 2002)

Quinlan, David *Quinlan's Film Directors* (BT Batsford, 1999)

Radio Times Guide to Films, 2004 Edition (BBC Worldwide, 2003)

Robertson, Patrick *The Guinness Book of Movie Facts and Feats* (Guinness Publishing, 1991)

Sikov, Ed *Mr Strangelove* (Sidgwick & Jackson, 2002)

Threadgall, Derek *Shepperton Studios – An Independent View* (British Film Institute, 1994)

Walker, Alexander *Peter Sellers* (Wiedenfeld & Nicholson, 1981)

Walker, John *Halliwell's Film Guide 2004* (Harper Collins Entertainment, 2003)

Walker, *John Halliwell's Who's Who in the Movies 14th Edition* (Harper Collins Entertainment, 2001)

Warren, Patricia *British Film Studios – An Illustrated History* (BT Batsford, 1995)

Robb, Brian J *The Pocket Essential – Ridley Scott* (Pocket Essentials, 2002)

Audio commentaries and features on DVD

Shakespeare In Love (Columbia Tristar Home Video, 1999)
Chocolat (Miramax Home Entertainment, 2001)

The Pink Panther Film Collection (MGM Home Entertainment, 2003)

The Omen Trilogy – 25th Anniversary Edition (Twentieth Century Fox Home Entertainment, 2001)

Useful internet sites

www.imdb.com
www.littlegoldenguy.com
www.bafta.org
www.bfi.org.uk
www.pinewoodshepperton.com

Each chapter in this book is introduced via a series of montage images. The pictures used in each section are as follows:

History
Lawrence Olivier in *The Entertainer* 1960
Shepperton House
A scene from Moulin Rouge 1953

Early Classics
Vivien Leigh in the lead role of *Anna Karenina* (1948) surrounded by fellow cast and crew
Alec Guinness as King Charles I in *Cromwell* (1969)
A haunting set for *Anna Karenina* (1948)
A scene from *Sanders of the River* 1934

Gritty Realism
James Fox and Dirk Bogarde, who play Tom and Hugo Barrett, in a moment away from filming Harold Pinter's claustrophobic story of manipulation and envy, *The Servant* (1963)
Tom Courtenay on location for *Billy Liar* (1962)
Director Bryan Forbes sharing a laugh with friend and producer Richard Attenborough, on location for their film, *The L-Shaped Room* (1962)

Best Sellers
Peter Sellers in *Revenge of the Pink Panther* (1977)
Herbert Lom in *Revenge of the Pink Panther* (1977)
Peter Sellers in *I'm All Right Jack* (1959)
Peter Sellers in *Heaven's Above* (1962)

Horror
Roy Castle in *Dr Terror's House of Horrors* (1964)
A scene from *Asylum* (1972)
Peter Cushing in *Dr Terror's House of Horrors* (1964)

Mind Games
Gregory Peck, Lee Remick, Billy Whitelaw, in *The Omen* (1975)

Epics
David Niven on the set of *Bonnie Prince Charlie* (1947)
On the set of *Oliver!* (1967)
On the set of *SOS Titanic* (1979)

Great Scotts
Sigourney Weaver in Ridley Scott's *Alien* (1978)
Tony Scott outside 'T' stage at Shepperton
Tony Scott enjoying the end of production party for *The Hunger* (1981)
Ridley Scott outside 'R' stage at Shepperton
Russell Crowe in Ridley Scott's *Gladiator* (1998)

Attenborough
Attenborough directing *Cry Freedom* (1986)
On the set of *Cry Freedom* (1986) with Richard Attenborough and Kevin Kline.

Branagh
Branagh looking through the stage - *Hamlet* (1995)
Branagh with Emma Thompson in *Henry V* (1988)
Branagh on the set of *Love Labours Lost* (1999)

Working Title Films
Hugh Grant in *Four Weddings and a Funeral* (1993)
A scene from *Bridget Jones Diary* (2000)
Rowan Atkinson in *Four Weddings and a Funeral* (1993)

Small Budget Big Box Office
A scene from *The Madness of King George* (1994)
A scene from *Bend it Like Beckham* (2001)

Shepperton Studios

Tracy Reed plays the beautiful Miss Scott, in
Dr Strangelove (1963)

Copyright

To the best of our knowledge the copyright holders of the pictures listed are as follows. Every effort has been made to contact the copyright owners for permission.

Film	Company	Page no.	Film	Company	Page no.	Film	Company	Page no.
The Omen	20 C Fox	162 & 163	Bonnie Prince Charlie	CANAL+IMAGE	192	The Servant	CANAL+IMAGE	97
The Omen	20 C Fox	164	Darling	CANAL+IMAGE	98	The Servant	CANAL+IMAGE	97
The Omen	20 C Fox	166	Darling	CANAL+IMAGE	99	The Sound Barrier	CANAL+IMAGE	34
The Omen	20 C Fox	167	Heavens Above!	CANAL+IMAGE	109	The Third Man	CANAL+ IMAGE	64
The Omen	20 C Fox	168 & 169	Heavens Above!	CANAL+IMAGE	119	The Third Man	CANAL+ IMAGE	65
The Omen	20 C Fox	321	Hobson's Choice	CANAL+IMAGE	70	The Third Man	CANAL+ IMAGE	65
Alien	20 C Fox	228	Hobson's Choice	CANAL+IMAGE	71	The Third Man	CANAL+ IMAGE	65
Alien	20 C Fox	233	Hobson's Choice	CANAL+IMAGE	384	The Third Man	CANAL+IMAGE	cover
Alien	20 C Fox	233	I'm All Right Jack	CANAL+IMAGE	109	The Wicker Man	CANAL+IMAGE	182
Alien	20 C Fox	233	I'm All Right Jack	CANAL+IMAGE	113	The Wicker Man	CANAL+IMAGE	183
Alien	20 C Fox	234	I'm All Right Jack	CANAL+IMAGE	115	The Wicker Man	CANAL+IMAGE	183
Alien	20 C Fox	235	I'm All Right Jack	CANAL+IMAGE	252	The Wicker Man	CANAL+IMAGE	184
Alien	20 C Fox	cover	Loot	CANAL+IMAGE	254	The Wicker Man	CANAL+IMAGE	184
Asylum	Amicus	135	Only Two Can Play	CANAL+IMAGE	110	The Wicker Man	CANAL+IMAGE	185
Dr Terror's House of Horrors	Amicus	134	Only Two Can Play	CANAL+IMAGE	116	The Wicker Man	CANAL+IMAGE	186
Dr Terror's House of Horrors	Amicus	135	Only Two Can Play	CANAL+IMAGE	117	The Wicker Man	CANAL+IMAGE	187
Torture Garden	Amicus	138	Only Two Can Play	CANAL+IMAGE	117	Gosford Park	Capital Films	328
Torture Garden	Amicus	143	Only Two Can Play	CANAL+IMAGE	118	Gosford Park	Capital Films	328
Torture Garden	Amicus	144	SOS Titanic	CANAL+IMAGE	193	Gosford Park	Capital Films	328
Asylum	Amicus	145	The Angry Silence	CANAL+IMAGE	84	Gosford Park	Capital Films	329
Tales from the Crypt	Amicus	146 & 147	The Angry Silence	CANAL+IMAGE	85	The African Queen	Carlton	cover
Tales from the Crypt	Amicus	148 & 149	The Angry Silence	CANAL+IMAGE	250	London Town	Carlton	30
Tales from the Crypt	Amicus	158	The Angry Silence	CANAL+IMAGE	253	London Town	Carlton	31
King of New York	Archway Prod	35	The Comedy Man	CANAL+IMAGE	95	Sanders of the River	Carlton	59
Bend It Like Beckham	Bendit Films	314	The Day the Earth Caught Fire	CANAL+IMAGE	139	Sanders of the River	Carlton	62
Bend It Like Beckham	Bendit Films	315	The Elephant Man	CANAL+IMAGE	150	Sanders of the River	Carlton	63
Bend It Like Beckham	Bendit Films	317	The Elephant Man	CANAL+IMAGE	151	The African Queen	Carlton	66
Bend It Like Beckham	Bendit Films	318	The Elephant Man	CANAL+IMAGE	320	The African Queen	Carlton	67
Bend It Like Beckham	Bendit Films	319	The Family Way	CANAL+IMAGE	102	The African Queen	Carlton	68
A Kind of Loving	CANAL+IMAGE	86	The Family Way	CANAL+IMAGE	102	The African Queen	Carlton	68
A Kind of Loving	CANAL+IMAGE	87	The Family Way	CANAL+IMAGE	103	The African Queen	Carlton	69
Billy Liar	CANAL+IMAGE	80	The Family Way	CANAL+IMAGE	104	Richard III	Carlton	72
Billy Liar	CANAL+IMAGE	82	The Family Way	CANAL+IMAGE	105	Richard III	Carlton	73
Billy Liar	CANAL+IMAGE	88	The L-Shaped Room	CANAL+IMAGE	81	Richard III	Carlton	74
Billy Liar	CANAL+IMAGE	89	The L-Shaped Room	CANAL+IMAGE	92	The Boys From Brazil	Carlton	173
Billy Liar	CANAL+IMAGE	89	The L-Shaped Room	CANAL+IMAGE	92	The Boys From Brazil	Carlton	173
Billy Liar	CANAL+IMAGE	90	The L-Shaped Room	CANAL+IMAGE	93	David Parfitt	Miramax	289
Billy Liar	CANAL+IMAGE	91	The Man Who Fell to Earth	CANAL+IMAGE	172	Dirty Pretty Things	Celador	327
Boulting Brothers	CANAL+IMAGE	38	The Servant	CANAL+IMAGE	80	Dirty Pretty Things	Celador	327
Bonnie Prince Charlie	CANAL+IMAGE	46	The Servant	CANAL+IMAGE	96	Cromwell	Columbia	58

Index

On location for *A Man for All Seasons* (1966),
Fred Zinnemann fourth from right

One of the happiest experiences of my professional life was the making of, *A Man for all Seasons* at Shepperton Studios, which was then managed by Adrian Worker. The crews and departments were top class and no request was too much trouble. It was a wonderful way to make a movie. There is still a glow twenty-five years later when I think of the lovely time we had.

Fred Zinnemann

John Mills as Willie Mossop in *Hobson's Choice* (1954). Filmed at Shepperton, this was his favourite film